Praise for the US edition

'In his rigorous and compelling book, Grinker examines the way advances in child psychiatry and cultural attitudes have changed the picture of autistics and limns his family's own hopeful story ... '

— *People Magazine*

'Thoughtfully written by a father and scientist trying to understand his daughter and illuminate her disorder.'

— New England Journal of Medicine

'[*Unstrange Minds*] makes the case that the rise in autism diagnosis is nothing more than an epidemic of discovery.'

— Slate.com

'Hands down, *Unstrange Minds* is the most useful book of the bunch for anyone who is interested in learning more about autism.'

— USA Today

'[Grinker's] cross-cultural approach is fascinating.'

— *Boston Globe*

'[A] fascinating book at many levels. It is very well written and enjoyable to read.'

— *PsycCritiques* (American Psychological Association)

'His daughter Isabel was diagnosed in 1994, and his warmth and compassion for autistic children and parents alike shines through in this immensely readable and informative narrative that looks closely at how culture influences the ways we understand, classify and treat autistic-spectrum disorders.'

— *Toronto Globe & Mail*

'In his new book *Unstrange Minds*, [Grinker] confidently traces how the press distorted terminology and misrepresented statistics to create a dangerous myth, and his credentials couldn't be better ... the most moving moments of *Unstrange Minds* occur when he recalls his life with Isabel. As he describes watching her around her preschool, he writes like an experienced memoirist … '

— *Time Out Chicago*

'In the emotionally powerful second portion, Grinker details the experiences of parents of autistic children in South Africa, South Korea and India, how their respective societies view the disorder (often negatively) and the obstacles surmounted to increase awareness of autism, its treatment and management.'

— *Publishers Weekly*

'Grinker's worldwide scope embraces the personal experiences of families with autistic children from the US to Africa and adds dimension and power to his position.'

— *Booklist*

'*Unstrange Minds* is a powerful survey of the parents of autistic children in South Africa, South Korea and India and how their societies view the disorder – and is written by an anthropologist and father of a daughter with autism.'

— Midwest Book Review

'An anthropologist as well as the parent of a child with autism, Grinker is perhaps uniquely placed to investigate the subject; and in *Unstrange Minds* he weaves cutting-edge science, personal anecdote and wry humour into a compelling journey of discovery.'

— *Irish Times*

'[I]mpassioned and thoughtful … [Grinker] makes a number of fascinating points about how doctors and health professionals understand issues pertaining to mental health and how cultural shifts can influence such understanding.'

— *Medscape Pediatrics*

'*Unstrange Minds* is a well-written, carefully presented work of scientific research, looking at the cultural implications of autism. It manages to address key points about autism today, both internationally and very personally. I believe that anyone touched by autism, whether physician, psychologist, teacher, or parent, should read this book.'

– Psychiatric Services

'Roy Richard Grinker's excellent book paints a unique biographical picture of his child's experience, conveys deep parental concern, and reminds us of the unmet needs of such children.'

– Simon Baron-Cohen, PhD, Director of the Autism Centre at
Cambridge University and author of *The Essential Difference*

'Roy Richard Grinker, a renowned anthropologist, walks across the roiling, highly charged world of autism and somehow manages to decipher what is real and what is not. The result is this big-hearted, uplifting, fiercely rigorous book – a genuine gift to readers who believe in the power of truth.'

– Ron Suskind, Pulitzer Prize-winning journalist and author of
A Hope in the Unseen

'In *Unstrange Minds*, Grinker uses the lens of anthropology to show how shifting cultural conditions change the way medical scientists do their work and how we perceive mental health.'

– Time Magazine

'*Unstrange Minds* is not only a compassionate account of the fights parents all over the world wage for their children with autism. It is also a beautifully written history … *Unstrange Minds* is as compelling as it is heartbreaking and wise.'

– Marti Leimbach, author of *Daniel Isn't Talking: A Novel*

'This is a wise and compassionate book, informed by academic rigor, deep personal feeling, and a sensitivity not only to the difference that is autism but also to the variety of human experience across cultures and classes. Grinker's research is as wide-ranging as it is open-minded, bringing together the precision of social science and the artistry of memoir, balancing the academic and the anecdotal to build polemical arguments about the nature and prevalence of autism. He speaks of how people have responded to the illness, and of how else we might respond, and in doing so challenges us to make a better world.'
— Andrew Solomon, author of *The Noonday Demon*

'A unique, extraordinary book ... Every reader – whether scientist, physician, psychologist, parent or teacher – will be moved and inspired.'
— Perri Klass, MD, author of *A Not Entirely Benign Procedure*

'... a fresh view of the challenges posed by this condition ... Grinker's exploration of cultural differences in attitudes to autism is very moving.'
— Nature

'Anthropologist Grinker's affecting investigation communicates a much-needed truth: autism is both a disease (biological) and an illness ... a life-altering experience completely at odds with society. Hope then comes like a bullet via vignettes of parents from America to Korea who've adapted to their children's "unstrange" worldviews.'
— *Library Journal*, selected for Best Books of 2007

'... scientifically rigorous and profoundly moving ... '
— American Heart Association newsletter

'Richard Grinker's descriptions of the perceptions of autism in other cultures are fascinating, uplifting, moving, and disturbing.'
— Temple Grandin, PhD, author of *Thinking Pictures*

Unstrange Minds

UNSTRANGE
MINDS

*A Father Remaps
the World of Autism*

~

ROY RICHARD
GRINKER

For Isabel

Published in the UK in 2008 by
Icon Books Ltd, The Old Dairy, Brook Road,
Thriplow, Cambridge SG8 7RG
email: info@iconbooks.co.uk
www.iconbooks.co.uk

Sold in the UK, Europe, South Africa and Asia
by Faber & Faber Ltd, 3 Queen Square,
London WC1N 3AU or their agents

Distributed in the UK, Europe, South Africa and Asia
by TBS Ltd, TBS Distribution Centre, Colchester Road
Frating Green, Colchester CO7 7DW

This edition published in Australia in 2008
by Allen & Unwin Pty Ltd, PO Box 8500,
83 Alexander Street, Crows Nest, NSW 2065

ISBN: 978-1840468-93-9

Typeset in 12 on 16pt Bembo by Marie Doherty

Printed and bound in Sweden
by ScandBook

Contents

from whose ...
remembrance might no patient
mind unstrange
learn ....

e.e. cummings

Pervasive Developmental Disorders [also called Autism Spectrum Disorders] are characterized by severe and pervasive impairment in several areas of development: reciprocal social interaction skills, communication skills, or the presence of stereotyped behavior, interests, and activities … [They include] Autistic Disorder, Rett's Disorder, Childhood Disintegrative Disorder, Asperger's Disorder, Pervasive Developmental Disorder Not Otherwise Specified … These disorders are evident in the first years of life and are often associated with some degree of Mental Retardation.

Diagnostic and Statistical Manual of Mental Disorders, Fourth Edition, Revised (DSM-IV-TR). Washington, DC: American Psychiatric Association, 2000.

Introduction

Bringing Autism into Focus

WHEN MY DAUGHTER ISABEL was diagnosed with autism in 1994, I knew little about the condition and knew no one else who had it. It was, after all, considered a rare disorder, occurring in only about 3 in every 10,000 live births.

A little more than a decade later, there's an autism crisis. Scientists now report rates of autism as high as 60 in 10,000 live births, and major news organisations, as well as members of Congress, are calling the sharp increase in diagnoses of autism an epidemic.

The epidemic, we are told, is devastating families.

Even those who are no directly affected by autism within their family circle are affected indirectly. The reports in the media, and speculation about possible causes of autism, have caused many parents and parents-to-be to become concerned. An increasing number of them are choosing to withhold much-needed vaccinations for their children out of the fear that they will contract autism, although a connection between vaccinations and autism has never been firmly established. The epidemic is taxing our country's ability to provide an appropriate education for all the children with special needs, and our paediatric clinics and hospitals are overwhelmed by parents seeking information about the disorder and help for their children.

And it is no wonder that people are worried. When Isabel was diagnosed, information on autism was scarce. But today, autism is making headlines, and the stories can be heartbreaking. The stream of information is increasing in momentum, and along with it, a sense of urgency and even panic.

I believe that this extraordinary momentum is a signal that we should stop, step back, and take a closer look at our fears about autism. Clearly, the reported rates of autism in North America and in Europe are way up. But what is causing the increase, and does it reflect a true epidemic, or is it a byproduct of changes in the way the statistics are gathered or the way the disorder is defined and diagnosed?

I'M AN ANTHROPOLOGIST, a social scientist who studies culture. Therefore, even though I study illness, my research does not look at chromosomes, antibodies, toxicology, vaccines, or the circuitry of the brain. Rather, I'm interested in the intersection between culture and illness – that is, how culture affects the way we define and classify illnesses. Psychiatry is a good topic for someone like me because, unlike the problems many physicians see from day to day – a rash, a virus, a tumour, a broken bone – most of the illnesses psychiatrists treat and study are incredibly hard to describe and open to multiple interpretations. Compared to other branches of medicine, psychiatric diagnosis is highly subjective.

Take pneumonia, for example. The most common severe form of the disease is caused by the bacterium *Streptococcus pneumoniae*. Whether it afflicts a slum dweller in Brazil or a rice farmer in Bangladesh, it is exactly the same disease. You can see the bacterium under a microscope, you can devise a way to treat it, and the treatment will be the same no matter where you are.

Now take a disorder like autism. You cannot see autism under a microscope or discover it through a lab test. The only evidence we have that someone has autism is the individual's behaviour. There is little agreement, even in a single culture, about exactly what it is or how to treat it.

So when we start to panic about the rise in the prevalence of certain conditions or disorders, it is good to remember that most psychiatric diagnoses are essentially just descriptions and classifications based on the behaviours particular clinicians have seen and chosen to emphasise at a particular point in time, and they can even reflect the personal and cultural biases of the individual clinicians. One clinician's description of a certain patient, and hence the diagnosis given to that patient, may vary considerably from another clinician's description of the same case, even when both clinicians are part of the same culture. Variations in diagnoses are even greater across cultures. Many societies, for example, do not even have a word for autism, and in others, the symptoms of autism are not thought to be abnormal as much as divine or spiritual.

Moreover, psychiatry – especially child psychiatry – however valuable, is an imprecise science that can change rapidly in response to new ideas, methods of training, and especially changing historical and cultural conditions. Many psychiatric diagnoses come and go – and hence rates of diagnoses go up and down, not unlike fashions. For example, several million Americans have been diagnosed with depression. But many people with depression, perhaps hundreds of thousands, would not have been diagnosed with it just 50 years ago. The increase in the number of those reported to be clinically depressed does not mean that depression is more common today than in the past, but only that our way of defining depression has changed. 50 years ago, the term was used to describe only serious, debilitating depressions that may have required long-term hospitalisations. Likewise, there exists the logical possibility that the incidence of autism has not increased but that we are defining it differently and counting it differently than in the past. Of course, the fact that some diagnoses become popular or fade away does not mean the conditions they describe are not real. Isabel would have the symptoms of what we today call autism whether she was diagnosed with autism, schizophrenia, something else, or nothing at all. It does mean, however, that what may be called an 'epidemic' is really a reflection of a change in the way a culture perceives a condition or disease.

Since rates cannot rise without diagnoses, it makes sense to ask how and why autism is getting diagnosed more. And since rates cannot rise without scientists to count the diagnoses, it also makes sense to ask how and why they are counting more cases. Finally, if culture does affect the way we view autism, we ought to look at autism around the world to see if it exists in cultures very different from ours and, if so, what people do about it.

When I began to look for answers to these questions, I discovered that the current crisis about autism in the United States is the culmination of a complex process that began several decades ago. It started with the first description of autism in 1943 and with the birth of child psychiatry after the Second World War, when scientists began using medical knowledge to understand children's behaviour. This process picked up speed when society began integrating a wider range of people into schools, the workplace, and communities, and it reached its maximum velocity – its 'tipping point', in the phrase made popular by journalist Malcolm Gladwell – when doctors began to use a set of criteria to diagnose autism that included people who, in the past, would never have been diagnosed with the condition at all.

This book therefore addresses the clear rise in the prevalence of autism – and, more precisely, the range of conditions now called *autism spectrum disorders* – by exploring the cultural factors that have changed our perspectives on children and mental disorders. The shift in how we view autism, in other words, is part of a set of broader shifts taking place in society. The growth of child psychiatry as a field of inquiry and area of practice, the decline of psychoanalysis, the rise of advocacy organisations, greater public sensitivity to children's educational problems, and changes in public policies (for example, the establishment of autism as a valid special-education code under the Individuals with Disabilities Education Act, or IDEA, passed in 1991) have together changed the way autism is diagnosed and defined. As a society, we have become more aware of children's behavioural and learning differences at earlier and earlier ages and more comfortable with diagnosis, medication, and psychiatric labels. Under the rubric of autism we now find a multitude of emotional and cognitive problems, problems that used to be given other diagnostic labels or that were even considered within the range of the normal. Doctors now have a more heightened awareness of autism and are diagnosing it with more frequency, and public schools in the United States, which first started using the category of autism during the 1991–1992 school year, are reporting it more often, developing ways to help children with autism, and directing parents to appropriate resources. Epidemiologists are also counting it better.

As a result, the statistics on autism that we have today are the most accurate we've ever had. There are more people with a diagnosis of autism now than at any time in history. After all these years, we have realised that autism is a major public health concern. Still, these rates may not be proof of an epidemic. Why? Because the old rates were either inaccurate (because cases went unreported or misdiagnosed) or based on different definitions of autism than the ones we use now. Indeed, before 1980, when the criteria we're familiar with today were first standardised by the American Psychiatric Association (APA), there was little agreement among clinicians and researchers about what was and was not autism. Today, in fact, autism is more than just one disorder; it is a spectrum of disorders that encompasses a wider range of people than ever before. Some of those considered autistic – or 'on the spectrum' – under this broader definition are so high functioning that in the past they might have been considered simply eccentric. Identical definitions need to be used if rates of occurrence are to be compared, but as it is impossible to go back into the past and gather statistics according to today's standards, there can be no comparison. And without a comparison, there can be no spike in the incidence of autism.

'Epidemic' is a powerful concept. It implies danger and incites fear, calling up associations with plagues that can sweep through the streets, something contagious in the air you breathe or in the food you eat, threatening the ones you love. With autism, the label of 'epidemic' sounds both frightening and tragic.

But what if, paradoxically, the rise in rates of autism as gathered by schools, epidemiologists, and public-health officials is evidence not of tragedy, but of good? What if the power of the term 'epidemic' lay not in creating new illness but in treating it and finding a cure? This book argues that the newer, higher, more accurate statistics on autism are a sign that we are finally seeing and appreciating a kind of human difference that we once turned away from and that many other cultures still hide away in homes or institutions or denigrate as bizarre. The result of the new rates is that we are fortunately seeing more research, more philanthropy, and more understanding of how families struggle to cope.

Just 30 years ago, my daughter Isabel might have been labelled mentally retarded, and there would have been little opportunity for her to find her place in the world. Our family would have been at a loss as to what to do. Isabel would probably have been placed in a residential institution with a minimal education plan, where the symptoms of her autism would have worsened. A mildly autistic child living at the same time at home would have been teased and bullied mercilessly, would have had little access to special-education services, and would have failed at school and suffered profound emotional distress. Paediatricians, mental health care practitioners, speech and occupational therapists, and educators still need to know more about autism, but they know enough now to make a big difference. They are diagnosing autism and providing therapy to children with autism at earlier ages than ever, and they are discovering how to use safe and effective medicines to ameliorate some of the symptoms of autism. Today my teenage daughter is mainstreamed into a high school classroom for part of the day. Numerous tests have shown that she has above average intelligence. She even plays cello in the school orchestra.

Autism is a lifelong disorder, but it's a better time than ever to be autistic. A child with a diagnosis of autism has access to more services and educational opportunities than ever before. As a result, there are parents whose children have rare chromosomal disorders that involve social and language deficits or mental retardation, including Down syndrome, who want them to be diagnosed with autism, though the early writers on autism never dreamed the term would be applied to these diseases. Perhaps this is not so surprising, since there is much less stigma attached to autism than there once was.

WHEN ISABEL WAS FIRST DIAGNOSED, in April 1994, and was two and a half, things were just starting to change for people with autism. Washington, DC, was beautiful that month. The cherry blossoms were in full bloom and there was even some good news in the world. In India, the Untouchables, or outcastes, were out in the streets for everyone to see, protesting for better jobs and pay. South Korea, a country whose people barely knew what a North Korean person looked like, had just accepted 100 North Korean defectors from Siberia. And in South Africa, President F.W. de Klerk conceded to Nelson Mandela in an election that would finally give blacks the political rights and representation they deserved. And in my little corner of the world, a suburb of Washington, DC, more and more children with special needs were being included in mainstream classrooms, being challenged and succeeding academically to a degree that few educators ever thought possible.

The changes in India, South Korea, and South Africa made visible the formerly invisible. Autism is becoming more visible too, and in some unexpected places.

IN THE WINTER OF 2005, Mamta, a young mother from Nainital in the foothills of the Himalayas, brought her three-year-old boy, Ohjyu, on the seven-hour train ride to New Delhi, despite her family's protest. She was convinced he had autism, even though none of the doctors in Nainital believed her. She was going to learn how to interact with him and help him learn even if it meant abandoning her husband and parents-in-law in their mountain village for months, an action many of her friends and neighbours thought was outrageous. Mamta could only imagine the insults hurled behind her back. Within days after arriving in Delhi, her son was diagnosed with autism and she had a treatment plan in place.

In KwaZulu-Natal, in South Africa, Suzanna and Golden Khumalo didn't know what to do about their six-year-old son, Big Boy. He had stopped talking, didn't respond to his name, made strange movements with his hands, and avoided all eye contact. Suzanna and Golden fought with Golden's parents, who insisted

Big Boy go to a *nyanga*, or witch doctor. But Suzanna and Golden were afraid of what the witch doctor might do. He would likely arrange goat sacrifices to please the ancestors, give Big Boy an emetic to make him vomit, and give him a laxative to expel the evil inside of him. Finally, Suzanna and Golden surrendered to custom and brought Big Boy to the nyanga. After they had spent three days in the doctor's village, he finally gave Big Boy a diagnosis. It was 'autism', he said, a word no one ever expected to hear from a nyanga's mouth. Suzanna and Golden now know a lot about autism. Suzanna even told me that in South Africa, 1 in 166 children have autism. She couldn't tell me where the figure came from – I knew there hadn't been an epidemiological study conducted anywhere in Africa – but she promised to find out. When I saw her in the parking lot of Big Boy's school the next day, she called out to me, 'It's from Brick Township, New Jersey!'

Just outside Lima, in 1975, a young Peruvian schoolteacher named Lily Mayo visited a church hospital where children and adults with autism were kept in cages. Over the adult cages the priests had hung a sign that read, *No Te Acerques Por Que Muerdo* (Beware, I bite). The villagers and the priests believed the children were either possessed by the devil or being punished for the sins of their parents. In the yards of state institutions, she saw naked boys tied to poles as punishment for biting themselves or banging their heads. Lily recalls those days from behind her desk at the Anne Sullivan Center in Lima, an autism treatment and education facility she directs. Her assistant, a 32-year-old man with autism, brings her papers to sign. In 2005, exactly 30 years after her first encounter with autism, Lily is writing agreements with some of Peru's largest corporations to hire young adults with autism, people who will become a visible part of their communities. Mayo finds it hard to believe so much had changed in just 30 years. 'It's like that old line,' she says: 'The past is a foreign country; they do things differently there.'

IT SEEMS AS IF NEARLY EVERYONE I meet these days knows something about autism. It's on the front pages of major newspapers and magazines, it's discussed on morning talk shows and in best-selling books, and celebrities lead high-profile fund-raising efforts. Considered a rare condition when first named by the child psychiatrist Leo Kanner in 1943, autism was thought to occur in fewer than 3 in 10,000 live births in the United States. Current estimates range from as few as 30 cases per 10,000 (about 1 in 300) to as many as 63 per 10,000 (about 1 in 158). Even the lower estimate of 1 in 300 tells us that autism is not a rare disorder, certainly more prevalent than cancer, diabetes, spina bifida, and Down syndrome in children. The US Department of Education figures show a national increase of 544 per cent in diagnoses of autism over a period of nine academic years (1992–1993 through 2000–2001), with startling increases in some states (for example, Alabama – 1,000 per cent, Arkansas – 2,000 per cent, and Kentucky, 2,000 per cent). The Department of Education in Wisconsin reported eighteen new autism cases among public school children in 1992–1993 but 1,823 new autism classifications in 2000–2001. The Autism Society of America, the major advocacy organisation for autism, estimates that 1.5 million Americans suffer from some kind of autism and predicts a figure as high as 4 million for the year 2014.

Federal, state, and local agencies in many countries, especially the United States, Canada, and the United Kingdom, have been mobilised to manage the heavy public health burden of autism. Special-education programmes are expanding; in the United States, new money is pouring out of the National Institutes of Health into autism research, and donors are contributing millions of dollars to parent advocacy organisations, private schools, and research foundations. In the United Kingdom, the National Autistic Society, founded in 1962, has grown considerably over the past decade to include more than 17,000 members and institute a telephone helpline that in 2007 took 38,000 calls. Even scientists who never before had an interest in autism, but work in a related area such as neuroscience or genetics, are joining an increasingly long parade of autism researchers. Between 2003 and 2004 the number of grant applications to the National Alliance for Autism Research, then the leading private foundation for autism research (before its merger with Autism Speaks), doubled. Through the Internet, people in remote areas of the world read news stories about the epidemic. Media reports consistently refer to autism with phrases like the 'hidden epidemic' and the 'mysterious outbreak', citing the 'exploding number' of autism cases, leading to fears that causal factors such as vaccinations, mercury poisoning, or other environmental exposures (a subject I do not discuss at length in this book) might be contributing to the rise in cases of autism. But is there really more autism, or are we just seeing it more? There are lots of theories around to explain the rise in diagnoses, none of them proven. Some scientists think that the 'increase' is due to more aggressive epidemiological methods that make it easier for researchers to count the right number of cases. Others think that the broadening of diagnostic criteria over the past two decades to include more symptoms, and a bigger range of severity of symptoms, has made it easier for physicians and psychologists to fit their clients into the framework of autism. Still others – though not most scientists – think that the number of cases of autism started to increase when a mercury-containing preservative called thiomersal (since 2002, present only in some influenza vaccines) was added to many common childhood vaccines in the 1930s and 1940s.

However, no single factor seems to account for the rise. Nor should any single factor be accepted at face value. For example, if we accept that scientists are counting cases more accurately than before, we should look into how and why they started counting them better. If we accept that new diagnostic criteria are responsible for the increase in prevalence rates, how and why did the new diagnostic criteria emerge at this time in our history? And if we believe that autism awareness is at an all-time high, how did this happen? At what point did autism shift from being just a terrible disease to an 'epidemic'?

Amid all the disagreement and debate about the origins and nature of autism, most experts will agree that autism is a highly variable syndrome that resists easy definition. There is a multitude of symptoms, appearing in different constellations in different people, and most of these symptoms will also change in form or severity throughout childhood and adulthood. In addition, some people diagnosed with autism are much more affected by autism than others. 'Autism' today is really an autism *spectrum*. The spectrum is broad enough to encompass both a severely mentally retarded autistic person without speech and a super-intelligent but socially awkward mathematician or physicist. Hence, many people today refer to the various manifestations of autism (Pervasive Developmental Disorder, Asperger's Disorder, and Autistic Disorder, for example) as 'autism spectrum disorders', or ASD. In fact, autism researchers are already beginning to suggest that there is no such thing as the singular 'autism', but rather many autisms, many distinct disorders, perhaps defined not only by their different symptoms but by the many different genes involved.

Most experts would also agree that nearly all their knowledge about autism spectrum disorders is based on research in North America and the United Kingdom and that little is known about autism in other parts of the world. Yet we know that autism is a brain disorder that can affect anyone in any culture. We also know that huge countries like China or India that seldom use the category of autism as a medical diagnosis are just beginning to do so more often – and to count their cases.

The dearth of information about autism in other cultures is a glaring absence of knowledge. We know how important it can be to study illnesses in multiple countries. World Health Organisation (WHO) studies on schizophrenia conducted in the 1970s, for example, showed that even though schizophrenia occurred with similar frequency all over the world, people with schizophrenia in developing countries did better over time than those in industrialised countries. They needed less care and fewer medicines, and they had fewer traumatic, psychotic episodes. We need similar information about autism around the world today to know if certain cultural conditions help people with autism improve their ability to learn, communicate, and participate in social and economic life.

THIS BOOK IS ABOUT how culture affects the way we view autism. It looks at autism as a global phenomenon and sees it not only as a biological disorder but as a group of symptoms that have become especially meaningful in particular times and places. The first part of the book chronicles the complex process through which autism became a widely diagnosed disorder in the United States and culminates in an analysis of the changing prevalence rates of autism. In the second part of the book we travel to a variety of different countries (South Africa, India, and South Korea, among others) to find out whether autism is also more visible today in the rest of the world and to see what the study of the disorder across cultures might teach us about our own experiences and interpretations of autism.

Over the past several years, I have met children and adults with autism in the Democratic Republic of Congo, South Africa, India, Korea, and the United States, and in all of these places autism, at first, looks the same. Whether in a rural South Korean village, Manhattan, or New Delhi, autism usually presents itself just after a child's second birthday with a core set of symptoms that includes a severe language delay, problems relating to other people, and repetitive or stereotyped behaviours. The symptoms change over the life of the individual, with some symptoms falling away and others emerging, but the same symptoms are found across cultures and, based on what we know about autism in the distant past, across time as well.

However, autism, like all disorders, does not exist outside of culture. It is culture that sees something as abnormal or wrong, names it, and does something about it, and all cultures respond to illness differently. For example, when I did research in central Africa with the Efe Pygmies, I found that a person with a serious or intractable illness would rarely go to a doctor alone; his entire family would go. They believe that the affliction within the individual is the expression of a larger underlying problem with the family, and so it is important to treat both the person and his relatives. I also learned, too late, that if I gave someone 28 pills (four a day for a week) to cure a bacterial infection, he would give one pill each to 28 different relatives. And so, when a boy not far from my village wouldn't talk or make eye contact, and began to have seizures, his parents assumed that the family's ancestors had attacked him. They gave him herbal medicines and sent him to a village far away, where he wouldn't have contact with any blood relatives. In urban South Korea, psychiatrists often diagnose children on the autism spectrum with Reactive Attachment Disorder (RAD), a mental illness often linked to child neglect, because RAD is the more culturally acceptable of the two diagnoses. Diagnoses of either RAD or autism are made at a very early age in South Korea, often before the second birthday, whereas in other countries, such as South Africa, children tend to be diagnosed when they enter elementary school at about age six. Despite being diagnosed early and living in one of the most medically advanced societies in the world, South Korean children with autism or RAD seldom receive medical treatment for the disorder, whereas South Africans – even poor, rural South Africans – find and make use of several different treatments.

There are also many differences within each country. In stark contrast to the big city, in the rural South Korean villages that I visited autism is a more common diagnosis than RAD. In addition, children with autism are known to everyone. They are often well integrated into community life, and, to some extent, they are accepted for who they are. In Seoul, however, a city of more than 11 million people, children with autism are often hidden from neighbours and seldom seen by relatives, in large part because of the extraordinary stigma associated with having a disabled child. In South Africa, whites tend to seek only Western medical care, while the Zulu and Xhosa peoples, in contrast, use a variety of healthcare systems, including Western medicine, traditional medicines, and healing rituals. In the United States, white children are diagnosed earlier than black children (6.3 years on average versus 7.9 years).

The study of these kinds of variations is the stuff of my discipline, cultural anthropology, a field that often studies the complicated relationship between culture and biology. The anthropologist Marshall Sahlins once compared the relationship between culture and biology to an artist and his or her medium, like Michelangelo and an unworked slab of marble. There is only so much one can do to the stone since its natural properties limit us. But it is culture that determines the decision to take the marble in the first place

– to select one section of stone from all others – and culture that determines whether the stone, meaningless until someone sees it and imagines its future, becomes a Roman column or the *David*. To paraphrase this idea in the context of medicine, illnesses may be biological, but they are never simply biological.

Ironically, the process of understanding autism itself parallels the work that anthropologists do, since the minds of people with autism are sometimes as hard to understand as foreign cultures. Anthropologists spend their days teaching about the customs of other cultures, many of which our students at the university level find irrational, even frightening. Our goal is to make the strange familiar. Indeed, with every day that passes, as autism advocates, parents, and researchers teach us about the complexity of human behaviour, autism seems less exotic and more 'unstrange', a word invented by the poet e.e. cummings in an untitled poem rebuking societies in the thrall of conformity.

But cultural anthropologists also try to make the familiar strange, seeking to turn our gaze homeward and see our own culture in a new light. And when we do, we find that scientists also belong to different cultures, and that their research is often a product of their time and place, their community's interests and values. As we'll see, the discovery of autism wasn't so much a discovery of new truths as a new way of seeing a group of cognitive and social differences. Although it's likely that autism has existed among humans for at least hundreds of years, until very recently no one thought to create a distinct category for it because our culture – our social, educational, and medical systems – was not ready for it.

Autism was first defined and described in the United States in the 1940s, but it took nearly 40 more years for the American Psychiatric Association to officially name and classify it in its bible of diagnosis, the *Diagnostic and Statistical Manual of Mental Disorders* (*DSM-III*, 1980), and to consider it something other than a childhood psychosis. It took the French psychiatric establishment another 24 years to officially state, in November 2004, that autism is a developmental disorder rather than a kind of schizophrenia, and it did so only because parents demanded it, not because the French psychiatrists had actually learned anything new. Science didn't change our culture, as much as culture changed our science.

ONLY A DECADE AGO, Mamta, Golden, and Suzanna had never heard the word 'autism'. Neither had the rural healer that Golden's parents consulted in Zululand. There is more awareness of autism now than ever before, and the Internet has made much of the difference. That is how Suzanna arrived at the figure of 1 in 166. And that is also how Suzanna learned enough about autism to fight for government services and find Big Boy the best educational setting possible. I envy the parent whose child has just been diagnosed with autism. When Isabel was first diagnosed in 1994, our local public school system regarded her as if she were from outer space. Autism was a strange word to most people. 'You mean like Dustin Hoffman in *Rain Man*?' people would ask. 'You mean she's *artistic*?' In 1994, newspapers and magazines ran autism stories infrequently. When they did, they usually talked about a truly unusual person, such as a 'savant', someone with miraculous talents – like the autistic person who located an error in one of Isaac Newton's mathematical calculations, or another who could recite from memory a dozen of Shakespeare's plays.

A person with autism is no longer an oddity. In a remote Appalachian mountain community, I met impoverished parents of autistic children, moms and dads who never went to high school, can barely read or write, and certainly have no Internet access. But they all knew the word 'thiomersal', the mercury-containing preservative that used to be in some vaccines. They had heard about it from parents in support groups they attend who had printed out dozens of pages from websites on vaccines and autism.

The parent whose child has just been diagnosed can find dozens of books on autism, many of them published in the past five years. And these books are becoming available in other countries too, where they are slowly but surely replacing copies of Bruno Bettelheim's 1967 book on the subject, *The Empty Fortress*. Societies that never had words for autism are inventing them, and parents throughout the world are founding autism societies.

If Isabel had been born ten years later, my wife Joyce and I wouldn't have felt so alone, and the teachers and staff at her school would have known how to talk to her, how to help other students interact with her, and how to teach her. The experienced county psychologist assigned to our local elementary school said that he'd never seen a child quite like her before, a child who, at first glance, looked normal – he said that she 'looked very intelligent' – and yet had little ability or desire to communicate, echoed whatever anyone said to her, repeated words and phrases from videos, and made little or no eye contact.

How was that possible? The truth is, in his job as a school psychologist in a mainstream school, he had met only a few children with a diagnosis of autism. In 1993, the state of Maryland told the US Department of Education that the public schools of the state had provided special-education services during the 1992–1993 academic year to only 28 children with autism (ages six through 21). Other states had higher numbers – California reported 1,605, Georgia 262, Florida 582, and New Jersey 446 – but some densely populated states had even lower figures, like Ohio, which reported only 22 cases. When Isabel was diagnosed, the public schools of the state of Maryland, from kindergarten through the community college and university level, claimed to have served only 300 people with autism under the age of 22 during the academic year

1993–1994 (a small number, but still an enormous increase over the previous year).

The principal of Isabel's elementary school was equally lost. She had already worked for twenty years in the school system and was responsible for sending in the annual child counts for the disabled children served in her school. Under the Individuals with Disabilities Education Act of 1991, the federal law guaranteeing that every child is provided a free and appropriate education in the least restrictive environment, disabled children in public schools have to be given a code, such as 'multiple disabilities' or 'traumatic brain disorder', and then the number of children in each category has to be reported to the US Department of Education. But the principal said she wasn't familiar with the autism code, since it was new, and that they were using autism only for kids who were mentally retarded because, as she put it, 'parents don't like the term mental retardation anymore.' Because Isabel had never been called mentally retarded, the principal was confused by the diagnosis of 'autism'. I realised only later, while writing this book, how pejorative a term 'mental retardation' has become, and how a diagnosis of autism gives hope to parents of children previously labelled mentally retarded. Mental retardation has become even more pejorative in the UK, where 'Learning Disability' is the preferred term for someone who scores in the range of mental retardation on intelligence tests. Many parents I've met have faith that autism means there is a 'normal' person imprisoned inside (echoing Bettelheim's 'fortress' terminology) and that, with the right therapy or medication, their child's true self will emerge.

Isabel was diagnosed just as autism diagnoses started their steep climb. By 2003 there would be more than 4,084 children (ages three to 22) coded with autism in the Maryland public school systems, a rate of 1 in 183 children.

A diagnostic label really does influence the way we view some-one. If Isabel had been diagnosed with schizophrenia, as might have happened in the 1950s and 1960s, the psychologist could have immediately recommended a mental institution where she could live, or assigned her to a class or school for mentally dis-turbed children. If she had been diagnosed as mentally retarded, as so many autistic people were and are, he would have been able to put her in any number of different classes for cognitively chal-lenged kids, since mental retardation is so common (as much as 1 per cent of the US population). What was our school supposed to do with a child who was just one of a few hundred kids in the whole state school system labelled with autism?

The key word here is 'labelled', because there were certainly thousands of people in Maryland with autism at the time the state reported just over 300 cases. Some, of course, were in private spe-cial-education schools, but if they received government assistance they would still have been counted. So where were all the kids with autism? The answer is that most of them were in school; they just didn't have the label 'autism'.

The category of 'autism' was introduced as a US Department of Education category for the annual 'child count' of children in publicly provided special education only in the 1991–1992 aca-demic year – and during that year only as an optional category – so before that time children with autism were called something else. Kids who entered the school system with autism, or with one of the other popular and vague diagnoses that were once given to people with autism, like 'non-specific developmental delay', 'brain dysfunction', 'obsessive compulsive disorder with brain dysfunc-tion', 'seizure disorder', or any combination of these terms, would often be given a code of 'mental retardation' or 'multiple disabili-ties' because these were the codes available in the school system at the time. Today we know better: Mental retardation – mild, moderate, or severe – often accompanies autism, but mental retardation, defined largely by IQ score, can exist in a host of different disorders without all the impairments in communication and reciprocal social interaction characteristic of autism.

Today, there are still only a small number of codes that schools use in their reports to the federal government: they include learning disorder, speech/language impairment, multiple disabilities, mental retardation, autism, and traumatic brain injury. There isn't even a code for Attention Deficit Hyperactivity Disorder (ADHD), one of the most common child psychiatric diagnoses in America. Children with ADHD, cerebral palsy, muscular dystrophy, and AIDS all receive the same code: 'Other Health Impaired (OHI).'

Of course, once the autism code was added, school autism figures rose quickly. Between 1992, a year after autism was added to the coding system, and 1993, the Department of Education statistics showed a national increase in autism cases of 23 per cent. Percentage increases can appear dramatic when you've just introduced a new category. For example, if in one year you jump from, say, 22 to 66 cases in Ohio, which has a population of 12 million, it might sound like an insignificant increase. But phrased differently – a three-fold increase – it sounds alarming.

By comparison, the same year autism was introduced, the Department of Education also added 'traumatic brain injury' as a reporting category. By 2000, the number of kids with 'traumatic brain injury' had risen by more than 5,000 per cent. This does not mean that there was actually a 5,000 per cent increase in traumatic brain injuries across the nation in the span of a few years; the new category simply opened up a way for cases of traumatic brain injury to be reported. Likewise, the new code for autism made a way for cases of autism to be reported. It also opened up a way for children with autism to begin to get appropriate help.

WHEN ISABEL FIRST ENTERED the school system as a kindergartner, she couldn't be mainstreamed. She couldn't sit still or
communicate with teachers or students, and she was simply too
disruptive. The psychologist thought about recommending placement in a class for children of normal intelligence with emotional disturbances, but dismissed that idea because her classmates
would then be mostly boys with attention and aggression problems – poor social models. Our psychiatrist concurred. Children
with autism, he rightly argued, need to be around children who
interact in socially appropriate ways. So instead, the school psychologist recommended that Isabel join a class of children with
multiple disabilities, such as cerebral palsy and a host of chromosomal disorders. We were convinced that Isabel was more intelligent and educable than the school thought. So we looked at a
local private school for children with mental retardation, autism,
and other severe deficits, called Ivymount, in the hope that they
would be able to place her in just the right environment. But the
Ivymount administrators said that Isabel was too high functioning
for them and that we should look at a school for bright but learning disabled children called the Lab School of Washington. When
we visited the Lab School, we were told, 'Your daughter is quite
impaired. You should look at Ivymount.'

Had Isabel been mentally retarded, there would have been more
options for her, public and private. Had her autism been more
mild, she might have been mainstreamed in the public school system or even enrolled in a private school for exceptional children.
But like many children with autism she was betwixt and between,
and no one knew what to do with her. There was not a single
private school in the greater Washington, DC, area that was appropriate for her.

Someone with a newly diagnosed child might have a similar
experience with these private schools, but now there are many

more good public placements available throughout the United States. In the mainstream schools in many counties, even in some of the most rural areas of the United States, such as the Appalachian Mountains, there are whole classes just for children with mild autism.

PARENTS STILL STRUGGLE to find appropriate placements for their autistic children. They fight with school systems, even hire lawyers and file complaints and lawsuits. But the 'epidemic' means that a newly diagnosed child is no longer a mystery, and no psychologist with even one or two years' experience could say today that he or she has never seen a child like Isabel. Whether or not we want to believe the idea that there is an epidemic, one thing is evident: Autism is more familiar and visible than ever before. And this is true no matter where you are, whether you're in a suburb of Washington, DC, or in Seoul, Cape Town, or the hills of northern India.

PART ONE ～

1

One in Three Hundred

SOMETIMES, AT NIGHT, ISABEL has a hard time falling asleep. It helps her if I sit in a chair in her bedroom. Looking at her then, from across the room, I see two different Isabels. There is Isabel awake – often hyperactive and isolated – and Isabel asleep, a beautiful child drifting into a calm night. And then I realise something unsettling: I feel more affection for the sleeping Isabel. She looks so peaceful and relaxed. And I wonder what this says about me. Do I love her less when she's a real person, awake and in the world?

When I can hear each breath, I know she's finally fallen asleep, but I sit for a minute more – just to make sure, I tell myself. The truth is, it's nice to be in the same room with her without having to work so hard. Isabel has always been a slim girl, but she has a round face that invites kisses. Joyce calls her cheeks 'bo-bo-bos', some Korean baby talk she learned as a child that refers to balls of fat in adorably plump babies. Before I leave her room, I kiss her cheek, and she's usually sweating, as children so often do in their sleep. I think about how much she has to struggle every day, just to deal with what to her must be chaos, and what to most of us is simply everyday life.

I try not to think about what other teenage girls are like – the ones I see outside our local middle school, gossiping and talking about boys – and focus only on Isabel. If I compare her to the rest of the world, she seems so impaired. But if I compare her with herself, and consider all the progress she's made, more than any doctor ever predicted, I'm suddenly filled with respect for her. I don't know how she keeps herself so happy.

It's at those moments I have an odd feeling of liberation. I remember that during my childhood one of my cousins described having a child with a severe disability as 'a prison sentence'. It doesn't seem that way to me because I cherish the idea of being with Isabel forever. Joyce and I are free of the stressful ambition of having Isabel go to a high-status high school or college, free of the anxiety about a child leaving us to live somewhere else or marry.

I am not a religious person, but there is something profoundly meaningful, if not spiritual, about being the father of a child with autism that has pushed me to consider lofty, abstract principles of life like truth, beauty, and goodness. I just have a hard time see-ing them during the day when I'm fighting with Isabel to stay near me on a pavement next to a busy street, pay attention to her homework, or turn off the television.

Now she's asleep for the night, her plush Panda bear under her right arm. When she wakes up, the everyday struggle will begin all over again.

It's the struggle of getting her to communicate, to learn, to say yes or no to a simple question, to come to the dinner table and sit with her younger sister, Olivia, to eat foods other than hot dogs and pizza, to stop putting her hands over her ears in response to some sound or frequency no one else can detect.

Especially in the early years, I'd lose my temper when I was frustrated by her inability to communicate. Joyce would lose her temper too. Our younger daughter, Olivia, would start to cry if we raised our voices. There are moments of intense emotion in any family, and most people regret them. But when you're facing something like autism, whether your child is severely affected or not, you've got to cut yourself some slack. I used to justify my expressions of anger and frustration by insisting that Isabel needed to be exposed to the full range of human emotions. The problem was that Isabel has usually responded to anger and loud voices and ignored gentle, quiet ones. I'd start out quietly, asking, 'Do you have to go to the bathroom? Yes or no?' But she'd only notice me when my voice got loud. 'Answer me!' The more I expressed my frustrations, however, the guiltier I felt, especially at night when I looked at her sleeping, so beautifully. How could I have been so mad at such an angel?

And if you knew how far she's come, you'd probably ask me the same question.

JOYCE AND I WERE MARRIED in the summer of 1990. I had finished my PhD in anthropology at Harvard University, having spent two years living with the Pygmies in what was then called Zaire, now the Democratic Republic of Congo. I was studying ethnic conflict and nationalism, nothing at all to do with mental disorders or autism. Joyce was a newly minted psychiatrist doing a fellowship at Harvard Medical School in medical anthropology, the branch of my profession that studies how culture affects the way we experience and treat illness.

Our first child, Isabel, was born in September 1991 in Minneapolis, where we had taken our first jobs. Isabel was extraordinarily beautiful, with an enigmatic face, a mixture of Korean and Caucasian features. She would have Joyce's lovely black hair, my pale skin, and eyes a grey-blue colour we thought genetically impossible, eyes framed by eyelashes so long they looked unreal. We never had a clue that anything was wrong until 1993, a year after we moved to Washington, DC, and Joyce gave birth to our second daughter, Olivia.

Isabel was two, and she couldn't talk.

WHEN I THINK ABOUT THE DAY Isabel was diagnosed with autism – as if that was the first day she really had autism – I'm reminded of how memories privilege events over process. We think of our marriages, for example, as a first date, an engagement, the wedding; we punctuate our children's lives with birthdays, or the first day of school. But the reality of our social lives is a gradual march of time, a complicated process of building relationships.

I trace the beginning of my knowledge about autism, and Isabel's identity, to a single event, a beautiful spring day in 1994, when a short, slightly overweight, affable child psychiatrist told us, 'Isabel has enough features of autism to be called PDD-NOS, Pervasive Developmental Disorder Not Otherwise Specified. It means that she's not severely autistic.' But, in fact, by that time we had already been worried about Isabel for more than six months and we were sure there was something different about her. The diagnosis was really just about someone we could trust telling us what we knew all along, even if we didn't admit it to ourselves.

Despite the joy of our second daughter's birth in November 1993, the year 1994 would begin poorly. In her first two years, Isabel had seemed to us like any other child, and at twelve months she had begun to make some of the sounds that seemed like the beginnings of words. But she was our first child, and so we didn't really have a standard for comparison. We thought she was fine. But when I look at our home movies today, I see that she never once tried to communicate with us; in none of the videos of Isabel between eighteen and 24 months does she say a single word.

She may not have tried to communicate with words or gestures, but she did interact with us, and she looked so normal. There's a pretty, happy, dark-haired little girl hugging and kissing us, playing hide-and-seek and ring-around-the-rosy in the living room of the house we rented in Chevy Chase, Maryland. I play an electric piano as she dances on her toes. Joyce tickles her, one hand on the camera, one hand on Isabel's belly, and they both squeal. Had there been someone else in the room watching, he would have thought to himself, 'Now there's a happy family.'

She used to carry Mickey and Minnie Mouse dolls with her everywhere. In one film, Isabel throws Mickey and Minnie on the floor outside of our bedroom, then goes inside and shuts the door. A few seconds later, she peeks outside the door to see if they are still there. Our new baby, Olivia, sleeps in her crib as Isabel meticulously arranges the dolls on either side of her and tucks her, Mickey, and Minnie into bed, as if they were three dolls.

It had been just the three of us, until now. Three, a unity so perfect that it blinds you. Only now, with Olivia here, an outsider in the way that all second, third, and fourth children are outsiders, did we start to look at Isabel with a worried eye. Olivia made us see Isabel anew, if only because we tried to assess how far we and Isabel had come, what kind of parents – and what kind of sister – Olivia was about to meet. And what we saw gave us pause, like when relatives come late to a dinner already in progress, and you stop what you're doing, take stock, and feel somewhat sorry for having begun without them. You make way, starting over. We looked at Isabel as if for the first time, and we began to see how different she was from other children her age. It was a bit like we had two new children.

A few months before Isabel's second birthday, and Olivia's birth, Isabel appeared to be losing what little language she had. That winter, in December 1993, while Joyce and I were focused on things other than Isabel – making dinner, changing Olivia's nappy, cleaning the house – our ears would occasionally perk up when we thought we heard Isabel say a word or two. We called these events 'Elvis sightings' because, even though we were never certain she'd actually said something, we were still excited. We may have just believed what we wanted to believe. But she had crawled and walked on schedule, was almost completely toilet rained, and apart from the speech problem, didn't seem unusual. We didn't notice that she made little eye contact.

Our new paediatrician in DC had been reassuring. He was a bland, if brusque man who insisted that Isabel was 'normal' and that there was nothing to worry about. He blamed the speech delay on the fact that Joyce and I spoke some Korean to Isabel at home – Joyce is Korean American and I have studied Korean – and had a Korean babysitter who spoke little English.

'Normal'. It's the word every parent wants to hear. Paediatricians are so well trained to use it that I've wondered if they get bored with it. I realise that in most cases they are right, that new parents often need reassurance, and that speech delays do sometimes occur in bilingual households. But there is that cynical side of me that imagines new paediatricians attending a training centre someplace where they learn how to look sweet, dress in Disney ties, bow ties, or scarves to look just a little ridiculous, and say things like 'He'll be *fine* so the hysterical mum will just go home.

It turns out that my cynical side is not that far off the mark. Years later, after interviewing dozens of families with autistic children in several countries, I repeatedly heard different versions of the same story – in India, South Africa, Korea, and in telephone conversations with parents in Trinidad, Croatia, Peru, Kenya, Namibia, and Venezuela. Typically, the mother is the one who brings the child to the paediatrician. He dismisses her concerns and makes her feel that she is overanxious, if not hysterical. If it is a boy, he says that boys always speak late; if it is a girl, he says she's just a polite child. Paediatricians are trained to be reassuring. But the directors of parent-run advocacy organisations will tell you that the number-one target for all their efforts in promoting autism awareness is the paediatrician.

And they are right to do so. Some paediatricians still think of autism as fairly uncommon, and they have been taught not to go searching for uncommon disorders – as the medical school saying goes, when you hear hoofbeats, look for horses, not zebras. Yet we know that the earlier autism is 'picked up', the better the potential outcome. Many paediatricians want to wait until things are really bad before giving a diagnosis – until, as one doctor told me, 'the delay is bad enough that the kid cannot do what is expected of him.' The problem is that little is expected of one- and two-year-olds, when the symptoms of autism sometimes appear, an age where paediatricians can dismiss parents' concerns because children develop at different rates.

To be fair, I also think that paediatricians are getting a bit of a raw deal. The paediatrician may say something like, 'He's probably just fine. We can't know yet if anything is wrong; for now, give your child a stimulating environment – take him to baseball games, go on a camping trip, do fun things together, and let's see how he's developing in six months.' The parents later retell the story with the bitterness of someone who has been called a liar or hysteric: 'Our paediatrician told us we should just go to a baseball game.'

Joyce did not like our first paediatrician, finding him too paternalistic. I thought the new doctor was too anxious, but Joyce had been given her name by physician colleagues, so she felt comfortable with her. 'We need to know if something is wrong with Isabel,' Joyce said. 'We need to pursue it.' The first exam proved that Isabel did not have a hearing problem (one of the first things you rule out when assessing a language delay), but the developmental checkup was inconclusive. She told us to come back in a few months. We were satisfied that she took our concerns seriously, but she certainly never used any diagnostic terms. Joyce and never talked about autism. It wasn't in the air; I didn't know anyone with autism.

We had an infant, a child with a mysterious developmental problem, and on top of it I was getting ready to come up for tenure, the make-or-break time in a professor's career, when you find out if you'll be given total, life-time job security or be fired. Joyce was working long and difficult hours as the director of the psychiatric in-patient unit at Georgetown. The stress was unbearable at times, and it took a toll on our marriage and on our relationships with our respective parents and parents-in-law.

Isabel, now 25 months old, made only fleeting eye contact. She began flapping her hands and arms occasionally and didn't respond to her name consistently. We were at a point where we demanded clarity and accuracy from doctors. A valid diagnosis of what was wrong with Isabel would be more satisfying than devastating. But neither of us thought any doctor would again tell us that Isabel was normal.

By this point, the time for Isabel's follow-up visit with the paediatrician had arrived. She noted the same symptoms we had seen but focused more on Isabel's speech. Her ability to talk, even to make sounds, had diminished since the last visit. The doctor paged Joyce at work the next day: 'I've been thinking about my exam with Isabel and I'd really like you to see a child psychiatrist who specializes in autism.' Joyce knew little about autism. In her entire psychiatric residency at Harvard's Massachusetts General Hospital, arguably the best residency in the United States, she had never once seen a case of autism.

THE PAEDIATRICIAN RECOMMENDED we see a speech pathologist at Washington Children's Hospital as well as a child psychiatrist. The speech pathologist determined that at the age of 32 months Isabel could say about 70 words, which might not sound so bad for a two-and-a-half-year-old, except that a typical child knows about 100 words by the age of two, about 500 by the age of three, and well over 1,000 by the age of four. More importantly, a typical two-year-old also uses what few words he or she knows to interact with others. Of Isabel's 70 words, all were nouns. A third were the names of *Thomas the Tank Engine* trains, a third the names of Disney characters, and the rest numbers and Korean nouns she learned from Joyce or our Korean babysitter.

The list didn't include 'mommy' and 'daddy'. Isabel was unable to create sentences or even issue commands. She couldn't tell us if she was hungry or thirsty. She couldn't even say 'yes' and 'no'. And except for pulling Joyce or me to the refrigerator when she was hungry, she didn't use gestures to communicate. Five months later, she had yet to learn a single new word. On the plus side, her articulation was great, so if she did learn language she would likely have no speech impediment, and the speech pathologist noted that Isabel seemed to be good at doing simple puzzles. Her visual and spatial memory looked strong, and this, we were told, was a sign of good intelligence.

The first child psychiatrist we saw was a disaster for us because he blamed Joyce for Isabel's autism. Joyce left his office angry, and I left feeling like I must be a horrible father. So we moved on to a child psychiatrist in Baltimore. We were lucky to be able to get these appointments, since there is a shortage of child psychiatrists in the United States.

By the time of the first meeting with our new psychiatrist, we had looked at a few books on autism and we had a strong suspicion of what was wrong with Isabel. In Baltimore, the psychiatrist sat calmly with Isabel on the floor, dolls and toys scattered around him. Isabel picked up a small, plastic brush for combing a doll's hair and started to brush the doctor's hair. Never the distant doctor observing the child like a scientist, he was engaged and comfortable with Isabel while she brushed him. He had in his office a *DSM-III-R* (*Diagnostic and Statistical Manual, Third Edition, Revised*), the current diagnostic manual at that time. He showed us the criteria for autism and related disorders, all classified under the heading of 'PDD', and then drew our attention to PDD-NOS, Isabel's diagnosis. But it seemed to me that Isabel *did* fit the criteria for autism. She couldn't make friends or communicate with words or gestures. She used repetitive speech and was preoccupied with lining things up in a row. So why didn't he say she was autistic?

He explained that while it was true that Isabel had most of the features of autism, she had them to a lesser degree than many of the other children he had seen in his years of practice as a child psychiatrist, and she showed no evidence of being mentally retarded (though the absence of mental retardation never rules out an autism diagnosis). In retrospect, I think he may have been afraid to give us a devastating diagnosis like autism when Isabel was so young and in some ways functioning at a higher level than other children he had seen. As a child psychiatrist from Fairfield County, Connecticut, told me recently: 'Things are different now. Even in the mid-90s, autism used to be like the "c" word [cancer], and I didn't use it if I didn't have to. So it was only the severe cases that got an autism diagnosis from me. The others got "PDD-NOS".'

In fact, I remember that, despite knowing little about autism, I felt happy that Isabel had PDD-NOS instead of autism. I didn't realise then that, over time, PDD-NOS would prove to be an ambiguous and cumbersome diagnosis, that it would morph into 'autism' or 'autism spectrum disorder', and that I'd rarely use the term PDD again. Today, Isabel is simply a child with 'autism'.

Isabel was enrolled in a small preschool in Chevy Chase, Maryland. Our psychiatrist recommended that we keep her there so that she could be with 'unimpaired' children, children who might serve as good social models. The topic of arranging one-on-one, intensive, in-home therapies came up only briefly. Then Joyce heard about the kind of preschool you just don't turn down, a hands-on, museum-based preschool at the Smithsonian Institution.

I remember well the mornings I brought Isabel to the Smithsonian. She used to linger outside the National Museum of American History, where her classroom was located, exploring the trees and gardens. Watching her there I realised for the first time that she had heightened visual skills. She looked around constantly, memorising everything.

On winter mornings, you could see the glow of sunrise above the Capitol building, sometimes turning the Washington Monument a light shade of orange or yellow or even purple, a colour so pale you weren't sure what it was. There are twenty-foot Saucer Magnolias around many of the museums, lindens and hollies, ginkoes and weeping birches, whose shapes and textures made Isabel stop and stare, not so she could avoid going to school, but, it seemed to me, to fix in her mind memories of the place she now spent all her days. I recall most vividly the occasional patches of *Corylus avellana* 'Contorta', one of the strangest looking trees you'll ever see. The *Corylus* branches, revealed in winter, twist and curl as if afflicted with a mysterious disease. It doesn't grow like a tree is supposed to.

Every day at the Smithsonian Early Enrichment Center the children went to at least one of the more than eighteen museums at the Smithsonian, or to nearby museums, such as the National Gallery of Art, extending across the Washington Mall. If they were supposed to learn about shapes, they went to the Hirshhorn

Museum and Sculpture Garden, the Smithsonian's museum of contemporary art, to find shapes in paintings or sculptures; if they were supposed to learn about insects, they went to the entomology department at the National Museum of Natural History. When they needed to learn about emotions – one of Isabel's most difficult tasks, largely because she didn't like to look at faces – they went to the National Portrait Gallery on a hunt for as many emotions as they could find. The Smithsonian was an ideal place for a child with strong visual and spatial skills, like Isabel, but few verbal skills. She had the opportunity to move around a lot, and she could be with unimpaired kids who modelled social behaviour for her.

I don't know for sure if the Smithsonian was the key to Isabel's development, but she started to communicate more, even if she was still socially awkward. Going out in public became more difficult for us as she began to try to interact with people – there were some embarrassing moments – but we were happy that she was interested in initiating social interactions. At Disney World in Florida, she walked up to strangers and tried to get them to repeat whatever sentence she was fixated on at the time. She would say something like, 'Mickey is a boy,' and then, 'Mickey is a _____.' She'd wait for the other person to fill in the blank, a practice she continues today with more complicated sentences. Outside a restroom near Cinderella's castle, she approached a man with a big beer belly, pointed at his stomach, and said, 'Baby inside.' He wasn't thrilled, but we applauded Isabel for using a preposition. At a hotel swimming pool, she snapped a stranger's bikini top. The woman, less good humoured than the pregnant man, lectured Joyce about being a bad mother.

Isabel would take phrases and distort them, sometimes to odd effect. One of these times – more recently – occurred after she had a blood test at a doctor's office when she was ten. She was so terrified of having her blood drawn, even a small finger prick for a typical blood count, that to do so would require several people holding her down while she screamed and flailed. As a result, we delayed one of her booster shots for two years. It was awful to see her this way, acting as if she were convinced she was about to be murdered. We got her to repeat the words 'It's just a little finger prick', in the hope that she could reassure herself. After one visit to the doctor, Joyce dropped Isabel off at my office on her way to work. The department faculty, having adjourned from a meeting, mingled in the lobby of the anthropology building as Isabel ran in crying, 'My prick is filled with blood!'

By the time Isabel was six years old and we entered the public school system, she knew about 200 words, mostly nouns and proper nouns, and was getting better at school routines. But it would be a tough and extended battle to get the school system to understand Isabel and figure out what type of classroom was most appropriate for her and how to provide it. That's a story better saved for later in this book. Any parent or guardian of a child with a disability already has an idea what that fight entails.

Our story is, in fact, a happy and hopeful one. Isabel has gone beyond what we imagined possible. She's now a teenager – a cellist, a good artist, a caring sister. She adores and takes good care of our two French bulldogs, Linnea and Natasha. She's made Joyce and me better parents, and she's made her sister, Olivia, a better, more compassionate human being. And autism doesn't seem so bad anymore, especially in comparison to the many other tragedies we read about in the newspapers every day.

We're not so embarrassed by Isabel anymore, not because she always acts appropriately in public, but because things have changed so much in American society since Isabel was born. Autism is less a disease to be hidden than a disability to be accommodated; it is less a stigma, reflecting badly on her family, than a variation of human existence. People pity me less for Isabel, and praise me more for her progress. Recently, at a shopping mall, when Isabel acted oddly, I told the cashier that Isabel had autism. The cashier repeated a romantic and popular idea whose origin remains a mystery to me. 'I've heard,' she said, 'that autistic people are supposed to be very beautiful.' I was stunned that this stranger knew about autism, let alone that she thought about autism so positively. In our community I hear not only about Isabel's achievements, but about how she contributes to the lives of others. Not long ago the parent of a 'neurotypical' ('normal') child in her grade told me that Isabel had made her son a better person, that her son had learned from Isabel that the concept of diversity isn't just a positive way to think about racial or ethnic differences, but about differences in learning and intelligence as well.

As time goes on I'm getting more comfortable with Isabel's disorder, more grateful for who she is and less mournful of the person she might have been without autism. And the difference between Isabel asleep and Isabel awake seems to be getting smaller. I'm comfortable enough now to write a book about her and about autism, something I never expected to do.

To be honest, for most of Isabel's life, I have had little to say about autism. Like most parents of children with autism, and perhaps any disability or disease, I knew enough. Enough to describe the basics to strangers when she did something embarrassing in public, enough to navigate the educational system in the county where I live, enough to convince doubting family members who insisted that, like Albert Einstein, who is said to have been speechless until the age of six, Isabel would one day outgrow her social and language problems. How much more did I really need to know?

Someone I never met changed my mind. In 1999, I began writing *In the Arms of Africa*, a biography of the anthropologist Colin Turnbull (1924–1994). A gifted writer, he made anthropology accessible to readers beyond the ivory tower, in books that were equal parts passion and science, emotion and intellect. As I wrote, I began to talk more about Isabel and autism with my students and colleagues. And the more she crept into my lecture material, the more I recognised that I, too, was trying to make anthropological perspectives understandable and relevant to a general public.

Turnbull used to say that anthropology can be a method both to convey one's personal involvement in a culture and to teach about the diversity of human experience. This book is guided by Turnbull's belief that anthropology is about much more than going away to distant cultures. It's also about coming home and seeing your own world, even your own child, in a new light. It's about finding that, in the end, the people who can teach you the most might very well be in your own backyard.

Isabel has taught me that the unexpected, even the beautiful, can emerge even from the undesirable, like a lotus growing out of the mud, its beauty and purity unsullied by its origin. That beauty can be found in a single person, inside of whom there is something – no, not something 'normal', but a brilliant light or an inner truth struggling to blossom.

So when people pity me for my daughter, I don't understand the sentiment. I work hard for Isabel, but I don't regret it or feel sorry for myself. At the end of the day, when I tuck her in, she's not a case of autism, or even a child with social deficits and language delays. She's simply my daughter. My job is to clear the land for whatever growth is to come, even if, sometimes, no one else believes it will happen, even if the growth is twisted like the *Corylus* in front of the Smithsonian.

WHEN ISABEL WAS FIRST DIAGNOSED, the experts we consulted told us that she was lucky to be alive in the 1990s, that in times past she would have been diagnosed with mental retardation or schizophrenia and institutionalised. Autism itself wasn't new, they said. What was new was the diagnosis and management of the disorder. Over the past decade, we've seen autism move from being a rare disorder to a common one. It seems like the 'epidemic' happened overnight. But it actually took decades to arrive. After all, Leo Kanner first identified and named autism way back in 1943. What did he see in the early 1940s that no one else had seen before? And why did it take so long for autism to become well known?

2

Theme and Variation

The 'Discovery' of Autism

WHEN THE AUSTRIAN DOCTOR Leo Kanner (1894–1981), the father of contemporary understandings of autism, took his first job as a psychiatrist in the United States, he had to go to an asylum. There was little else he could do. Almost all psychiatric work was done in big institutions, many of them warehouses for the 'chronically insane'. During Kanner's medical school years, the American Psychiatric Association was still called the Association of Medical Superintendents of American Institutions for the Insane.

Most of these institutions were less than 30 years old, but by 1904, two in every 1,000 Americans lived in one. By mid-century, more than 500,000 Americans lived in mental institutions, more than three in every 1,000. The patients, many of them violent and with signs of psychosis, were often locked in barren cells, strait-jacketed. Not surprisingly, they usually got worse the longer they were there. Most asylums were depressing and inhospitable, unsanitary and with poor ventilation. And the psychiatrists, working in miserable conditions and having little hope of actually helping anyone improve, questioned the goals of their discipline. Was it simply to decide who was abnormal and then separate them from society, or was it to treat people and make them productive members of society? They were demoralised and found themselves denigrated by the medical establishment as second-rate caretakers. In 1928, the psychiatrist Werner Heinz poked fun at himself and his colleagues, saying that those doctors who decided to become psychiatrists were 'afraid of failing', 'physically and intellectually inadequate'. They enjoy the asylums, he joked, because 'they stand out there less'.

This was the same period during which my grandfather, Roy R. Grinker, Sr, became a psychiatrist. His career spanned most of the 20th century, from the early 1930s to his death in 1992, and for much of that time he was, like Heinz, cynical and pessimistic about psychiatry's future. For a time, he thought the only hope for psychiatry was psychoanalysis. At least psychoanalysts tried to treat patients, usually fairly healthy patients, people who were capable of making real progress. Psychoanalysts listened, too, rather than shutting their patients away in silent cells, and they believed the patients had something important to say. In 1935, my grandfather founded the Department of Psychiatry at the University of Chicago, with an annual salary of less than $10,000, just weeks after he returned from Vienna and his expensive analysis with Sigmund Freud ($25 an hour, equivalent to $330 in today's economy, all paid for by the Rockefeller Foundation).

But there wasn't much they could do for the most severely ill patients, other than sedate them, and little would change until May 1954, the month Smith, Kline, and French introduced Thorazine, the first antipsychotic medicine. Before that time, doctors used hypnotics such as chloral hydrate and paraldehyde, or mixed them together in a colourful concoction many doctors called the 'Green River'. It wasn't metabolised by the liver, so the patients exhaled it, and because it had a fruity odour, it attracted insects. 'You would always know the patients with schizophrenia,' my grandfather told me, 'because they'd be the ones with flies buzzing around their faces.'

Leo Kanner was born Chaskel Leib Kanner, at home, to orthodox Jewish parents in a small Austrian village called Klekotow in 1894, and he would struggle with these names for the rest of his life. He hated the sound of the name Chaskel, a Yiddish version of Ezekiel. Nor did he like Leib, so he changed it to Leo. And in the United States, despite the fact that he kept telling people that Kanner should be pronounced 'Connor', only one person ever got it consistently right, a longtime Irish patient of the Phipps asylum in Baltimore who always called him 'Father O'Connor' and said he was ready to give confession. In his retirement, Kanner would often ask himself whether all the fuss over names and naming in the world was really worth it.

Kanner described his father as abnormally short, socially awkward, obsessively dedicated to Talmudic studies, and eager to absorb large amounts of useless information on just about anything in the world. Had his father lived in the 21st century, he might well have been diagnosed with Asperger's Disorder. Kanner recalled that his mother played with his father's unusual skills as if he were a toy and enjoyed having him perform his amazing memory in public. If she had a skill, it was the art of opposition. She strayed from Jewish tradition often, and eventually she placed her son in a public, non-Jewish high school, where he excelled in science but felt isolated and unusual. He was the only Jew in the school.

Kanner, his four other siblings, and their parents knew that for the children to get anywhere in life, they had to leave Klekotow. So at the age of twelve Kanner went to live with his uncle in Berlin. He was soon followed by the rest of his family. The Kanners lived simply, managing a small hotel while Leo's father became a middleman in the rag business, and lived in a small ghetto occupied by Galician immigrants.

Now that Kanner didn't live near his paternal grandparents, he visited them as often as possible. He never understood why he liked them so much, but it could be because they were as socially awkward as he and his father. They were both emotionally flat to a fault, matter of fact, seemingly incapable of showing much feeling. In later years, Kanner would remember how odd it was that their personalities and emotions seemed unchanged during and after tragedies – as when their son (Leo's uncle) was called to military duty during the First World War, or when their seventeen-year-old daughter (Leo's aunt) died from typhoid. When his grandfather died, Kanner didn't shed a tear. He wrote in his unpublished papers, now lodged at the American Psychiatric Association, that both grandparents were 'paradigms rather than real people of flesh and blood'. How can you love or mourn people, he reflected, who were almost shadows of real human beings, people whose feelings never break the surface?

So Kanner was a lonely boy raised by bizarre, unexpressive people. And he often felt himself to be on the margins of society. Is it any wonder, then, that as an adult, he would be so sensitive to the needs of the handicapped, and so acutely aware of the social deficits that would become the hallmark of autism diagnoses?

Kanner did prosper in Berlin, and, though sidetracked by military service during the First World War, he eventually went to medical school at the University of Berlin. In 1924, newly married, a freshly minted MD with no experience in psychiatry – and no specialty, for that matter – Kanner decided to go to America, largely for economic reasons. In Germany in the early 1920s, the inflation rate was so high that people tried to spend their paychecks the same day they received them: the money earned one day would be worth less the next.

In 1924, Kanner took a job as assistant physician at the State Hospital in Yankton, South Dakota, a town not much larger than

Klekotow. In a disreputable field of medicine like psychiatry, you had to start somewhere. In 1879, ten years before South Dakota became a state, the governor of Dakota Territory had selected 1,700 acres in Yankton as the site for the new hospital for the insane. It became the state hospital, with an initial population of seventeen patients, a number that rose to almost 1,300 patients by the time Kanner got there. Situated in the middle of the prairie, the hospital was a beautiful place with expansive lawns lined with petunias, gladioli, and giant cannas. The main building is still there – and it is named after Kanner – but it has little to do with psychiatry (despite being a stressful place). Today, the Kanner building is where Yankton residents get their driver's licenses renewed.

In those days, one became a psychiatrist not by doing a psychiatric residency but simply by working in a mental institution. There were no social workers, no trained nurses, just six doctors, a few dozen farmer's children who worked as attendants, and 1,300 patients. There were open cottages for the better patients, but many, such as those who were incontinent or violent, were locked in buildings that reeked with disinfectant. Kanner called it the 'snake pit', after a well-known book at the time about mental illness. He was frustrated by psychiatry's inability to treat anyone, and he was ambivalent about diagnostic labels. On the one hand, he deplored the fact that there were only a handful of diagnoses available. Unlike the nearly 300 listed in the American Psychiatric Association's manual of mental disorders today, psychiatrists had only a small number of terms to work with, such as dementia praecox (schizophrenia), manic-depressive psychosis, paranoia, senility, epilepsy, and the most popular, 'disorder undiagnosed'.

On the other hand, he disliked labelling because he found it dehumanising. In a rare burst of anger, he once stormed out of a colleague's case conference. The patient, who had hallucinations, was an anthropologist of the Near East whom Kanner referred to in his papers as 'Miss Geral'. The attending doctor said in front of the patient, 'I cannot decide if she is Praecox or Hysteria.' Kanner said in a rage, 'She's *Miss Geral*,' took her arm, and escorted her back to her room. He ranted on about how surveys named diseases and their frequency but did nothing to cure them. In an article that I do not think was ever published (it was described to me by his former colleague, Leon Eisenberg), entitled 'Surveys: No Cure-All', Kanner said that psychiatrists could count all they wanted, but in the end someone had to care for the patients.

In photographs, Leo Kanner appears an awkward man with poor posture, just slightly taller than his five-foot-two father. He's bald, looks exhausted, and has droopy eyes, resembling what I imagine Edvard Munch's subject in *The Scream* might have looked like after he finished screaming. But beneath the gawky, sad surface was a man who combined great confidence and ambition with caring, especially when it came to the welfare of children.

Kanner had reason to be sad. His father died just before the start of the Second World War, and it was to be the only natural death in the family. The Nazis shot his mother while she was napping in a rocking chair, his three sisters and their families were murdered in concentration camps, and his brother, Klias, a lawyer, committed suicide as the Nazis approached the small town in which he lived. The only survivors were Leo's sister, Dora, born while Kanner was in South Dakota, who escaped with her husband and eventually became a librarian at Hebrew University in Jerusalem, and a brother, Wolf, who fled to Shanghai, where he worked as a pharmacist for seven years before returning to Austria to become a violinist with the Viennese Philharmonic Orchestra. One wonders if Kanner's commitment to helping the disabled and marginalised came, at least in part, from his hatred of the Nazis, who wanted to exterminate the sick and disabled – or, as the Nazis themselves called them, 'life unworthy of life'.

Kanner's personality was much like his father's, defined in large part by his strange memory. He could recite by heart long poems learned in childhood by conjuring up a mental image of the exact page of text he read in school, but it was the words he was reciting, not the meaning. He could repeat the poem if asked to do so, but he wouldn't bring it up, or be able to recite it, in reference to a particular context, as when one recites a portion of a Shakespeare sonnet in a romantic gesture. I'm not saying that Kanner had autism – his social skills and his extraordinary compassion and empathy for his patients argue against such a conclusion – but he did have some traits that may have helped him identify with the patients with autism. Scientists today call these subtle traits 'subclinical'.

He used to teach courses for public school teachers who needed recertification. Once, when he and a colleague were on a street in Baltimore, a woman approached him and said, 'Dr Kanner, you'd never remember me, but I took one of those teacher's classes you gave, about ten years ago.' Kanner not only knew her name but proceeded to tell her the names of the four students who sat directly in front of and behind her and to her left and right. Leon Eisenberg, the colleague who was with him that day and who is the former chair of psychiatry at Harvard, told me, 'He's the only person without autism I've ever met with that kind of memory.'

In 1943, a New York psychoanalyst named Abram Blau wrote a paper in which he argued that whereas there were numerous words, proper and slang, for the penis, there were few words, and virtually no slang words, for the analogous organ in women, the clitoris. Based on this assumption, Blau made grand arguments about the universal symbolic importance of the penis to humanity. Kanner, as evidence-based as anyone in psychiatry at that time, was furious about Blau's assumption, based on no data collection at all, and quickly wrote a paper with the dry title 'A Philological Note on Sex Organ Nomenclature', which he published in a psychoanalytic journal. In it, Kanner listed dozens of words for the clitoris, from languages all over the world, and all of them, he claimed, from memory. He destroyed Blau's argument.

AFTER FOUR YEARS IN SOUTH DAKOTA, Kanner had earned his stripes, and more. Indeed, his brilliance and clinical skills were easy to see. His first publication was a paper on the American Indians he had treated at Yankton, one of the few state hospitals in the United States that would treat them, and it received national attention. Kanner argued that Indians didn't have as much insanity as the rest of the population, probably because the incidence of syphilis, one of the main causes of insanity in those days, was inexplicably low in Indian communities.

His observation seemed so simple in retrospect, but no one had thought of it before. That was the first sign of his clinical genius. Kanner received so much attention that the German physician Emil Kraepelin, the founder of modern scientific psychiatry – and probably the most famous psychiatrist in the world at the beginning of the 20th century – decided to visit Yankton during his trip to America. Kanner soon became a professor at the Johns Hopkins University in Baltimore, working under the Swiss psychiatrist Adolf Meyer, perhaps the most well-respected psychiatrist in the United States at that time and founder of the first child psychiatry ward in any children's hospital in the world.

Kanner is, of course, best known for describing autism, but in Maryland, where he would spend the rest of his life, many would remember him for his care of the mentally retarded. In the mid-1930s, unscrupulous lawyers had arranged for 166 mentally retarded residents of a state institution to be released, most of whom were placed as unpaid domestic servants with Baltimore families. Kanner decided to track them down.

At some level, even at such an early stage in psychiatry, he must have understood the need to avoid bias in scientific studies, and he was determined to find every one of the former residents. Through sheer hard work, he found 102 of them. Eleven had died before the age of 30, seventeen had tuberculosis or venereal disease, twenty were prostitutes, eight were in mental hospitals, and six were in prison. One woman had married three different men. The 166 had produced 165 children, many of whom were in orphanages or had died of neglect. Kanner's report made the headlines of the *Baltimore Sun* ('Scheme to Get Morons to Work in Homes Free Charged') and the *Washington Post* ('Record of Misery Traced in Freeing of Moronic Girls') and led to much greater protections for the mentally retarded.

During the mid-20th century, while doctors were advocating euthanasia for the 'feebleminded', and the Supreme Court continued to support forced sterilisation of the mentally disabled, Kanner wrote: 'Let us try to recall one single instance in the history of mankind when a feebleminded individual or group of individuals was responsible for the retardation or persecution of humaneness and science.'

In his article 'Autistic Disturbances of Affective Contact', published in 1943 and now famous, Kanner described eleven very different children (all born in the 1930s) who, he believed, were nonetheless similar, sharing something he called 'infantile autism'. But Kanner did not invent the word 'autism', and he wasn't the first to use it in psychiatry.

Coming from the Greek *autos*, meaning 'self', the term was used as an adjective by Swiss physician Eugen Bleuler in 1912 to describe the behaviour of some people, then diagnosed with schizophrenia, who were disengaged from everything except their internal world. Before Kanner, 'autistic' referred to a *symptom*, not a syndrome. Sigmund Freud talked about the word 'autistic', too. He contrasted the 'social' with what he called the 'narcissistic', but was quick to point out that by 'narcissistic' he meant the same thing as 'autistic', 'in which the satisfaction of the instincts is partially or totally withdrawn from the influence of other people'. Freud didn't like the word 'autistic' at all, but it's not clear why. He may have objected to the fact that by the early 1920s some physicians had started to use the word 'autistic' to refer to daydreams and fantasies; Freud thought the word, if it was used at all, should refer to an impairment in *social* functioning. It's amazing that Freud was so perceptive, so long ago.

Although many other features of autism would be introduced into the psychiatric literature in the decades to follow, most of Kanner's descriptions are still relevant today – a testament to his acute observation skills. This is uncanny, historian Chloe Silverman has said, since virtually all the old descriptions of any other mental disorder sound so unfamiliar and antiquated today. Kanner argued that these children were fundamentally different from people with schizophrenia. Their disorder didn't look like schizophrenia to him because they didn't seem to hallucinate or have delusions, and besides, schizophrenia rarely emerged in early childhood. But, ironically, Kanner's remarks in 1949 on the relationship between autism and schizophrenia would make it much more difficult for autism to emerge as a full-fledged and common diagnosis. He noted, 'I do not believe that there is any likelihood that early infantile autism will at any future time have to be separated from the schizophrenias.' He couldn't have been more wrong.

Large numbers of people with autism would be diagnosed as 'schizophrenic childhood type', even into the 1970s, because that was the only official category of the American Psychiatric Association in which the word 'autistic' appeared. 'Schizophrenia childhood type' included people with symptoms of autism, especially 'withdrawal' and mental retardation. Kanner believed that autism, or 'infantile autism', as he often called it, was its own distinct syndrome, but he wondered if this infantile autistic condition was a precursor to schizophrenia, early evidence of what would come later. In practice, clinicians distinguished autism from schizophrenia with the name 'infantile autism' and occasionally

'Kanner's syndrome', but the official name for autism was still 'schizophrenia'. Two of Kanner's original eleven patients had come to him after having already received a diagnosis of schizophrenia from another doctor.

Because Kanner thought his patients had had autism since birth, he refused to call their condition 'withdrawal', writing, 'It is not a "withdrawal" from formerly existing participation.' In other words, these children had never been engaged with the social world. Kanner didn't think the condition was the same as mental retardation, either, because most of the eleven children he examined had, he believed, normal or above normal intelligence. The eldest of his patients, Virginia, born in 1931, could not talk, but she achieved an IQ score of 94 on nonlanguage items of the Binet and Merrill-Palmer intelligence tests. The psychologist who did the testing wrote, 'Without a doubt her intelligence is superior to this.' Another child, Alfred, spoke rarely, and when he did he confused his pronouns and repeated the same sentences over and over with the same inflection. Nonetheless, a psychologist was able to complete a Binet IQ test with him. Alfred received a score of 140. Anything over 140 is considered near genius. Kanner wrote of the eleven, 'They are all unquestionably endowed with good cognitive potentialities,' and he frequently used the word 'intelligent' to describe them as a group.

KANNER BEGAN HIS DESCRIPTION this way. 'Since 1938, there have come to our attention a number of children whose condition differs so markedly and uniquely from anything reported so far, that each case merits – and, I hope, will eventually receive – a detailed consideration of its fascinating peculiarities.' These were indeed unusual children, but there were many more he excluded from his article. The group he excluded comprised many children with symptoms of autism but who also had seizures or were mentally retarded.

Kanner was interested in defining a new syndrome, so he needed to set the boundaries of what would and would not qualify as autism. From the perspective of 21st-century psychiatry, his definition of autism was quite narrow. Today we know that about half of all people with autism are mentally retarded and that about a quarter of children with autism, mainly those who are more severely impaired, develop seizure disorders in their teens. But to anyone else, it might have looked as if the criteria for autism were broad. The children he included in his syndrome were extraordinarily diverse. Any other psychiatrist would have called the nonverbal children in Kanner's group mentally retarded or brain damaged, and the few that were verbal might have been diagnosed with schizophrenia.

All eleven of the patients described in Kanner's report had difficulty relating to other people, a condition Kanner called 'extreme autistic aloneness'. This was, for Kanner, the determining feature of autism. In addition, most of the children had speech delays or unusual language (they echoed what they heard, or they reversed pronouns, using 'you' when they should use 'I'), had fantastic rote memories, and had an obsession with sameness and repetition. Most were highly skilled at one or two tasks, such as classifying animals or memorising addresses or train schedules. He saw these similarities where others might have only seen the differences.

His first patient, born in 1933, was named Donald. Donald had a great memory even at the early age of twelve months, and as he grew he became even more precocious, learning to recite the 23rd psalm when he was two. At two and a half, he could name all the presidents and vice presidents of the United States forwards and backwards. He had the kind of unusual memory that doctors in late 19th-century France had called 'hyperamnesia', but this extraordinary memory was seen as an impairment as much as a skill.

His parents noted that Donald was happiest when alone, didn't ask or answer questions, and didn't engage in conversation. By the time he was four, Donald made stereotyped movements with his fingers, shook his head from side to side, whispered to himself, and arranged and spun objects on the floor. When Kanner met Donald, then five years old, he couldn't get him to make eye contact. Donald occasionally used language pragmatically, but only the same exact phrases, and he asked the people he spoke with to say exactly what he wanted them to say. For example, he said to his mother, 'Say "Don, do you want to get down [from the bed]?"' His mother would say the phrase, and then Don would say, 'Now say "All right",' and his mother would say it. He was clearly bright, performing mathematical calculations, but in odd ways. If his mother asked him 'What is 10 minus 4?' he would draw a hexagon.

Frederick, six years old when Kanner met him, was withdrawn as well, but he was very different from Donald. Frederick could make only unintelligible sounds, showing no sign of awareness that there were adults around to talk and play with him.

Richard, age three, was presumed deaf. Like most of the other eleven children, he was thought deaf because he neither talked nor responded to questions. And, like many of the others, he showed signs of normal cognitive development – or at least this is what the parents retrospectively argued – until he was about two. Then, as his mother wrote to Kanner, 'It seems that he has gone backward mentally gradually for the last two years. We have thought it was because he did not disclose what was in his head, that it was there all right. Now that he is making so many sounds, it is disconcerting because it is now evident that he can't talk ... He gave the impression of silent wisdom to me.' By the time Kanner saw Richard he didn't speak to people and made only short staccato sounds, such as 'Ee! Ee! Ee!'

Barbara, eight years old when she arrived at Johns Hopkins, had an ordinary spoken vocabulary at age two but excelled at spelling, reading, and writing. She seemed unable to comprehend the principles of basic mathematics, though she could perform mathematical calculations by memory. With seemingly no desire to please anyone, she only passively agreed to do some psychological tests, playing with her hands and tongue throughout. Barbara read beautifully, at the level of a ten-year-old, but couldn't answer any questions about what she had read. She liked to draw, but her drawings were stereotyped, with no evidence of imagination, significantly different from what a typical eight-year-old would produce. How could she and a mute child like Richard be classified with the same disorder?

Richard, a boy named Herbert, and a girl named Virginia were all mute, but seven others articulated their words precisely. The problem was that they didn't use language to convey meaning. The parents, so pleased that their children could repeat numbers, nursery rhymes, prayers, lists of animals, or even songs in foreign languages, grew discouraged when it became clear that their children could do little with language beyond naming, memorising, and echoing what other people said. None of them could consistently use pronouns correctly. A child might ask for milk by saying, 'Do you want milk?' because that is exactly what he heard his mother say.

Now if Kanner had seen just one of these patients, he might not have been so interested. But this was another story – eleven patients, eight boys and three girls, all so different – some quite verbal and some mute – yet all socially and linguistically impaired. It was certainly worth a case report. Kanner saw each child as a unique individual – a function of the fact that his teacher, Adolf Meyer, had insisted on studying the whole person – yet he recognised that they seemed to have something in common. It wasn't mental retardation, epilepsy, or any obvious neurological disease. It was something else, something yet to be named. And given how different these children were, it took an extraordinary observer like Kanner to find their shared features and see an overall shape to their variations rather than just an arbitrary collection of symptoms.

In retrospect, it seems that his task was actually very simple. All the children shut out or ignored anything that impinged on their aloneness. And when each set of parents thought back to their child's infancy, they recognised that isolation in subtle absences. When Barbara was an infant, for example, she never seemed to change her position or look up when her parents approached her crib. This is something even four-month-old babies do. But, like 16th-century anatomists who never noticed there were valves in our veins, even though they were right in front of their eyes, all the other doctors completely missed autism. They weren't looking for it. They didn't have a reason to. Or perhaps they simply didn't have the autistic-like traits that Kanner had inherited from his grandfather and father – and thus, the particular lens through which he viewed these patients. When Kanner looked at these children, he saw a version of himself.

In addition to the social isolation of these children, Kanner noted in all of them an 'anxiously obsessive desire for the maintenance of sameness that nobody but the child himself may disrupt'.

They hated changes in routine, in the arrangement of furniture, or even the path taken from one place to another. Many would eat only a small number of different foods, refusing to try new foods or even to accept the same foods prepared in different ways. There were also sensory problems. Most of the children were highly sensitive to particular noises, such as running water or the sound of a toilet flushing.

Finally, the children were all concrete thinkers. In fact, no matter how intelligent someone on the autism spectrum might be, he or she probably has difficulty with abstract or symbolic thought. Their strengths are visual and concrete rather than verbal and conceptual. They might do wonders with an abacus, but they are unable to apply mathematical principles to a real-life situation. In Lima, Peru, a few years ago, the police launched a massive search for a missing teenage girl with autism named Carmen. An autistic boy from her school ran down the street to the police yelling, 'I found Carmen! I found Carmen!' He hadn't actually seen her. He was holding a photograph of her he'd found in the classroom. The concrete thinker is not unlike the famous Mr Spock from *Star Trek*. In a risky situation, if Captain Kirk used the expression, 'If we play our cards right … ' Spock would ask, 'Why do you want to play cards?'

Today, as I read Kanner's vivid descriptions of the eleven children, written in 1943, I see my own daughter on almost every page. Though I thought Isabel was developing normally until the age of two, a look back at our home videos shows how little eye contact she made in infancy and how seldom she tried to communicate with us. Even today, she plays the same way, finding and maintaining sameness wherever she can, whether it is by repeatedly drawing the same picture over and over again, or rewinding a video or DVD to watch the same fragment of a scene multiple times.

She is reluctant to try new foods, and she's able to discern the smallest change in the way I prepare something. When we were in Spain, we had to hoard and bring packets of Heinz ketchup from McDonald's to other restaurants, since the Spanish brand of ketchup tasted different. The sound of a toilet flushing caused her so much discomfort that we had to get new toilets, trying out every one until we found one that made a sound Isabel could handle. She gets upset if I wake her up in the morning using any words but the same repeated pair, 'Get up, get up'. And she's so concrete that if I forget myself and say something like, 'I'm so tired I could die', she becomes terrified that I am, in fact, going to die. Fortunately, she has now learned to ask, 'Is that just an expression?' And, like Donald, who answered mathematical questions by drawing pictures, she insists on making indirect connections. On a social studies exam, the teacher asked, 'Who invaded France after Charlemagne's death?' The correct answer was 'The Vikings'. Isabel wrote, 'Daunte Culpepper' and stood by her answer, despite the teacher's protest. Daunte Culpepper was the quarterback of the Minnesota Vikings.

Kanner's ability to see shared features in this diverse group of children is truly remarkable, and his basic definition of autism still holds today. But he erred by excluding many children – such as children with mental retardation and epilepsy – from the diagnosis because they didn't fit into a coherent pattern. Kanner didn't think people with autism were either mentally retarded or had seizures (despite the fact that one of his original eleven patients with autism, John F, did have seizures).

He also made a crucial public relations error that made it difficult for psychiatrists to accept autism as a distinct syndrome. He ended his article by saying that autism was a biological disorder: 'We must, then, assume that these children have come into the world with innate inability to form the usual, biologically provided affective contact with people, just as other children come into the world with innate physical or intellectual handicaps … For here we seem to have pure-culture examples of *inborn autistic disturbances of affective contact*' (emphasis in original).

How many psychiatrists were going to listen to something so ridiculous? For one thing, with almost every psychiatrist under the sway of psychoanalytic thought in the 1940s, believing that nearly every mental disorder was caused by psychological disturbances, Kanner's hypothesis had little chance of being accepted. For another, psychiatrists thought that if a mental illness was caused by biology and genetics it was untreatable, while psychogenic illnesses, those caused by psychological disturbances, could be treated with psychotherapy, virtually the only treatment at the time. They weren't likely to believe that autism or any other mental illness was untreatable because that would make psychiatry irrelevant.

So the answer to the question, 'Was Kanner seeing a new disorder?' has to be answered both yes and no. Yes, it was new, because no one had ever noticed how such varied characteristics fit together into a single pattern. Kanner gave it a name and made it a syndrome. But no, it was not new, because the symptoms were probably as old as humanity.

PEOPLE SOMETIMES ASK ME: 'If there is no autism epidemic, then where were all the autistic children before now?' Older friends and colleagues say, 'I know children with autism now, and I see them at the shopping mall or on the street, but I never saw them before. Where did they come from?' My first reaction is to ask: 'Well, where were all the people with schizophrenia and bipolar disorder before *those* categories were constructed?' Autism is new because over the past century we've described mental disorders more precisely, differentiating one from another, and giving them names.

So did autism exist before it had a name? Yes, in the sense that there were people who, today, we would call autistic; no, in the sense that the concept of autism as a distinct illness didn't exist and so we didn't see it. We saw epilepsy or schizophrenia, mental retardation or brain dysfunction, but not autism. Autism also exists today without a name. There are still cultures in the world today that do not have a name for autism, or that do not even see as pathological the symptoms we call autistic; there are the so-called 'marvellous children' of Senegal, called 'Nit-ku-bon', or the Navajo Indian children with autism in the American Southwest, who are seen simply as perpetual children.

The cluster of symptoms we now know as autism has probably been around for a long time, but no one really knows for sure. And even assuming that there were such people, no one knows how many there were. Maybe the best way to explore the idea of autism in history is to ask whether, if we could travel back in time to the 19th century or earlier, we would find people who fit our current diagnostic criteria.

It is difficult, if not impossible, to make diagnoses from historical evidence, but it's worth discussing briefly some of the evidence for autism in the distant past, if only to note that aspects of what we call autism today existed long before the invention of modern psychiatry. Several hundred years ago in Europe, there were people who exhibited symptoms we can now associate with autism. However, what we have are stories, some of them fanciful, and it is difficult to know if any of the descriptions are accurate.

In the Middle Ages, we find tales of alien children found in forests or hiding in ditches. There were the 'green children', for example, a boy and girl described by William of Newburgh in 12th-century England. He said their skin was green, they could

not communicate, and they didn't know how to follow social customs. The British psychologist Uta Frith has described the 13th-
century legend of the Little Flower of St Francis. In this story there
is a character named Brother Juniper who cannot understand that
people might have an opinion that differs from his, a hallmark of
autism. So when, for example, he commits a crime by cutting off
the foot of a pig to give to someone who is ill and hungry, he joy-
fully confesses to everyone who confronts him, and with no sense
of regret; he is repeatedly asked why he cut off the pig's foot, but
since he thinks concretely, like someone with autism, all he can do
is simply recall the steps he took to cut it off.

There are many records in Russia, from the 16th through the
19th centuries, of so-called 'blessed fools', children and adults who
were preoccupied with repetitive behaviours, needed to be confined so they didn't wander away, and had seizures. They were
often mute, and if not mute were echolalic (repeating back verba-
tim whatever they heard, but not initiating independent speech)
or spoke gibberish. Frith noted that in those days 'blessed' really
meant 'feebleminded' or 'innocence in the eyes of God'. There is
the case of Pelagija Serebrenikova, who, in 16th-century Russia,
was, like many other mentally retarded or mentally ill people at that
time, considered to be the 'village idiot', but was also seen more
positively as a blessed or holy fool. When Pelagija was not chained
down, she carried rocks to the river and threw them in one by
one. Then she'd go into the water, remove the rocks, and start all
over again. But because she was 'blessed', she wasn't expected to
follow all the conventional rules of society. The fact that many of
the blessed fools had seizures, Frith pointed out, suggests that they
had autism rather than schizophrenia, since the frequency of seizures in schizophrenia is relatively low.

But the reality is that there is little we can do to find out about
autism or other childhood-onset mental disorders in pre-19th-

century Europe. Majia Nadeson, a historian of autism, noted that because children weren't usually admitted to European asylums, scientists had few opportunities to observe and document their symptoms. In addition, until the 19th century, when public schools expanded in Europe, most children did not attend school, perhaps the best place to compare children with each other. So it wouldn't have been easy for scientists to identify children who deviated from a norm, even if they had wanted to. But perhaps most importantly, until the 20th century Europeans and Americans accepted or even indulged eccentric children, especially if there was a social or economic role they could play in their communities.

However, symptoms of autism can be seen as well in the small industry of books and articles about wild or feral children published over the past 200 years. We now know that few or none of these children were actually wild or lived with animals. Yet, many societies believe in feral children. As of this writing, there is even an elaborate website called feralchildren.com that provides a lengthy list of children thought to have been raised by animals, or at least to have spent a significant amount of their early childhood alone in nature. The most famous cases include Wild Peter, found in what is today Germany in 1724; Victor, whose story was depicted in Francois Truffaut's famous film *L'Enfant Sauvage*; Kaspar Hauser, found in 1828 in Nuremberg; and the girls Kamala and Amala (possibly sisters), found together in 1920 in a forest in India.

It is also intriguing that Linnaeus, who in the 18th century established himself as the father of scientific classification, included in his scheme of things a feral child from Hesse, found in 1344; the Lithuanian 'bear-boy', found in 1661; and an Irish 'sheep-boy', found in 1672. He listed these children under the category *Loco ferus*, with subtypes that included *mutus* (mute) and *hirsutus* (hairy). Many such creatures were displayed in carnival atmospheres all the way into the modern age, when other 'exotics', such as the so-called Bushmen and Pygmies of Africa, were displayed at World's Fairs. We only know about these children through a few historical documents, explorers' reports, and folktales, but there is reason to believe that most, if not all, of the children who appeared to have been raised by animals were children with autism who had lived for perhaps just a few days in the wild before being discovered.

If they did have autism, they were probably abandoned by their parents (although severe emotional deprivation cannot cause autism, autism can motivate parents to abandon their children). They were then found a short time later, appearing so dirty that the discoverers assumed they must have been alone for years, raised by animals. (Curiously, of the 105 cases of feral children that I found reported in the press or in the literature of earlier times, 73 were boys and 32 were girls, a sex ratio not totally out of line with what we might expect in a random sampling of about 100 autistic children.)

There is also early evidence of autism from science. Darold Treffert from the University of Wisconsin is certain that autism is not a new disorder, but that it was in the past simply subsumed under the categories used for mental retardation, such as 'feeble-mindedness or 'idiocy'. He supports his view with the descriptions of what the British doctor J. Langdon Down called 'idiot savants' in 1887 (from the French *savoir*, 'to know'). Down, after whom scientists named the chromosomal disorder Down syndrome, wrote about a variety of different 'feebleminded' children, so-called savants, who had great musical, artistic, or mathematical skills. One child, according to Down, was clearly mentally retarded but had memorised large portions of Gibbon's *The Rise and Fall of the Roman Empire*. (Such people exist today, and have a diagnosis of autism. Leslie Lemke, at fourteen, blind and with cerebral palsy, played Tchaikovsky's Piano Concerto No. 1 perfectly after hearing it once on television; he is a virtuoso pianist despite never having taken a lesson. Kim Peek, the man on whom the character of Raymond Babbitt in the 1988 film *Rain Man* was based, has memorised, among other things, 7,600 books.)

What most intrigued Treffert about J. Langdon Down's patients was the group that didn't seem to fit easily into any category. These were children who did not have what was thought to be the physical appearance of someone with mental retardation (and many appeared to have normal intelligence), and whose deficits didn't seem to have been present from birth, and weren't caused by an accident, a problem during labour, or some other physical trauma. Down termed their disorders 'developmental'.

The children Down described often developed normally and then regressed, losing speech and what he termed 'mental growth'. Some seemed to understand language but couldn't respond. When they did talk, they confused pronouns, even talking about themselves in the third person. These children were strikingly similar to the group of children with autism we're familiar with today, who are sometimes diagnosed with 'autism with regression'. Another group of children that Down called 'developmentally disordered' didn't regress. They had been disordered from the start, moved their hands or fingers in stereotyped and repetitive ways, and were, he said, 'beautiful'. Of them, Down wrote: 'Living in a world of their own they are regardless of the ordinary circumstances around them, and yield only to the counter-fascination of music.' These children also fit into our modern conception of autism. But despite calling these children's deficits 'developmental', Down continued to classify them as mentally retarded.

As recently as the 1908 publication of the first of what would become eight editions of Alfred Tredgold's classic *Textbook of Mental Deficiency*, many of the serious mental disorders we know today were lumped into a small number of categories, including 'idiocy', 'lunacy', 'insanity', or 'feeblemindedness'. These, in turn, were part of a larger category of 'defectives'. The tenth edition (1963), edited by R.F. Tredgold and K. Soddy, outlined three grades of deficiency, ranked from most to least severe: idiots, imbeciles, and the feeble-minded. Well into the mid-20th century, the term 'feebleminded' was used in England to refer to someone with a below average IQ – uneducable, but still able to work in some capacity. The American equivalent to the British 'feebleminded' was the term 'moron'. Tredgold described children who were seemingly normal after the first year of life, but who then became remote and unresponsive to their environment and often mentally retarded. They exhibited repetitive, obsessional behaviour, sometimes giving the appearance of a 'fantastic ballet'. The children ritually touched objects and seemed abnormally attached to objects or parts of objects – for example, they might play with a single wheel of a wagon rather than the whole wagon. The descriptions are consistent with what we today call autism.

WHILE KANNER WAS HARD AT WORK writing his famous 1943 article, another description of autism emerged independently in Kanner's own homeland. Hans Asperger, another Austrian, was examining autistic children and used the word 'autism' to describe them. Asperger, from whom we get the name for Asperger's Disorder (one of the autism spectrum disorders), saw something in these children that he termed 'autistic psychopathy in childhood'. He called them 'autistic psychopaths'.

The two psychiatrists never met. Asperger (who published in German) and Kanner (who published in English) apparently knew nothing of each other, perhaps because of the absence of communication between the United States and Austria during the Second World War. Asperger apparently did little work on the subject after his lab was destroyed by Allied bombing. It's too bad because he, much more than Kanner, believed that autism was a spectrum, and it took another 35 years for the idea of the spectrum to take off in the United States and the United Kingdom.

Asperger (1906–1980), twelve years younger than Kanner, was born in Vienna and, like so many child psychiatrists then and today, became a paediatrician first and a psychiatrist second. Kanner and Asperger were similar in several ways. They were both educated in the same German medical tradition. Both were influenced more by the classifier and empiricist Kraepelin than by Freud, so they were more interested in describing disorders than in trying to find their elusive causes. They were also both described by their families and peers as loners.

From the start, Asperger was convinced that autism was the result of a complex interplay between biological (genetic) and environmental factors. 'Predisposition,' he wrote, 'is not fate but rather a possible fate.' But he tended to side with biology. He was confident that future studies would show that 'the autistic personality is neither biologically nor genetically related to schizophrenia'.

Kanner's life story suggests the reasons why he was able to see a single syndrome in a diverse group of children. They were a reflection of a part of himself. But how was Asperger able to see it too? And why did they see it at the same time?

Child psychiatry was emerging on both continents simultaneously, and it was a mixture of medical and educational theories. In Austria, there was a field called 'remedial pedagogy', a totally different enterprise than just remedial education. It was about using medical research to describe and then treat learning disorders. Kanner, working under Adolf Meyer, and Asperger, working in a biologically based paediatric clinic, didn't get caught up in Freudian psychology. They didn't even use common Freudian terms like 'id'', 'ego', and 'superego'. In Asperger's clinic, the doctors didn't distinguish between psychotherapy and education; they were one and the same. Asperger simply seemed fascinated with people, especially boys, who weren't severely affected by mental illness but still were, somehow, abnormal.

We know a lot less about Asperger's life and personality than Kanner's, but we do know that Asperger had become involved with supervising boys' groups and camps – the Austrian equivalents of Boy Scouts – and this made him interested in figuring out why some boys didn't join. Who, he wondered, were the misfits, and what was wrong with them?

Today, most mental health professionals think that Kanner and Asperger were treating different kinds of patients. Kanner's name is associated with the classic, severe form of autism. Asperger's is associated with more mildly autistic, or at least highly intelligent and highly verbal, children. In the late 20th century, researchers in child development started calling Asperger's kind of patient 'little professors', children with enormous vocabularies and a mature taste in art. As Asperger put it, in the context of art, 'Autistic individuals can judge accurately the events represented in the picture, as well as what lies behind them, including he character of the people represented and the mood that pervades a painting.' To paraphrase: These 'abnormal' children had a skill for appreciating visual media that most 'normal' adults never achieve. 'Asperger's Disorder' would eventually denote not just a higher functioning form of autism but a distinct kind of higher functioning autism; in other words, most children with Asperger's are higher functioning, but not all children who are higher functioning have Asperger's.

In his 1944 article describing the syndrome, '"Autistic Psychopathy" in Childhood', Asperger said that four children between the ages of six and eleven seen in his clinic looked like 'they had just fallen to earth', that despite being highly intelligent and highly verbal, they rarely made eye contact and were teased and bullied at school. Some had small movement disturbances, such as walking on their tiptoes. Their skills were intellectual in nature. So, for example, Asperger described a young boy so infatuated with chemistry that he spent all his money on experiments; another who, as a freshman in college, noticed an error in Isaac Newton's calculations; and yet a third whose fascination with building and taking apart model spaceships took him away from any social life and even, Asperger believed, reality.

There are some important differences between the children described by Asperger and Kanner. Kanner had noted in his descriptions that autistic children were good with objects, meticulously arranging them, whereas Asperger said that his patients were generally clumsy. Asperger's patients were more exceptional in their mathematical and verbal skills. In fact, today, many psychiatrists think that 'Kanner's autism' (usually called 'autistic disorder') and Asperger's Disorder represent two different phenotypes on a continuum of social deficits. So if Kanner was the father of autism as a diagnostic category, Asperger was the father of the concept of the autism spectrum.

In many ways, however, Asperger's and Kanner's patients seem more similar than different. Asperger presented only four patients in his famous article on 'autistic psychopathy', all of whom were quite verbal. Two performed complex mathematical calculations at a young age. Yet because of their behavioural problems, Asperger found it difficult, if not impossible, to do accurate intelligence testing on them. If you look beyond their islands of 'intelligence', you find that the children were just as socially impaired as any of Kanner's cases. They were just as 'unmanageable' in school, had poor eye gaze, and exhibited unusual repetitive behaviours. Six-year-old Fritz, for example, spoke 'like an adult' in early childhood and was highly skilled at mathematics, but was referred to Asperger's hospital after the local school considered him to be 'uneducable'. He did not play with other children, he beat rhythmically on his thighs, and he banged tables, hit walls or other people, threw himself into puddles, licked tables, and played with his spit. He ate whole pencils. Nevertheless, educators, clinicians, and the media today present 'Asperger's Disorder' as a very 'high-functioning' form of autism.

The most important feature of children with Asperger's Disorder is that they do not have delayed speech. In fact, they sometimes talk too much. But they do have a lot of trouble communicating and interacting socially, in large part because they have highly circumscribed interests and do not seem to care if anyone else shares the interest. Children with Asperger's Disorder are often very intelligent, and they are certainly knowledgeable about the one or two subjects they like.

One child I know, a nine-year-old boy named Andrew, talks about medieval castles and has difficulty stopping, even when you walk away from him. When in public – on an airplane, at a concert, or in a restaurant – he cannot tolerate sitting next to anyone but his mother or father. When I interviewed his family recently in Wisconsin, we went to a 1950s style diner, in which the only seats available were at the counter. He walked up to the few people eating there and said, while looking down to his left away from the counter, 'Excuse me, ladies and gentlemen, I would appreciate it if you would move because I do not like sitting next to strangers.' That kind of action may not seem typically 'autistic'. His verbal abilities far exceed anything my daughter Isabel – or almost anyone with classic autism – is capable of. But he has just as much trouble communicating effectively. Both have strikingly similar social impairments, and neither can talk about abstractions. Andrew and Isabel both lack imagination, have highly restricted interests, and are preoccupied with a small number of behaviours or forms of play.

These children, like most on the autism spectrum, also have deficits in empathy, or what is sometimes called 'theory of mind', defined by autism specialist Simon Baron-Cohen as the ability 'to infer the full range of mental states (beliefs, desires, intentions, imagination, emotions, etc.) that cause action'. To use Baron-Cohen's examples, someone on the autism spectrum would not be able to comprehend that Little Red Riding Hood thinks that her grandmother is in the bed when it's really the wicked wolf, or that Snow White thinks the old woman is giving her a good apple when it's really poison. Neither Kanner nor Asperger used the contemporary phrase 'theory of mind', but their subjects had difficulty understanding that other people might have different thoughts than they had. Whether the absence of theory of mind should be a criterion for autism, or is exclusive to autism spectrum disorders, is debatable (the American Psychiatric Association does not list it as a criterion). I'm certainly confused about what theory of mind means and whether it can be learned. I've spent hours trying to help Isabel develop it, even on occasion teaching her how to lie, because if she could lie she'd have learned that two people can have different ideas about the same thing.

Kanner's descriptions became much more well-known than Asperger's much more quickly, perhaps because he wrote in English, and by the early 1950s, mental health professionals had started conducting research on autism and had published dozens of articles. Lorna Wing, a British expert on autism – and the parent of a child with autism – introduced Asperger's work to an English-language audience in 1981, changing the name from 'psychopathy' to 'Asperger Syndrome'. As a result, there were few publications on Asperger's Disorder until the 1980s, and the American Psychiatric Association didn't even formally recognise the disorder until 1994.

In addition to introducing the world to Asperger's observations, Wing presented cases from her own practice to corroborate the existence of a distinct syndrome. But her great contribution was to show that Asperger's patients, while all similar in terms of their social impairments, exhibited a range of deficits. The patients were the empirical evidence that Asperger syndrome was related to autism on a broad spectrum.

Since Wing's original 1981 publication, there has been a tremendous amount of debate about the validity and reliability of criteria for Asperger's Disorder, much of it centring on the question of how to distinguish it from 'autism'. But most researchers today agree with Wing that autism is best conceived as a spectrum of problems. For it seemed to Wing that the core features of autism – a triad of impairments in social interaction, communication, and imagination (with repetitive interests and activities) – occurred in a wide range of people. And when they did occur, they were so variable in their severity that one person with autism might be profoundly mentally retarded and totally nonverbal while another might be a physics professor.

Like the colour spectrum, in which there is no clear-cut division between, say, red and orange, or blue and purple, the autism spectrum offers no obvious borders between different kinds of people with autism. Human beings, and especially scientists, are classifiers, so we're compelled to break up the spectrum into seemingly discontinuous segments, like individual colours, and we name them PDD or autism or Asperger's Disorder, or even high-functioning and low-functioning, mildly impaired, or severely impaired. This doesn't mean that those diseases actually exist as separate entities. It simply means that the classification helps us in some way to explain what autism encompasses. Already, researchers are beginning to talk about 'autisms' rather than 'autism', and it is likely that new autism spectrum disorders will be described in the near future to reflect different deficits. As two experts in the field, Michael Rutter and Eric Schopler, put it, 'There is no one basic deficit because the disorder reflects varying patterns of organic brain dysfunction rather than any single disease state.'

The idea of the spectrum was validated by a series of family studies conducted in England by Lorna Wing and Sir Michael Rutter, most published during the late 1970s and early 1980s. Their scientific papers described what were called 'autistic probands', a kind of genetic loading of autism in families that resulted in the presence of variants of autism among relatives. Some relatives might have severe symptoms, like mutism, whereas others were aloof or simply socially awkward.

Silicon Valley is alarmed about Asperger's Disorder. Steve Silberman, a journalist who wrote a widely read article in 2001 in the magazine *Wired* called 'The Geek Syndrome', suggested that the high-technology industry is filled with people with Asperger's Disorder. Bill Gates is one of the most common recipients of the diagnosis in everyday conversation. There is no scientific evidence that rates of Asperger's Disorder are higher in any particular geographical area, profession, or socioeconomic cluster, but the anecdotal reports are compelling. At George Washington University, where I teach, the professors have fun guessing which of the physicists and mathematicians they know are autistic.

Boys with Asperger's Disorder – and they outnumber girls by about ten to one – tend to excel at mathematics and have a superb systematising ability. According to the psychologist Simon Baron-Cohen, systematising can be defined as the 'drive to understand a system and to build one', systems like maths, computers, astronomy, music, anything governed by a finite, limited set of laws – even bus routes and sports rules constitute systems. Universities, Baron-Cohen noted, are great places for autistic systematisers to live and work, because the social eccentricities of physics and maths professors cause few problems in that setting. He thinks that some of the men of history who had great minds – and made great contributions, like Einstein and Newton – may have been autistic, even though typically people with a diagnosis of autism who are capable of doing mathematical calculations are incapable of applying the mathematics to real-world situations.

The same holds true in Silicon Valley and major research institutions, places loaded with systematisers. The well-known writer with autism, Temple Grandin, has called NASA 'the largest sheltered workshop in the world'. We could throw out lots of other names for speculation too, like the chess champion Bobby Fischer or Vincent van Gogh. These famous figures were alienated and socially awkward. They were insensitive to the subtleties of human expression, finding it difficult to tell the difference between truth and humour, between honest expressions and sarcasm, between a normal contraction of the eyelid, a blink, a knowing wink, or a facial tic.

Because many people with Asperger's Disorder are indeed intelligent, they sometimes go undiagnosed; and if they are diagnosed, it happens later than in classic autism, because they do not have delayed speech and are not mentally retarded. One of my eighteen-year-old college students was diagnosed with Asperger's Disorder when he was sixteen. Still, many children with Asperger's Disorder can be just as impaired and socially disabled as someone with classic autism. A psychiatrist I know has a brother with Asperger's Disorder who is quite verbal but so socially impaired that he cannot work. He received the diagnosis when he was in his mid-30s. At first, the oversight occurred because the diagnosis of Asperger's Disorder didn't exist; once it did, it took years before anyone thought of diagnosing him with it. Oddly, in retrospect, no one – not his parents, his child psychiatrist brother, or any of his doctors – made the connection.

THERE IS NO EASY ANSWER to the question of whether the concept of autism should be more or less inclusive. Big, popular, inclusive categories like 'autism' can be good for advocacy, awareness, and acceptance. But they can also mask variations and lead, at times, to a 'one size fits all' approach to a group of distinct disorders. If he were alive today, Kanner would probably object to how inclusive a category autism has become.

The subcategories of autism are beneficial, however, because the spectrum has grown so much that it can be hard to keep track of who belongs on it. And the more we learn about the various manifestations of any given phenomenon, the more likely we are to produce new words and categories to describe them. The Lese and Efe people, with whom I lived in central Africa, have only three colour words: red, black, and white. They see all the colours the human eye is capable of seeing, but they have no reason to invent more colour categories. Pink, orange, and dark yellows are called red; brown, green, blue, and purple are black; and very light colours are white. If they need to be more specific they might say, 'white like a banana', or 'black like a leaf', and everyone knows what they're talking about. Psychiatric classification is similar: We used to have just a few words for mental illnesses – almost everything was schizophrenia, mania, hysteria, neurosis, or senile dementia. Those categories, as they used to be defined, were large enough to encompass most psychiatric symptoms. Today we have hundreds of diagnoses, but it's not because people have hundreds of psychiatric symptoms they never had before. It's because the science of the mind, brain, and behaviour – and our educational systems, more attuned than ever to individual differences – demand specificity.

I'm amazed by how often families of people with autism use the same scenario to explain the similarities and differences in autism: They say that if you walk into a room filled with people with autism, the first thing you notice is how similar everyone is; the second thing you notice is how different they are from each other. It's like the way you see a pair of identical twins when you first meet them, on the one hand, and the way you view them once you get to know them, when their distinctive features come to light, on the other. I think the reason this statement about autism resonates so much with the families I've met is that they want to see the autistic person as an individual rather than a disease. This is the sentiment Leo Kanner so bravely expressed during the public diagnosis of 'Miss Geral' in Yankton. Spend enough time with two people who have autism, and you will find countless differences between them; spend enough time with one person with autism, and you will find a unique personality, someone with likes and dislikes, his or her own temperament, and his or her own sense of humour. And in making these observations of variations on a theme, you will be doing exactly what Leo Kanner and Hans Asperger once did.

Neither Kanner nor Asperger truly *discovered* autism. They *described* it. Autism wasn't a new disorder, born in the 1930s. Like virtually all disorders it didn't emerge and get observed, described, and named all at the same time.

Kanner and Asperger got autism into the scientific literature, and they did so at a time when psychoanalysis was still the dominant mode of psychological thought. Would anyone listen to them? As it turns out, many experts did listen, but what they chose to hear wouldn't help children with autism or their families. In fact, it made their lives worse.

3

Stigma, Shame, and Secrets

IT WAS SOMETIME DURING THE WINTER OF 2001.

'Is this the Grinker residence?' the woman on the telephone asked. 'I'm Mrs. J, a parent at Ivymount calling about the school auction.'

I said, 'I don't have a child who goes to Ivymount, but I know the school. It's a great school for kids with autism, right?'

The woman on the telephone was flustered and quickly corrected herself. 'Oh! I said the wrong school name. I meant Woodcrest. Your daughter Olivia goes there, right?'

Now she had it right, but she felt she'd made a terrible mistake.

'I misspoke. I do have a son at Ivymount,' she said, 'and another child at Woodcrest, but no one at Woodcrest knows about him. Please keep this confidential. It's not something I share with people.'

Here was a well-educated, well-liked, stay-at-home mother from Washington, DC, trying to keep her son a secret.

AS I THOUGHT ABOUT THE PHONE CALL, I began to sympathise with Mrs. J. Raising a child with autism is difficult, and even more difficult when parents try to include their children in community life or mainstream activities. Maybe that's why she hides her son.

Or maybe it's because she's embarrassed, as if his disability reflected badly on her, her family, and her social status. I have long assumed that poorer families, or those with little education or social status, would feel more stigma from a disability than better-off families. Many underprivileged people in the world depend on the achievements of their children to improve the family's social and economic status. A family that is already disadvantaged has more to lose from having a child with autism. But Mrs. J isn't disadvantaged, and she doesn't hide her child solely because an association with autism might hurt her status.

She was probably responding to a deeply held cultural belief, one that developed during the middle of the 20th century with the rise of psychoanalysis, and especially with the work of Bruno Bettelheim. I can only imagine the agony of having a child with autism during the heyday of psychoanalysis. Not only did parents learn that their children would be mentally disabled for life, but they were told that they had inflicted the injury. The most loving mothers concluded that they must have done something horribly wrong to have made their child withdraw into a protective shell. One mother recalled the meeting when Bettelheim diagnosed her son with autism in the late 1960s. 'You were in the judgment seat, and he was your judge, your prosecutor, your everything. He was going to send you to mother hell because you made this kid autistic.'

I know something of those parents' guilt. When Isabel was diagnosed with autism, I felt guilty too, but for what I don't know. I automatically questioned myself and Joyce: What did we do wrong? Did Joyce not take care of herself during pregnancy? Were Joyce and I so preoccupied with our work that we had failed to help Isabel attach to us properly? What parent doesn't wonder if he or she did something to cause the autism? Bennett Leventhal, a child psychiatrist at the University of Illinois, told me, 'The parents of my patients are so afraid that they are to blame that they won't even ask about it. Without fail, I have to bring up the issue myself. And when I tell them they aren't to blame, they are visibly relieved.'

After I spoke with Mrs. J, it occurred to me that autism is really two illnesses. It's all the symptoms we're familiar with, plus the stigma and exclusion that society attaches to it. At first, one might think that since most people with autism don't often look particularly different from other people, there would be less stigma. The paradox is that handicaps that are invisible can actually create more burden, stigma, and shame than those that are easily seen, a point that was once made by the writer Susan Sontag in her 1988 book *Illness as Metaphor*. She said that people throughout the world tend to pass moral judgments on illnesses that have few obvious physical signs, illnesses with symptoms and causes that are confusing to people or that may be incurable, such as mental illnesses, tuberculosis, and many cancers.

'Nothing,' she wrote, 'is more punitive than to give disease a meaning – that meaning being invariably a moralistic one. Any important disease where causality is murky and for which treatment is ineffectual, tends to be awash in significance.' Recent examples of such moral judgments include the association of HIV infection with promiscuity or criminal drug use. Genital herpes was called, on the August 1982 cover of *Time* magazine, 'The New Scarlet Letter'. As anthropologists Nancy Scheper-Hughes and Margaret Lock put it, the second illness, the illness's double, forces the patient, 'now twice victimized, further into the cage of his or her illness: shunned, silenced, and shamed *in addition* to being very sick'. Stigma is a branding, a way that society marks us for transgressing the bounds of what is considered normal.

I've interviewed some people who would agree with Sontag. Seung-Kyong, a woman I met in a suburb of Seoul and who has a son with autism, said, People who see our children say,

'Why is a normal child acting so strangely? There must be a problem with their parents. Aren't the parents sending him to school?' Children with autism often misbehave, so the first thing you think of when you see a kid with bad discipline is that there is a problem with their school or ability to learn or that they have a bad mother. I really think the parents of children who are not severely physically disabled, like the parents of the children with autism I know, suffer more than the parents of physically handicapped children.

The philosopher Ian Hacking, who recently gave a series of lectures on autism at the College de France in Paris, wondered aloud which was worse: the child who never speaks and has no social life, or the child who seems *almost* normal? He didn't think there was any real answer to the question but posed it as a philosophical exercise. At least the profoundly impaired person clearly has a disability. There may be little dispute about how to take care of the person. But what of a child with autism who speaks, is even capable of having a friend or two, but periodically becomes violent, or sometimes needs hospitalisation and strong medication? This was the situation, Hacking said, for Jeanne-Marie Prefaut, who, in the 1999 book *Maman, pas l'hopital!* (Mama, No Hospital!), described how she murdered her daughter who had a mild form of autism. Hacking was obtuse, and speaking in French, but it seems that he was suggesting that had Prefaut's daughter been more severely impaired, and institutionalised, the murder might not have taken place.

The family who can rationalise, and afford, placing their child in an institution may experience less stigma. In Kenya, Monica

Mburu, an autism parent and advocate who lives in Nairobi, told me, 'If you are poor, there is no way to hide your child. But if you are rich, and you have more rooms, you can keep your child in a room. And even if people know you have this child, no one will say anything to you. Neighbours don't want to cause you any more trouble than you have already. But if you bring your child outside, you are at the public's mercy.'

There are widespread rumours, none of them well substantiated, however, that in South Africa, Kenya, and Uganda, among other African countries, police have discovered children with autism chained to beds, in part, perhaps, to restrain them from hurting themselves, but mostly to hide them from the community. Parents in Kenya told me that the police recently found a fifteen-year-old autistic boy in the coastal town of Mombasa who had been tied to a tree in a fenced backyard while his mother went to do errands. And after Monica Mburu did a radio show about autism, listeners called in to alert the police to a twenty-year-old man with autism in their neighbourhood in Nyeri. The police then rescued the man, who had been shackled to a chair. The neighbours said the parents never mentioned that they had this son, and though the neighbours claimed they had never seen the man, someone must have, since they all knew he was there. Kenyan television reported that he had been shackled for perhaps years and that, as a result, he was unable to move his upper arms. He was taken to a Nairobi hospital so that orthopedic surgeons could release the tendons in his shoulder joints, which had become fused together because his arms had been tied back for so long. He was subsequently returned to his parents.

Where did the stigma come from? How did parents, especially mothers, end up being blamed for autism? The answers to these questions are not terribly complicated; they begin, simply enough, with psychoanalysis, a subject I learned about in my childhood.

I was taught about the history of psychoanalysis the way many people are taught about their family trees.

Leo Kanner believed that children with autism were born that way. They had not purposefully withdrawn from their parents or from human society in general; they were already withdrawn at birth.

This should have exonerated parents from blame. But Kanner, and Asperger too, provided evidence for those who wanted to hold parents responsible, observing subtle shades of autism in their patients' fathers and mothers, and wondering if there might be a connection between parent and child other than a genetic one. Psychoanalysts, who dominated American and European psychology at the time, and who argued that the relationship between mother and child is the prototype for all later social relationships, seized upon this idea. They argued that people with autism were socially impaired because they had abnormal or failed relationships with their parents, especially their mothers.

Despite the peer pressure he received from colleagues who were psychoanalysts, Kanner himself was uncertain about causation. On the one hand, he entertained the idea that the link could be psychological – cold parents produce cold children – but on the other hand he still believed that autism was innate. He also considered the possibility that the parents were cold but that it was genetics that made them that way. Asperger was more convinced that the link between parents and autistic children was entirely biological, involving a complex relationship between genes and environment that had little to do with parenting. After all, many children with autism, even many identical twins, had normal siblings. Still, Asperger wrote that in the process of studying 200 children with autism over a ten-year period, he 'got to know their parents and other relatives of theirs and found abnormal traits in their relatives'.

Kanner introduced the fateful term 'refrigerator mother', which came to define many psychoanalysts' views on the causes of autism, including Bruno Bettelheim's. It came from a single phrase in Leo Kanner's first description of autism as a syndrome, a phrase Kanner would forever regret, in which he said that the parents of the first eleven autistic children he studied kept their children 'neatly in a refrigerator that did not defrost'. For Asperger, the cold parent of an autistic child was simply more evidence of the role of genetics; for psychoanalysts like Bruno Bettelheim, it was evidence of bad parents.

By the way, it turns out that Asperger was right. Today, psychiatrists routinely teach their students that schizophrenia and bipolar disorder are the most genetically determined of all mental disorders. But autism has just as strong a genetic component, if not an even stronger one. Scientists estimate that the concordance of Autistic Disorder (the classic form described by Kanner) in identical twins – meaning the percentage of people with the identical DNA who both have the disorder – is at least 60 per cent, higher than the concordance for coronary artery disease, depression, or breast cancer. Three twin studies showed a 70 per cent concordance rate for 'Autistic Disorder' in identical twins, but 0 per cent in fraternal twins. And when scientists measured concordance along the whole autism spectrum, including those who would have a diagnosis of Asperger's Disorder or another Pervasive Developmental Disorder, the concordance rate increased to 82 per cent among identical twins versus only 10 per cent among fraternal twins.

Kanner and Asperger also noted that the parents of children with autism all tended to have something else in common, something that would be mentioned repeatedly by future researchers:

They were all highly educated. They therefore tended to have professional careers, and they often hired nannies to take care of their children during the day. Because Kanner was living within a world increasingly ruled by psychoanalysis, he wondered (but never actually investigated) whether autism might in some way be linked to the ambitions and emotional (and sometimes physical) distance of well-educated parents.

Four of the eleven fathers in Kanner's sample were psychiatrists, not a very representative sample of the general American population. The remaining seven fathers included two lawyers, a clothing merchant, a chemist, a plant pathologist, a professor of forestry, and a mining engineer. Nine out of the eleven mothers had college degrees, which was unusual for the 1940s. In 1943 fewer than 4 per cent of American women over the age of 25 had completed a four-year college education. Believing that the parents of children with autism were more highly educated than the parents of his other child patients, Kanner looked for more 'unsophisticated families' to study, but with only partial success. Of the first 100 cases, the average education was a bit more representative of the country, but still high: 74 per cent of the fathers and 70 per cent of the mothers held college degrees, and 38 per cent of both groups combined had graduate degrees. Did more educated, ambitious people tend to be colder, more distant parents?

As a result of Kanner's observations and those of other researchers following in his footsteps, scientists began to study social class in a variety of mental illnesses to find out if certain illnesses were more or less common in certain segments of society. Even today a few autism researchers continue to question whether there is a significant relationship between autism and social class, and there is increasing suspicion that autism, especially Asperger's Disorder, occurs more often in the offspring of scientists, mathematicians, and computer experts. A 21st-century psychiatrist would quickly understand that what Kanner saw was a referral bias, meaning that the people most likely to consult a Johns Hopkins University psychiatrist were well-educated professionals, including fellow psychiatrists. Nonetheless, Kanner didn't dismiss the sample as biased, and a lot of ink was spilled over the next decade to explain that socioeconomic and educational levels were unrelated to the incidence of autism but were related to whether people sought psychiatric advice or not. People of higher socioeconomic status tend to avail themselves of medical interventions more often than people of lower socioeconomic status, and they are more willing to participate in research protocols.

The same referral bias can be found in other parts of the world. In India, autism diagnoses are made infrequently, and when they are, the patients tend to be the children of affluent, well-educated parents. These are the families that seek high-quality medical care and can pay for it, and who visit the expensive specialists who were trained abroad. These parents have Internet access, travel internationally, and read English-language publications. No wonder then that when I went to the only school for children with autism in New Delhi, ten out of ten fathers and four out of the ten mothers I interviewed were college educated; half of the men had advanced degrees, and two had PhDs. I interviewed only one child there who had received a diagnosis of Asperger's Disorder, and – big surprise – his mother is a chemist with a PhD from Harvard, and his father is a physicist with a PhD from the Massachusetts Institute of Technology.

During the 1960s, Leon Eisenberg of the Johns Hopkins University studied the fathers of children with autism, mostly because he noticed that the psychoanalytic literature neglected the role of the father in producing psychopathology in children. The typical case was a man whom Eisenberg called Mr T, who had a son named Billy. Mr T told Eisenberg, 'I am interested in my work to the point of detachment from other things.' Eisenberg said that Mr T and his wife decided to have children not because they wanted them but because it was the socially appropriate thing to do. They had twins, and when one died in infancy, Mr T began drinking heavily and became even more distant. According to Eisenberg, Mr T and his wife were so frightened of losing the surviving twin, Billy, that they kept him 'almost completely isolated from human contact, which was viewed solely as a source of bacteriological contamination'. When Billy was hospitalised for psychosis, Mr T visited, but 'he was stiff and distant toward his son.'

Eisenberg concluded that, based on observations of 100 fathers, 85 were 'obsessive, detached and humourless … Perfectionist to an extreme, they are preoccupied with detailed minutiae to the exclusion of concern for over-all meanings. Thus, though a number are scientists, none is a major contributor to his field.' One of the fathers, in describing his personality, used as an example his own father's bizarre behaviour. It seems that his father, a professor, had been in a terrible train wreck. The car he was in was tilted at twenty degrees from vertical, and when the emergency squad finally cut through the metal to rescue him he was still working away on a manuscript he was writing.

The two hypotheses, that bad parents, especially mothers, cause autism, and that autism is associated with high socioeconomic status, are actually hard to shake, despite the fact that research like Eisenberg's could just as easily support a biological, genetic argument. Indeed, a lot of genetic research is being conducted today on the behavioural similarities between 'normal' parents and their autistic children. We are now told over and over again that autism is a genetically based brain disorder. But we are also told that genes alone don't make mental disorders, and that our brains are strongly influenced by environmental factors, including interaction with our parents and other relatives. So it's not surprising that people still wonder if parents are partly to blame for autism.

Parent blame came up when I interviewed a child psychiatrist in wealthy Fairfield County, Connecticut. She found it fascinating that so many of her patients' fathers were absent during important evaluations and consultations. She said, 'The typical Wall Street dad calls up and says, "I have to be in the city; can you just put me on speaker phone?" I see the mothers, usually well dressed, beautiful women with $1,000 handbags, and the dad is on the speaker phone, never seen and only heard,' like, she said as she laughed, 'the boss in *Charlie's Angels*. For many of the kids I've treated – I've never even met the father.' She said jokingly, 'One day, I'm going to discover that there's just this one guy on the line, that these are all his kids, and that's why they're so similar.' She knows that autism, and many other childhood mental illnesses, have a genetic cause, but she wonders about the effect of the distant father. 'Parents cannot cause autism – that is totally impossible,' she said. 'But children with autism can still have good or bad parents.' We have graduated from the refrigerator mother to the speaker-phone dad.

What psychiatrists did not anticipate was the recent genetic, clinical, and epidemiological studies that strongly suggest that the social deficits characteristic of autism spectrum disorders are not only common in the general population – albeit in minimal, subtle forms that cause no alarm or major social problems – but that they are more prevalent in the relatives of people with autism. There are even Magnetic Resonance Imaging (MRI) studies that show that 'normal' people and their autistic relatives share similar abnormalities in specific parts of the brain responsible for motor planning, imitation (motor cortex and basal ganglia), and the processing of social information (somatosensory cortex).

I GREW UP IN A SECTION OF CHICAGO called Streeterville. Now, when I see the upscale shopping mall on Michigan Avenue called Water Tower Place, just two blocks from where I grew up, I remember the small but perfect park that used to occupy its lot. Bordered by high, dark red fences, the private, gated park accessible only by key, was a rare piece of green among concrete, giving the illusion of being detached from the city. Looking to the west, above tall oaks, you could see the old Chicago water tower ascending, with its pale yellow blocks of Joliet limestone. It was a playground for the children of the upper middle class and a cemetery for our pets. It was a site of both privilege and protection.

Few children frequented the park more than Tim, a mentally retarded boy who lived nearby. Tall and stocky for his age, with curly light brown hair, he was the first and only disabled child I would meet in my densely populated neighbourhood. Tim didn't have a mean bone in his body, but he scared us all to death. He drooled, his speech was impaired, and he had a head tremor. With poor control over his arms and legs, and unable to monitor the location of his own body relative to others, he often bumped us accidentally or stepped on our toes.

I often wondered, with some resentment, why I was bullied more often than he was. I realise now that the other boys at the park avoided him because they were afraid of him or repulsed by him, and because he couldn't engage in any kind of conversation with them. I avoided him too. Though we were well aware of him, we pretended not to see him, as if he were simply a part of the landscape.

And then, in the summer of 1973, when I was eleven, Tim wasn't there. I found out many years later that he had been sent to a residential institution. No one talked about him – not my parents (at least they didn't talk about him to my sister and me), and not the other children. It was as if he had never existed. I felt uncomfortable talking to Tim's parents; the family was, for me, tainted by the disability. I couldn't understand why they had ever brought him out in public.

In retrospect, I marvel at this silence and other similar silences. My family seldom spoke about misfortune or tragedy or even commonplace ugliness, including homelessness, poverty, and alcoholism – this despite the fact that my father devoted his life, as his father and father's father had, to helping miserable people become normally unhappy.

We lived in a rich, discursive world that revolved around interiority, an imagined world with imagined tragedies like killing your father and marrying your mother, rather than real ones. Psychoanalysts gathered at our house for parties and sometimes bared their own unconscious fantasies as if they were commonplace. When I was thirteen or fourteen, one 70-year-old guest told me that he unconsciously wanted to be a woman. They were like members of a nudist colony that somehow wandered off into the world of the clothed.

It was an environment dominated by Freudian theory, and in particular the idea that parents are ultimately responsible for their children's psychopathology. In this kind of intellectual environment, in this urban neighbourhood of educated professionals, children with special needs were kept inside so as not to reflect badly on their parents.

I suspect that in rural environments children were less easily hidden, but downtown Chicago apartments were not as transparent; we didn't always know what our neighbours were up to, and that suited us. If we ever did hear about a child who saw a psychiatrist, or even a speech therapist or academic tutor, our parents told us never to mention it to anyone. I thought that childhood mental illnesses and learning disabilities were shameful and embarrassing.

Psychoanalysis did a lot of good. It helped Americans become more open to seeking mental health care. It promised people the capacity for self-understanding and improvement. People believed it would help them to resolve the emotional conflicts their parents had saddled them with in childhood, so that they could live a more well-adjusted life, and often it did help. But parents were also held responsible for nearly every aspect of their children's lives. It was a time when even the great psychologist Erik Erikson, a guru in the history of American childhood studies, yielded to the advice of his good friend Margaret Mead and sent his son Neil, born with Down syndrome, to an institution within days of his birth. Afraid that Neil would tarnish his family's reputation and his career, Erikson and his wife kept his existence a secret from the rest of the family, including three of their four other children, for more than two decades.

Those children in our neighbourhood who were physically or mentally disabled were, I believed, sent to prison-like schools far away from our part of the city. I imagined that those who did live at home went to a school in a dilapidated, dark grey Victorian mansion not far from my middle school that seemed to be perpetually in winter and which my friends as I referred to as 'the Munster house'. We'd hold our breath while running by, so we wouldn't catch a disease, or simply walk on the opposite side of the street to minimise the chance of meeting someone from the school. I never saw anyone enter or leave the house, and to this day I do not know if it was, in fact, a school. But that's where the disabled kids were, I was sure.

Then there was Bruno Bettelheim's Orthogenic School on the south side of Chicago. I knew about it because my father used to take me on tours of Hyde Park and the University of Chicago to show me where he had spent his childhood and college days, and the area seemed to me far enough away to be another city entirely.

This fuelled my fantasy about a child prison because I had heard that children actually resided there but that their parents were not allowed to visit.

My children and their friends lead a much less sheltered exist-ence than I did. For them, difference and diversity go beyond race and ethnicity to include developmental disabilities, dyslexia, Tourette's syndrome, ADHD, and autism, among others. They know many children who take stimulants or antidepressants for anxiety or attention problems. Parents today often talk candidly about medications and diagnoses and are conversant with the idea that there are many different kinds of intelligence and a wide range of emotional development among children. The culture of psychoanalysis, as dominant as it was during my childhood, didn't allow for this kind of openness.

THE STIGMA AND THE SHAME didn't start with Bruno Bettelheim, though he certainly popularised the psychoanalytic idea that bad parenting caused autism. Rather, it started with the way Americans welcomed psychoanalysis.

When Freud first visited the United States in 1909, and deliv-ered five lectures at Clark University, he was astonished by his warm reception. He was also sceptical. Freud had come to America believing that he was bringing the equivalent of a plague. He assumed that Americans, considered by most Europeans to be prudish and puritanical, would be reluctant to embrace a the-ory that was founded on frank discussions of sex and sexuality. Americans accepted psychoanalysis so easily, he thought, that they must be simplifying it, or at least using it for some unexpected and particular purpose.

He was right. The sociologist Sherry Turkle has argued that psychoanalysis took hold among mental health professionals in

America, and in American intellectual and popular life more generally, because psychoanalysis fit perfectly with American individualism. In the context of rapid urbanisation, social dislocation
(including immigration), and the decline of the religious in favour
of the secular, people were no longer defined by their immediate
community and its values. Psychoanalysis focused on the individual, the *plastic* individual, on the capacity for self-improvement.
American individualism, Turkle said, 'tends to represent the individual as a virtuoso or entrepreneur of his or her own self.'

This appealing focus on the possibility for change is both eman-
cipating and daunting because if we're capable of changing for
the better we're also capable of doing harm. Although the most
orthodox Freudians might argue that reality matters less to personality development than fantasy, most claim that psychopathology begins with disturbances in parent-child relationships. It is not
surprising, then, that some of the first writing about the causes of
autism blamed parents.

Most parents believed their doctors and were devastated.
Marriages, in-law relationships, and families as a whole were
irreversibly damaged. One of the psychoanalytic leaders of
Chicago, Franz Alexander, who founded the Chicago Institute for
Psychoanalysis in 1932, believed strongly in parental responsibility. In fact, my grandfather thought that Alexander set child psychiatry back by at least a decade and made it difficult for anyone
to mount a successful attack against another Chicago figure, the
leader of the mother blamers, Bettelheim.

Bettelheim wasn't a medical doctor or analyst by training (he
held a doctorate in psychology from the University of Vienna). Yet
he became one of the most well-known and influential 'experts'
on child mental health, especially autism, in the world. In 1967,
Bettelheim wrote in his book *The Empty Fortress* that autism was

caused by both biology and environment. But the cases he presented argued instead that autism was caused by bad mothers.

The parents of children with autism, he said, were detached, cold, and suffered from their own psychopathology. In his view, although the disorder was biological in nature, a parent's negative attitude toward the child would cause the biological disorder to manifest itself. Bettelheim ignored empirical evidence that contradicted his own hunches and instead paid attention to psychologists like Harry Harlow, who argued that abnormalities in early infant-mother interactions could produce disturbances in attachment.

Harlow conducted experiments, now famous among animal rights advocates for their cruelty, with rhesus monkeys. He showed that baby monkeys separated from their mothers and placed with mechanical monkeys preferred cloth monkeys to monkeys made of wire, even when the wire monkeys had milk bottles attached and the cloth monkeys did not. Harlow also showed that monkeys deprived of nurturing mothers in their early infancy suffered long-term emotional effects, whereas monkeys deprived of social contact in their adulthood suffered little. These studies validated the Freudian idea that the child-mother relationship determines the kind of social relationships a person establishes in both childhood and adulthood. Soon psychiatrists and psychoanalysts throughout the world would look at autism through Bettelheim's eyes.

In 1956 the Ford Foundation awarded a grant of $342,500 to Bettelheim for the study of autistic children (though he also called them child schizophrenics) at his Orthogenic School. The goal was to study a group of children 24 hours a day to learn what sorts of treatments were most effective. Eleven years later, in 1967, he claimed to have studied 40 autistic children intensively and to have made significant progress 'thawing out' the children who had been frozen, replacing what he poetically called their mothers' 'black milk' with proper nurturing. Having removed the children from their hateful environments, the school's staff, Bettelheim believed, was able to provide the emotional support and accessibility necessary to draw them out into the real world. He claimed that these children, most of whom lived at the school five days a week, gained under his supervision and safety the emotional potential for acquiring a self. Bettelheim used their progress in the school as evidence of the harm inflicted by parents in the home.

In the 1990s, one of Bettelheim's biographers, Richard Pollak, whose brother had been a student at the Orthogenic School, examined the school records and uncovered a different story. Between 1956, when the grant was made, and 1963, when it expired, Bettelheim admitted only six children who were officially classified as autistic. Between 1944 and 1973, only thirteen of the 220 children admitted to the school were classified as such. The clinical files are inaccessible, so there is no way to know whether all thirteen would qualify for the diagnosis by today's criteria, but this small sample size is sufficient evidence to question the veracity of Bettelheim's findings. *The Empty Fortress* itself is based on only three cases. Yet during the promotion of the book, in all major newspapers and on nationally televised programmes such as *The Today Show* and *The Dick Cavett Show*, the school was touted as a home for autistic children, a home that could keep these children safe from the long arm of the unloving parent. And in these contexts Bettelheim repeated the same claim parents read in the book: 'Throughout this book I state my belief that the precipitating factor in infantile autism is the parent's wish that his child should not exist.'

Two other books on autism, published at about the same time, got little mention in the press: Bernard Rimland's *Autism: The Syndrome and Its Implications for a Neural Theory of Behavior* (1964), which outlined the biological and neurological aspects of autism, and Clara Clairborne Park's *The Siege* (1967), a beautifully written memoir of raising an autistic child. Though they were more accurate depictions of autism, they couldn't compete with Bettelheim. He was simply too good a writer, and with his Viennese accent − the sign of an authentic expert in psychology − too good a self promoter.

It is possible that the three case descriptions presented in *The Empty Fortress* − Laurie, Marcia, and Joey − are cases of autism, but it is also possible that they represent actual instances of child neglect that produced short-term autistic-like symptoms. If that is the case, the parents' emotional disturbances cannot be generalised to all parents of children with autism. We simply don't know. It is clear, however, that Bettelheim did a magnificent job crafting his descriptions to highlight the parents' problems. He saw tormented parents disengaged from their children and assumed they hated them. But Bettelheim was more than likely witnessing the parents' reaction to their children's autism, not the cause of it. It's a classic example of confusing causes with consequences.

According to Bettelheim, Laurie's mother caused her daughter's autism by keeping her job throughout her daughter's infancy, entrusting her care to nannies. Marcia's mother was widowed early in marriage and subsequently married a man she did not truly love and who did not want children. He gave in, however, despite telling Bettelheim's staff that the baby 'was really of no interest to me'. Joey, the third and last case, spoke a lot more than Laurie or Marcia but was almost completely unable to communicate. This was because his mother 'thought of him as a thing rather than a person'.

Bettelheim noted that these children had unimpaired siblings. But he skirted the question of how such neglectful parents could have also raised siblings that were not autistic by saying that parents treat different children differently. These supposedly sick parents were, in his view, capable of overcoming their own psychopathology to properly parent a normal child. Bettelheim used the parents' honesty against them. When they told him that they were ambivalent about having children, for example, or that they felt their work and home lives competed with each other, he suggested they were mentally disturbed.

He went on to compare autistic children to Nazi concentration camp prisoners. He suggested that a variety of psychotic responses can be caused by the feeling of being unable to escape from a situation in which one's life is in jeopardy and completely outside of one's control. Not all people responded in the same way to this situation, he argued, but people with autism and some concentration camp victims responded by developing an inappropriate and shallow affect, by engaging in little or no eye contact, and by closing themselves off to the external world. Suicide was a common response in the concentration camps, one Bettelheim, a Holocaust survivor, chose for himself in 1990.

Bettelheim thought the primary difference between people with autism and the prisoners was their prognosis. Adult prisoners (that is, people with fully formed personalities) could recover from the abuse by drawing on the years of memories and experiences before their imprisonment, but children with autism had been abused from the start and were never given half a chance to build their capacity to fight the hate. Of one mother of an autistic boy, Bettelheim wrote, 'The only real difference between the SS guard and the mother of the autistic child is that the mother gets to the child much earlier in life.'

We now know that children who are horribly neglected or abused, or even prisoners who are brutally treated, do not become autistic. Otherwise the Puritans, who treated their children as the corrupted, sinful souls they believed them to be – the parents sometimes attached wooden rods to their infants' backs, so they couldn't crawl like animals – would have produced generations of autistic people. Why didn't the children in Shakespeare's time, swaddled and hung on walls for hours, become autistic? The answer, of course, is that parents do not cause autism. Abused or abandoned children, homeless children, or children raised in overcrowded orphanages may exhibit some symptoms of autism, but certainly not the core features, and their problems are more treatable and often reversible. Autism, in contrast, is a brain disorder and a lifelong disability.

PSYCHOANALYTIC VIEWS ON AUTISM left a legacy, largely through the work of Bettelheim, that is evident in the discomfort and guilt we still feel about presenting our children with autism to the world. That legacy is stronger outside of North America and Europe, especially in France and Argentina, where there are more psychoanalysts per capita than anywhere else in the world.

If, one day soon, you find yourself in a remote part of the world, take a visit to a local library and look for books about autism. If they do have a book on autism, it will almost certainly be Bettelheim's *The Empty Fortress*.

4

Blaming Mothers

T<small>WO YEARS AFTER THE PUBLICATION</small> of *The Empty Fortress*, the ideas behind it were the subject of a major motion picture, the Elvis Presley film *Change of Habit*. Elvis plays a young doctor, singer, and community activist running a clinic in Spanish Harlem. Mary Tyler Moore plays Michelle, a plainclothes nun who has been trained as a nurse and speech therapist. She is assigned by the church to work with Elvis, despite the risk that she will be tempted by worldly pleasures outside the convent, such as Elvis himself. The film revolves around the tension she experiences as she faces this temptation. She must choose between God and Elvis (if only life was that simple!), the religious and the secular. Elvis is a Christ figure, working with the sick and poor, ministering to them through caring and through music. Indeed, the real miracles are performed not by God but by Elvis, who is the only truly selfless and compassionate character in the film – certainly more compassionate than the church elders, who have little but disdain for the secular world.

One of his patients is a young, mute girl, Amanda, who shows no emotion, rocks back and forth, resists being touched, makes poor eye contact, and clutches a Raggedy Ann doll. The aunt who brings her to the clinic (it is important to note that the mother has abandoned the child) assumes she is deaf, but the speech therapist, Mary Tyler Moore, says to Elvis, 'I think she's autistic.' Though she tries her best, she cannot get the girl's attention. Elvis steps in, realising that, as a result of her mother's departure, Amanda does not know how to love.

'It's not gonna work Michelle. She's hiding behind a wall of anger. It's not gonna work. I'll take over and we'll try rage reduction.' It is important, he claims, to rid her of her 'autistic frustration' over her mother's abandonment of her. Elvis takes Amanda's doll and she begins to scream.

'You've got to learn how to start loving people,' he tells her. 'I'm gonna hold you until you get rid of all your hate.' She struggles, but he holds on. 'Then you can start to give love and take love. I love you. I love you Amanda. I love you. I love you. I love you.' In less than 30 seconds, she speaks her first word, 'mad', followed by her second word, 'love'.

PSYCHOANALYSIS DIDN'T INVENT mother blame. Negative stereotypes of mothers have existed in many times and cultures. Just think about how many different kinds of bad mothers have been identified in American history alone: the professional or rich woman who never sees her kids, the teenage mother, the Jewish mother, the stage mother, the overprotective mother, the overly permissive mother, the hysterical mother. But it's only in the past century that American scientists, like Bettelheim and his predecessors, began to systematically exploit the concept of the bad mother.

When mothers weren't being attacked for being too cold, they were being attacked for being too affectionate. In 1894, the guru of child guidance, L. Emmett Holt, decided to go on the offensive. The Dr Spock of his generation, Holt ordered mothers to stop showing too much warmth toward their children and discouraged breast-feeding. Thumbsucking and infantile masturbation should be prohibited, he said, even if it meant binding the child's elbows to a metal rod to prevent it.

By the 1920s, there was an explosion in the number of childhood experts in America who similarly urged mothers to apply so-called 'scientific methods' to their childrearing. What they meant by the word 'scientific' was not that their methods were based on experiments using the scientific method, but that the advice was coming from scientists.

John Watson, a child-guidance expert from the Johns Hopkins University popular during the 1930s, wrote that mothers of his generation were uniquely unqualified to raise children because they were too kind to them. He sarcastically dedicated his biting 1934 book, *Psychological Care of Infants and Children*, 'To the first mother who brings up a happy child'. He wrote, 'Once a child's character has been spoiled by bad handling, which can be done in a few days, who can say that the damage is ever repaired?' Watson urged mothers to treat their children as young adults, not to kiss or pet them, not even to bandage their wounds (which young children need to be taught to do themselves). Doing otherwise, he believed, would make children become weak and unable to succeed in the competitive workplaces in America. Watson's movement to withhold affection was established at almost exactly the same time that the first of Kanner's eleven patients was born. We have to wonder if the manner in which the parents presented themselves to Kanner – as ambivalent or unaffectionate – was affected by what they saw as the parental attitudes that were appropriate for the time.

By the 1940s, when psychoanalysts first began to emphasise the importance of affection, emotional contact, and nurturing to good childrearing, psychologists either ignored the psychoanalysts or treated them as if they were insane. After all, psychoanalysis was a theory intended to explain the inner workings of the mind – fantasy and unconscious desire – but not to serve as a guide to actual parenting behaviour. Breastfeeding declined so dramatically that during the 1950s and 1960s the majority of new American mothers left the hospital formula-feeding their babies, and those that did breast-feed stopped within a few weeks.

But the tide was turning. By the late 1950s, experts would urge parents to be as nurturing as possible to their children. The media published largely unsubstantiated rumours of widespread child abandonment, stories of women giving up their children because they could not support them or because they wanted to pursue their own careers. Many now argued that symptoms of psychological distress were caused by problems in the home and that women should stay at home, breast-feed, and indulge their children.

The widespread concern with family and childrearing in the postwar years is underscored by how often child-guidance experts warned Americans of the fragility of children's futures and the vital role mothers played in fostering the proper sexual development of the child. A small misstep in parenting could scar your child for life. If you were too repressive or too quick to toilet train, your child could become frigid and anxious about sex; or your child could resist the repression by becoming a nymphomaniac or a homosexual. One result of the concern was that parents turned to extrafamilial institutions, like the Boy Scouts and Girl Scouts, Sunday schools, and, of course, psychotherapy and psychoanalysis, to seek help in finding their way through the confusing maze of parenthood.

The scientific advances that have taken place in the second half of the 20th century have been extraordinary, but they've done little to demolish the belief that early childhood experience determines later life. During the 1990s, a small number of high-profile experts on child development, such as the psychiatrist David Hamburg (former president of the Carnegie Foundation) and Donald Cohen of the Yale Child Study Center, began to champion the view that neuroscience had proven the importance of early infant nurturing to brain development, especially in the years from birth to three. They were joined by Hillary Clinton, Rob Reiner, and other celebrities, and numerous journalists argued that the first three years of life were critical in determining whether a child would become, as Reiner put it, 'a toxic or non-toxic member of society'. They sought increased funding for child welfare and a reform of Head Start that would fund child care before the age of three.

During this time, a *Chicago Tribune* science writer, Ron Kotulak, wrote an influential book arguing that brain science could shape a variety of policy reforms in the United States, and the White House listened. In *Inside the Brain: Revolutionary Discoveries of How the Mind Works* (1996), Kotulak argued that poor brain development, caused by poverty, television, and single-parent households, among other things, contributed to violence. He didn't just say that people raised in poverty or abusive households were more likely to commit violence; he argued that in such conditions the brain itself, during the years between birth and three years old, created the 'chemical pathways of aggression'.

Remarkably few neuroscientists joined the parade. This was because, as John Bruer, the president of the James S. McDonnell Foundation, noted, their work was being distorted for political purposes. Bruer's critique is valuable because it begins to undermine the long held conviction that the ages between birth and three, that is, the ages *before the onset of autism*, determine a child's future.

In his book *The Myth of the First Three Years*, Bruer argued against three popular myths of neuroscience, none of them supported by neuroscientists themselves: first, that brain synapse growth is so exuberant in the first three years of life that later years are insignificant in comparison; second, that the critical window for brain development between birth and three is so limited that once the window closes there is little anyone can do about deficits that may have been caused by a poor environment; and third, that organisms raised in warm, rich, and stimulating environments between the ages of birth and three have more synapses in their brains than organisms raised under harsher, more isolated conditions.

First, there is virtually no brain science that links parent-child attachment in the first three years of life to brain development. Although research based on behavioural observation suggests a connection between children's attachment to their parents in the first three years of life and later childhood behaviour, the research indicates that this is only true when the environment remains stable. If the environment changes – economically, socially, geographically, and so on – even in later childhood, so does the child. Although early experiences may predispose people to certain problems, they do not determine everything.

Second, there is cross-cultural evidence that children treated in ways we might consider abusive (for example, Guatemalan villagers protect infants from the evil eye by isolating them in dark huts for more than a year) grow up to be teenagers little different from their peers.

Third, although the synapses do grow faster in the first three years of life than in subsequent years, the growth is under genetic, not environmental, control. For numerous psychiatric disorders, such as autism, schizophrenia, bipolar disorder, and Attention Deficit Hyperactivity Disorder, genes keep an especially tight rein on the child's outcome. Psychiatrists are also identifying distinctive patterns in the pruning of synapses after age three in different mental illnesses. This pruning, which continues throughout childhood and into young adulthood, is a normal process of discarding excessive synapses and neural pathways and occurs in all children. But the pattern of pruning in people with Attention Deficit Hyperactivity Disorder, for example, looks quite different from the pattern of pruning in people with schizophrenia. At the

National Institutes of Health, Judith Rapoport and her colleagues splice together a succession of multiple brain MRIs of a research subject, taken on the same machine over many years, and play them like a film. The animation shows the pruning in motion, and Rapoport can often correctly guess the diagnosis of a subject just by watching the process.

Fourth, the research on the so-called 'window of opportunity' is based largely on animal research – for example, on the developmental impact of early blindness in mice. There are critical periods of language acquisition, but they are not in just the first three years of life and, at any rate, are for the most part unrelated to nurturing. Almost all children, even those with significant language delays, learn to speak a language fluently whether or not they are cared for.

Science actually tells us little about how to raise or educate our children. But the selective appropriation of science by certain science writers and high-profile scientists tells us a lot about the continuing preoccupation with blaming mothers.

ALTHOUGH MOTHER BLAME for autism today may seem anachronistic in the United States, the refrigerator mother hypothesis is alive and well in many parts of the world. A study published in an international scholarly journal, *Infant Mental Health*, in 1999 would make Bettelheim proud. A team of Korean psychiatrists and one American psychiatrist described children who at first were given a diagnosis of autism but who, the authors argued, had actually suffered from a disturbance in their attachment to their mothers, a disturbance they blamed on maternal neglect and maternal psychopathology. Although there was no evidence of abuse, the authors suggested that the mothers and children were disengaged from each other. It is an excellent example of how easily the refrigerator mother hypothesis can be resuscitated.

In this study, 25 children (23 boys and two girls) between the ages of two and four (all living in 'intact nuclear families') and their mothers were seen at Yonsei University Hospital in Seoul, South Korea. The mothers had come to Yonsei complaining that their children had poor eye contact, did not respond to their names, preferred solitary play, and had little or no ability to speak. They did indeed show problems in social interaction, language, and cognition, and also attachment to their mothers. Some of the children had stereotypic repetitive movements or self-injurious behaviours such as hand-flapping, toe-walking, head-banging, and hand-biting. All 25 mothers reported that the children had appeared to be developing normally up to twelve to fifteen months of age.

The investigators asked each mother to play with her child for twenty minutes while they were observed through a two-way mirror. Fathers were neither observed nor interviewed and are not even mentioned in the research report. This is because Korean fathers are customarily not involved in child care, in large part because they work long hours at least six days a week. The researchers saw mothers who, as they described it, lacked social skills, failed to join in play, appeared insensitive to their children's cues, and engaged mostly in parallel play. The mothers expressed little emotion, but some got slightly angry when their children would not play with the toys offered to them.

I watched one of the tapes a couple of years ago when I visited Yonsei University, and what I saw was the mother's *reaction* to her child's autism. I saw a mother demoralised by months of futile and unrewarding attempts to communicate with her child. The researchers saw a bad mother. Not necessarily morally bad, but bad because of depression or other psychopathology. Instead of seeing mothers depressed or anxious as a result of their children's problems, and guilt-ridden already by native attitudes toward disability and mothering, they saw mothers who were making their children sick. And instead of acknowledging that these mothers were behaving in an artificial situation, in a setting away from home with doctors watching, the researchers saw evidence of inadequate caregiving environments.

When the researchers observed the same children playing with trained play therapists, the children performed much better. In fact, their communication skills and moods improved so markedly over just two or three play sessions that the researchers started to question the diagnosis of autism. The speed with which these children improved – improving even during the diagnostic procedure itself – is indeed remarkable, if not unbelievable. Over a period of one year, eight of the 23 children had play therapy, and three of these, the authors reported, 'recovered normal language'. Since the authors assumed that autism was untreatable in any way, they interpreted the children's progress as confirmation of the absence of autism and the presence of an attachment disorder.

The researchers might have easily concluded that these three children were simply less impaired than the rest. They might have guessed that speech and play therapies ameliorated some of the symptoms of autism, or that their progress was an effect of the passage of time. But the authors of the paper did not consider any of these possibilities. Instead, even in the absence of any evidence of abuse or neglect, or any chaos within the family, all they saw was bad mothers. In fact, twenty of the mothers took a psychological test and got high scores for depression, anxiety, paranoia, and other symptoms. Indeed, as we'll discover later, Korean psychiatrists commonly diagnose an attachment disorder in children with symptoms of autism.

Yet, rather than heap too much blame on the women themselves, the authors turned their research into a cultural critique. Korean women in general, they argued, suppress emotion more than women in other countries do and handle stress by withdrawing from social situations; when they do express emotion, they said, they do so through somatic symptoms, especially *Hwa-byung*. Hwa-byung is a Korean disorder that cannot be described easily in English. It is a kind of depression with bodily complaints such as fatigue and soreness associated with old age along with a persistent feeling of a mass lodged in the stomach. Hwa-byung is thought to be caused by inhibiting anger: anger about the Japanese colonisation of Korea, the Korean War, and other injustices. The authors of the paper suggested that older women, the mothers and grandmothers of the women whose children were seen in this study, responded to the stresses of colonisation and war by withdrawing from their children, the women who are now mothers themselves. Having inherited their own mothers' limitations, these women now negatively affect their children's development. Quoting a famous line in psychoanalysis, the authors said these children were the victims of the 'ghosts in the nursery', that is, the pathology of the child's grandparents and ancestors.

In addition, the withdrawal of mothers from their children throughout Korea, the authors argued, has been exacerbated by the progress that Korean women have made in the workplace, as professional careers take them away from their children. They even faulted the current emphasis in Korea on English education. Never mind that nearly all Korean children take English lessons and watch instructional videos. The researchers wrote, 'We inferred that these mothers also used videotapes as a way of avoiding direct interactions with their children.' I've found that this perspective is shared by a number of Korean psychiatrists, many of whom urge the mothers of children with social and language deficits to quit their jobs.

MOTHER BLAME has been especially prevalent in France this is because of the hardy influence of psychoanalysis – though it's

somewhat less intense than it used to be. As one French psychiatrist said to me, 'In this day and age, the rest of European psychiatry
thinks France is in the Middle Ages.' There is a kernel of truth in
this comment. French child psychiatry may not be in the Middle
Ages, but it does exist in its own cultural context. Psychoanalysis
in the United States succeeded because of a preoccupation with
self-improvement, the growth of child-guidance movements, and
popular concerns about postwar changes in the American family.
In France, psychoanalysis succeeded for very different reasons. But
the result for the parents of mentally ill children, and children with
autism, would be the same.

The French initially rejected psychoanalysis for the same reason
that Americans embraced it: the focus on the autonomous self.
In the early 20th century, while Americans were insecure about
identity – mourning the loss of stability and tradition and searching for a new sense of personhood – the French were secure about
identity. They were basking in the victory of the bourgeoisie over
the workers at the end of the 19th century, sure of the country's values and character. French elementary-school textbooks
opened with illustrations of the Gauls, Charlemagne, and every
other famous leader in French history holding hands in a chain
leading to the present, and ending with the name of the student
who owned the book. According to Sherry Turkle, 'Psychoanalysis
threatened this reassuring sense of continuity by insisting that civilization (even French civilization) is the origin of our discontents
and that the past can live within us as an insidious rather than
benign presence.'

By the end of the 1950s, there were only 150 psychoanalysts
in France as compared to several thousand in the United States.
Psychiatry in France wouldn't even become a discipline separate
from neurology until 1968, the year that many mental health professionals in France reversed their position and made psychoanaly-

sis the preferred therapy for mental illness. Philosophers, literary critics, and social scientists would make it the preferred theory in arts and letters as well. By the year 2000, France could claim an estimated 10,000 psychoanalysts, more than any other country.

Why the sudden shift? Politics. Workers' wages were terrible. Unemployment was high. In just a decade, the number of students in France had tripled, and they were graduating without jobs in sight. In 1968, massive strikes were instigated by workers and students, bringing the economy to a halt, and the public generally supported the protests. Even soccer players revolted, chanting in their own demonstrations, 'Football for the Football Players!' Although the strikes were eventually quelled, and people returned to work, the 1968 riots signalled a changing French society. Like the United States years before, France was becoming more secular, more urban, and more insecure about its national unity. Not surprisingly, city workers became nostalgic about the innocence and beauty of the countryside, and intellectuals fantasised about regaining the purity of the noble savage, uncontaminated by capitalism or other evils of civilisation. One of the most salient arguments of this new philosophical and social movement in France was that human beings are shaped, distorted, and corrupted by culture, not by nature.

In that same year, the great filmmaker François Truffaut released his film *L'Enfant Sauvage* (The Wild Boy), a reenactment of Jean Itard's 18th-century account of studying and teaching Victor, a harmless boy of eleven or twelve who had been captured by three hunters who came upon him in the woods near Caune in southern France. He was naked and covered with dirt and sores and had a large scar on his neck, as if he had been attacked or carried by a wolf. After several escapes and captures, the boy eventually comprehended and accepted an offer of shelter in a *canton* called St Sernin, which committed him to a hospital for treatment. Not quite four foot six, the boy did not speak. He rocked back and forth and twitched. By all appearances, Victor had been raised by wolves, or at the very least had been living for years in isolation from the rest of humanity. His case would provoke a sustained commentary on society's relationship to nature and the role of language in forming the self.

Eight years earlier, Truffaut had told *The New Yorker*, 'Morally, the child is like a wolf – outside society.' Now Truffaut was depicting the transition from animal to human in the context of French protests against government and capitalist elites and their resistance to the role these entities played in shaping humanity.

The year is 1799. In the opening scene, the filthy, wild boy, shown from a distance, sits on a branch high in the trees, rocking back and forth like an autistic child. A peasant woman gathering mushrooms in the forest notices what appears to be a wild animal and alerts local hunters. Once captured, the scarred, mute boy becomes the talk of France, and for three years he remains in a hospital while scientists observe and describe his physical appearance and mental defects. He was said to have a heightened sense of smell and to react only to certain sounds, especially those relating to food; a door slamming wouldn't startle him, but the sound of a nut being cracked would. He was bipedal but walked with an odd and rhythmic gait.

A young scientist working at an institution for the deaf and mute, Jean Itard, played by Truffaut himself, arranges for him to come to Paris. In Paris, the child is tormented by scientists, curious observers, and cruel children, and then Itard takes him to an intermediate point between nature and culture, the Parisian countryside. There, Dr Itard can interact with Victor against the backdrop of nature. Although they work together in Itard's home, nature is a constant presence. It appears in the form of bright, inviting windows, outside of which one can see the fields and forest. The camera returns repeatedly to the window as if to tell us that nature both defines Victor's identity and pulls him back. The black and white film is visually stunning, perhaps because Truffaut wants us to understand that, as for most autistic children, Victor's relationship to the world is initially visual and spatial rather than linguistic.

Victor is not just a child. He is a stranger – a stranger to language, love, and kinship. Although Itard tries to provide them to Victor, teaching him language, holding Victor and stroking his hair, giving both the tenderness and discipline of a father, their relationship is fragile. The film ends on a positive note, however, as Victor fights an unjust punishment that Itard has concocted for him. Itard believes that Victor's rebellion against authority signals the beginnings of a sense of morality, the beginnings, therefore, of humanity. Protest and resistance are thus the keys to the emergence of the self.

Enter Jacques Lacan, a sometimes impenetrable but brilliant writer and psychoanalyst, whom every American psychoanalyst has heard of but few have read, and even fewer have understood. Like the student demonstrators of 1968, Lacan was critical of all institutions, including government, education, and medicine in general. What Lacan did for the French Left in 1968 was to provide them with an intellectual framework to think about how society impinges on our freedoms without our even being conscious of its power. That framework was psychoanalysis.

In Lacan's scheme, children develop by learning the difference between an 'I' and a 'you', and they learn this unconsciously through language, by having to communicate with someone else. This is why Victor's social, psychological, and moral development emerged only with language. It is precisely through language – in words and concepts – that society shapes the individual mind in its own image. Lacan thus brought Freud and Marx together into a single theory: the Freudian concept of the unconscious and the

Marxist idea that individuals are subjected to large-scale systems of power without their awareness. One result of Lacan's sudden popularity was the development of a strong antipsychiatry movement in France, because, unlike psychoanalysis, psychiatry was part of neurology, neurology part of medicine, and medicine part of the establishment.

Psychoanalysis continues to dominate the French mental health system, especially in the area of child mental health. Among all European countries, the idea that parents are responsible for autism is thus strongest in France, though it appears elsewhere in Europe too, as the psychiatrist Victor Sanua found in a 1986 survey. At that time, 54 per cent of the psychiatrists in Europe indicated that parental psychopathology was a causal factor in autism, as compared to 35 per cent of psychiatrists in the United States. In France, since autism is generally seen to be a problem that lies with the family – and with the mother, in particular – there are only a few centres with expertise on autism as a genetic or brain disorder. Parents usually consult the national health-care system's psychiatric clinics, which are run by psychoanalytically trained child psychiatrists or paediatricians.

Furthermore, the French use their own manual of classification of childhood mental disorders, the *Classification Française des Troubles Mentaux de l'Enfant et de l'Adolescent (CFTMEA)*. The rest of the world uses either the American Psychiatric Association's *DSM IV*, the World Health Organisation's *International Classification of Diseases (ICD)*, or both, because mental health professionals want to standardise, as much as possible, their diagnostic criteria. Until November 2004, the CFTMEA classified autism as an 'infantile psychosis', but French psychiatrists and psychoanalysts also use the diagnosis 'psychic disharmony', a vague phrase that is used to describe cases of high-functioning autism. This diagnosis corresponds roughly to the *DSM-IV* diagnosis of PDD-NOS but also refers to the inability of mother and child to connect emotionally. The diagnosis of autism as infantile psychosis in France is usually reserved for children who fit the more narrow definition of autistic disorder, as first described by Kanner, and not the broader definition of the autistic spectrum used in the *DSM IV*. As a result, epidemiologists in France suggest that the prevalence of autism (as it is defined in France) is lower than in other parts of the world.

French analysts are not concerned with making their discipline appear scientific, as so many American analysts have tried to do; they seldom interact with psychoanalysts outside of France, and generally they do not read foreign works in translation, other than those written by the founders of psychoanalysis. They live in their own isolated world of symbols and metaphors. Many French analysts draw on the work of the great psychologists and ethologists as well, such as Konrad Lorenz's work on imprinting, in which he showed that baby animals attach themselves to objects in their environment from birth, and Harry Harlow's primate experiments. It should be pointed out, however, that *adult* psychiatry in France is not dominated by psychoanalysis. It resembles psychiatry in the United States and the United Kingdom and involves a well-established and sophisticated scientific research infrastructure that includes epidemiology and clinical trials of psychiatric medications.

Part of the problem with French child psychiatry is that French analysis has long divided mental disorders into two broad categories: psychosis and neurosis. For many in France, neurosis, while the source of conflict and emotional distress, is a part of typical human functioning brought about through the normal process of a child's separation from its mother. As a result of that separation, children develop their own sense of self independent of the mother and learn how to use language creatively, since, for Lacan, the self is actualised through language. Psychosis, in contrast, comes about from the improper separation of a child from its mother and involves an entirely different relationship to language. The psychotic's separation from the mother is incomplete, so language never really develops as a creative, generative vocabulary and grammar. It is fixed and repetitive, and it is not social. As one consequence, psychotics have a skewed identity and sense of self.

Given this framework, it is not surprising that autism was, until November 2004, officially classified as a psychosis in France. It was changed to a 'developmental disorder' largely in response to international pressure and the work of parent advocacy groups in France, notably the Autisme-France Association and the French Autism and Infantile Psychoses Federation. But this does not mean that French child psychiatrists universally accept the change. A few months after the change was made, an editor of a medical textbook showed me the page proofs of a chapter written by a French child psychiatrist that contained a section about autism in France. In it the author had written that autism is a psychosis. So, as a courtesy, I e-mailed the editor to make sure he knew that the classification he was about to publish was out of date. He told me he had asked the French author to change it, but that the author had refused.

The parents who run the French parent advocacy organisations believe that the problem in France is that children with psychiatric symptoms are generally referred to psychoanalytic treatment instead of to an educational sector. When the psychoanalyst assesses the child, he or she is concerned with managing symptoms, determining the cause of the symptoms through family history, and helping the child to acquire a sense of self. The analyst will also, in effect, treat the parents, since they are perceived to be part of the cause. He is not necessarily concerned with determining how the child's cognitive strengths and weaknesses can be described and then fitted into an educational programme. As one French psychiatrist told me in an interview, 'We wait for desire to appear.'

But parents don't want to wait. They want a diagnosis and an educational plan and are beginning to fight back. The parent associations draw on the English-language literature on autism to argue that there is no evidence that autism is related to parental psychopathology. They have a strong case.

DURING MY CHILDHOOD, my father, Roy R. Grinker, Jr, a psychiatrist and psychoanalyst, was on top of the world, with a practice flush with analytic patients. Psychoanalysis as a *theory* is still popular in nonscientific academic circles in the United States and throughout Europe, especially among literary critics, but psychoanalysis as a method of treatment is on the decline. During my adulthood, the number of analysts in training in the United States has dropped dramatically, and my father, like most analysts, is now lucky if he has one or two bona fide analytic patients.

There are many reasons for the decline, among them a preference for new and effective drugs over talk therapy and evidence-based medicine that relies on neuroscience, clinical trials, and the scientific investigation of falsifiable hypotheses rather than abstract, unfalsifiable theories like those that fill the psychoanalytic literature. There is also a shortage of people willing to spend the enormous amount of money and time necessary to complete a traditional analysis. In France, where there are more psychoanalysts than in any other country, they blame the decline of psychoanalysis in the United States on the American obsession with quick fixes. And in Argentina, where there are more psychoanalysts per capita than in any other country, they blame the decline on the rise of what the anthropologist Andrew Lakoff has called 'pharmaceutical reason', the American attempt to standardise diagnoses for managed care, treat illnesses with medicines rather than talk therapy, and explain the human mind in terms of genetics and neurobiology.

If you go to a bookstore in the United States today, you won't find any books that tell you that your autistic child is psychotic, that he should be institutionalised, or that bad parents cause autism. But those ideas still get communicated to parents, even if indirectly, in parts of the United States, even in Washington, DC, where in 1994 Isabel had her first psychiatric consultation.

When our paediatrician, worried that Isabel had autism, referred us to a well-known psychoanalyst and psychiatrist, we were enthusiastic. But his office was a run-down, musty studio. The whole pockmarked place looked like an archaeological find in need of preservation. And so did he. I saw him as a relic from times past, but a famous relic, one who had fashioned himself into something of a guru. I had heard that sometimes you had to wait months for an appointment. Only two weeks earlier, while waiting in line at a local photography store, I had noticed a stack of black and white glossies bearing his image, resting behind the counter, probably prepared for a book signing.

'Is there any mental illness in your families?' he began.

He asked us both to describe our educational background, and then he didn't look at me again for ten minutes. He had turned to Joyce.

'Can you tell me about your pregnancy?' 'Your labor?' 'Did you breast-feed?' 'How often?' 'Any problems?' 'Was it difficult for you?' 'Did you want to stop earlier than you did?' 'Did you enjoy breastfeeding?' 'How many hours do you work per week?' 'Do you think you could cut back on your hours?' 'Did you drink or smoke during pregnancy?' 'Were you happy with a daughter or did you want a son?' 'Do you have much free time for yourself?'

Finally, Joyce interrupted.

'You know, I'm not comfortable with this line of questioning, especially since you've yet to ask a single question about Isabel, the reason we're here.'

He agreed to change the subject to discuss Isabel. He said that she had a 'regulatory disorder', which, he noted, some people like to call autism. Our paediatrician had called him an autism expert, but he clearly didn't like the word. He said that the term was being used promiscuously. By 'regulatory', he meant that Isabel had failed to bond with Joyce, and that Joyce had failed to regulate Isabel's sensations and emotions. It's a psychoanalytic way of describing the mother's inability to contribute to a child's development. I suddenly realised that we were from different cultures or times. Wasn't the idea that mothers were to blame for everything dead and gone?

Joyce's tone of voice was impatient and irritated. 'I also wonder why you are treating my husband as if he is not a member of this family. Why aren't you asking him about his work hours, his schedule?'

He replied, 'It's just that at this age the mother is the most important person, and that's you of course.'

Joyce quickly countered, 'Are there scientific data to suggest that a developmental disorder like my daughter has – whatever you want to call it – will be affected by my job status? If you can tell me that by quitting my job and staying at home with her she will develop better, I will do it.'

He smiled and said all he could really say in his language. Thinking about it today, I almost feel sorry for him: 'Young children just like the warm and fuzzies from the mom.'

Next he said he wanted to watch us play with Isabel, but Isabel was standing at the door to the waiting room trying to turn the knob. It was locked. We stood on either side of her, struggling to get her engaged with us, showing her toys, tickling her, doing just about everything we could. But she just wanted to get out. The doctor told us we weren't doing it right. And that's the last thing I remember about him.

5

The Rise of Diagnosis

IN 1920, LIGHTNER WITMER, a pioneer in experimental psychology from Philadelphia, published the first detailed case report of a psychotic child. The boy had 'no desires except to be let alone'. He had a great rote memory and excellent visual and spatial skills (for example, he could do puzzles well), but he focused on only a small number of activities. Though he was able to have limited conversations with his teachers, when he spoke to them he reproduced the exact accent and intonation of their voices. He was diagnosed with schizophrenia.

In 1959, a little boy named Arnold, age four and a half, was brought to Bellevue Hospital in New York City for psychiatric treatment. His parents told the doctors that he didn't speak, was a loner, couldn't control his bowels, and played with the toilet. This is how Arnold's doctor described his condition: 'He was mute or echolalic, though he knew and could repeat the words of innumerable popular songs. He had severe tantrums in which he would withdraw completely, suck his thumb, make odd, guttural sounds and be completely inaccessible … His development was apparently unremarkable until the age of 11 months when he began to rock in his crib … There were no indications of organic pathology.' Arnold was immediately diagnosed with schizophrenia.

These cases, nearly 40 years apart, are just two among many scattered throughout the psychiatric literature and represent autism of the form described by Kanner. They are among the clearest cases of autism you'll ever find. They were almost certainly misdiagnosed.

The two cases help us understand why autism was an invisible illness for so long. Twenty years after Kanner's initial description, many children with autism were no longer diagnosed as idiots, imbeciles, or the feebleminded. But they were still misdiagnosed. They now had brain dysfunction, mental retardation, epilepsy, schizophrenia, autistic schizophrenia, childhood schizophrenia, childhood-onset schizophrenia, and child psychosis, among other diagnoses.

The lack of clarity in diagnosis is not surprising, given that child psychiatry was still in its infancy; there were still only a few hundred child psychiatrists in the United States by the early 1970s. It was a low-prestige medical specialty with few widely agreed upon diagnoses. Attention Deficit Hyperactivity Disorder, which is today the bread and butter of child psychiatry, didn't even become a legitimate diagnosis until 1980.

One of the most influential mid-century child psychiatrists, Lauretta Bender of Bellevue, argued that children with autistic symptoms generally grew up to become adults with schizophrenia. This seemed a logical progression to her because so many adults with schizophrenia are socially withdrawn as children and as adults show a variety of cognitive deficits. For example, they have difficulties thinking abstractly and reading social cues. In the 1950s, she claimed to have on file more than 600 cases of childhood schizophrenia at Bellevue alone, and by 1966 she reported having studied 2,000 children with schizophrenia.

Occasionally, in adults, so called 'schizotypal personalities' can be confused with Asperger's Disorder. But childhood schizophrenia is one of the rarest of mental illnesses worldwide. Judith Rapoport, chair of child psychiatry at the National Institute of Mental Health

(NIMH) and one of the world's leading experts on childhood schizophrenia, has spent the past eighteen years looking for as many cases of childhood schizophrenia as she can find. Of the thousands of cases referred to her from doctors throughout the country, and the 300 most likely child schizophrenics she brought to NIH for six-week-long evaluations, only 88 cases have been confirmed. Some psychiatrists today believe that childhood schizophrenia doesn't exist and that Rapoport's cases could be accounted for by psychoses associated with bipolar or borderline disorders.

Why, then, did doctors confuse autism with schizophrenia? How could Bender have documented so many cases of childhood schizophrenia? During the 1960s and 1970s the only mention of autism in the American Psychiatric Association diagnostic guidelines was the adjective 'autistic' in the criteria for 'Schizophrenia, Childhood Type'. In other words, if you were going to use the official categories, a diagnosis of autism was, de facto, a diagnosis of schizophrenia.

American psychiatrists pleaded with their students to understand that the signs of schizophrenia are apparent even in early childhood – in the inability to emotionally connect with others, and in mutism – though these symptoms might not look exactly like the symptoms of schizophrenia in adults. However, numerous follow-up reports in the 1950s and 1960s showed that few of the so-called childhood schizophrenics became adult schizophrenics. Instead, the early 'autistic' symptoms persisted. Delusions and hallucinations seldom showed up, either during puberty or afterward. In addition, many who were diagnosed in childhood with schizophrenia were rediagnosed in adulthood as mentally retarded. Still, the diagnosis of autism eluded psychiatrists.

Kanner, as I noted earlier, did little to distinguish autism from schizophrenia. In addition, he excluded from his diagnosis of autism any patient for whom he could find some other cause of symptoms of autism. So did almost everyone else who accepted autism as a valid diagnosis. There were certainly rumblings from some researchers that brain abnormalities were behind autism. But if someone had, say, a chromosomal disorder, with or without physical deformities, the scientific consensus was that the patient couldn't be diagnosed with autism. Nor could he be called autistic if he had epilepsy. And until the late 1960s, if he was mentally retarded he was quite unlikely to be called autistic. In contrast to children with mental retardation or a brain injury, children with autism were thought to have good intellectual potential.

That was until Stella Chess came onto the scene.

STELLA CHESS WAS A PSYCHIATRIST who started working at Bellevue Hospital in 1964 during a rubella outbreak. Rubella, or German measles, was an uninteresting disease. It gave children a rash and a fever, but they recovered. Australian ophthalmologist Norman Gregg, however, suspected there might be more to it than that. Following an outbreak of rubella in Australia in 1940, Gregg had noticed that many babies were born with cataracts. Searching for a possible correlation, he finally settled on rubella as the culprit. He became a laughingstock. Everyone believed that rubella was harmless, and scientists thought foetuses were totally protected from such diseases in the womb. (Ironically, protection against rubella is now part of the Measles, Mumps, and Rubella vaccine, which many people – but virtually no scientists believe can cause autism.) It would be years before Gregg was proven right about the link between the cataracts and rubella.

In the late 1960s, thousands of babies were being born with birth defects throughout the United States. Many were blind and deaf, some had brain damage, and others had severe cardiac problems. Like Gregg's Australian patients, these babies had been born to mothers who had rubella while pregnant.

In 1971, the state of New York asked Chess to do psychiatric assessments of children with congenital rubella because many had developmental delays. 'No one wanted to do that research,' Chess told me, 'because rubella was just so boring. I don't even know why I did it. Maybe I sensed there was something important to be found.' For those who were congenitally blind or deaf, the reason for the delay was clear. But there were others, who were not blind or deaf, who had profound delays that were unexplained. They appeared to have autism. But when Chess diagnosed them with autism, it was her turn to be ridiculed.

'People had a fit,' Chess recalled. 'They said that autism couldn't possibly be caused by a disease like rubella. Most of my colleagues were convinced that the cause of autism was genetic, or bad parenting, or both, but not anything else.' Yet her data were so good, her writing and presentations so persuasive, and her reputation so solid that she changed people's minds. Chess and her colleagues believed that autism could be diagnosed in a much wider range of individuals than those included in Kanner's initial pool of eleven children. Mental health professionals finally listened to her.

Unfortunately, at the time Chess began to publish her results, psychiatry was still defined largely by psychoanalysts. How did we go from seeing autism as either a subset of schizophrenia or a result of bad parenting to seeing it as a neurodevelopmental disorder? The answer to that question lies in how psychiatry has changed over the past 50 years.

Two crucial and interrelated contributing factors were the rise of biological treatments for psychiatric illnesses during the 1940s and 1950s, and the standardisation of psychiatric diagnoses through the publication of various editions of the *DSM*. One treatment was prefrontal lobotomy, which involved drilling two holes into the skull and severing the prefrontal cortex from the rest of the brain. Thousands of lobotomies were performed in the United States during the 1940s, many at George Washington University, where I now teach, and the surgery was widely thought to bring sanity to the insane, or at least to make the aggressive and unmanageable patients living in mental institutions more docile. For pioneering the surgical technique for the lobotomy, Antonio Egaz Moniz of Lisbon, Portugal, won the 1949 Nobel Prize for Medicine and Physiology. By the early 1950s, children were being lobotomised, especially those who were described as living in fantasy worlds – children then called schizophrenics, but who would today almost certainly be called autistic. In 1950, Walter Freeman of George Washington University reported operating on a four-year old boy. 'The aim has been to smash the world of fantasy in which these children are becoming more and more submerged,' he wrote. He said that it was easier to sever the child's fantasy life than to attempt to socialise him.

In 1952, French scientists showed that chlorpromazine (with the brand name Thorazine) was effective in managing hallucinations, and in 1957 Swiss doctors developed the first tricyclic antidepressant, imipramine (with the brand name Tofranil). The new medications made it possible for institutionalised patients to return home and be treated on an outpatient basis. Psychiatrists were reluctant to treat children with these medicines – the antipsychotics had never been tested on children, and they had a lot of side effects – but older children with autism, children who had symptoms of psychosis or were violent, could now be controlled. Teenagers could be educated in special schools, provided they were given their medications. The mere existence of the antipsychotic drugs prompted research on biological treatments for mental illness.

At Bellevue, for example, Bender and her colleagues started administering LSD (Lysergic Acid Diethylamide) to what she called 'autistic schizophrenic children'. She had previously used electroshock therapy on more than 100 such children, and she had also induced seizures chemically with a cardiac stimulant called Metrazol, with inconclusive results. By the 1950s, however, Bender had an even larger pool of what were called 'autistic schizophrenic' children to choose from for her experiments, and believing that children showed fewer side effects to medications, she argued that children before puberty could be given larger doses than adolescents. She found that LSD had a paradoxical effect on the children at Bellevue. Rather than causing hallucinations, the LSD calmed the autistic children. They seemed happier, more spontaneously playful with balls and balloons, and much less hostile (I should note that when I was in college, students who took LSD also became playful with balls and balloons). The children were also more receptive to fondling and affection. The experiments stopped quickly, however, possibly because of public concerns about the use of psychedelic drugs during the 1960s.

Because there were now new and effective treatments for serious mental illnesses, the field of biological psychiatry began to grow, and the US government did what it could to help that process along. In 1962, the Food and Drug Administration required that new medications be tested in rigorous clinical trials prior to being marketed. Scientists had to prove that a drug was not only safe, but also effective against a particular disease, in order for that drug to be approved. As a result, psychiatrists began to develop more precise classifications of mental illnesses, and by the 1970s they were conducting research on the biological and genetic bases of mental illness.

Child psychiatry's shift to a more medical, less psychoanalytic model of diagnosis and treatment invigorated the discipline. There were more doctors willing to specialise in child development. Membership in the American Academy of Child and Adolescent Psychiatry, the largest organisation of child psychiatrists in the world, began to grow rapidly. The academy had only 400 members in 1970, approximately 1,200 in 1980, 3,300 in 1990, and 6,700 in 2000, before levelling off at about 7,400 in 2005.

A new generation of child psychiatrists was demanding more reliable, more scientific methods. As with the drift in the definition of schizophrenia, they began to see mental illnesses as *brain disorders* rather than as disorders of the self. And, as scientists, they wanted psychiatry to develop definitions and classifications of disorders that everyone could agree on. This marked an important change in the study of autism because the emphasis on definition led to more case descriptions. The more child psychiatrists and others became aware of the symptoms – and clusters of symptoms – of autism, the more autism began to look like a unique syndrome separate from schizophrenia, epilepsy, or the other all-purpose categories. There were still relatively few autism researchers, but as child psychiatry grew as a medical specialty, those researchers began to elaborate on the neurobiological and behavioural features of autism, such as altered responses to sensory stimuli and uneven gross and fine motor skills.

It wasn't easy to develop good definitions. Child psychiatrists have the difficult task of applying diagnostic criteria to growing and developing children. Diagnosing a mental disorder in a child is like describing a moving target. It is virtually impossible to produce a list of criteria for a mental disorder that will be relevant at all developmental levels. A temper tantrum in a two-year-old is considered part of the 'terrible twos', whereas the same behaviour in a school-aged child might be reason to send him to the principal's office. Likewise, a two-year-old with autism who makes poor eye contact could be seen as simply shy, while the same deficit in a six-year-old would be seen as a serious problem.

It was Sir Michael Rutter, a British psychiatrist, who, with a simple classificatory scheme, made one of the greatest strides toward making autism both a coherent and a conventional diagnosis. In several articles published in the early 1970s, he proposed four major characteristics of autism that could be observed and measured: onset by two and a half years of age, impaired social development, impaired communication, and unusual behaviours (like lining things up, insistence on sameness, or stereotyped body movements). Rutter was by no means defining autism as a single or homogeneous condition like Down syndrome. But the four criteria could still be used as a starting point for all definitions of autism.

Autism became a conventional diagnosis in psychiatric practice during the 1970s, though it was not as common as it was to become. The American Psychiatric Association had not yet made it an official diagnosis. In 1980, in the new edition of its diagnostic manual, the *DSM-III*, the APA no longer lumped autism together with schizophrenia as a psychosis, instead calling it a pervasive developmental disorder. Receiving official status meant autism was bound to become a more popular diagnosis.

A similar story can be told about other disorders, such as Post-Traumatic Stress Disorder (PTSD) or Attention Deficit Hyperactivity Disorder (ADHD). Before 1980, children with the symptoms of what we today call ADHD were seen as bad kids whose problems, often blamed on their parents, caused them to do poorly in school, and in some cases to become criminals or develop drug addictions. After 1980, when it was first included in the *DSM*, ADHD quickly went from being rare or unknown to becoming the most common childhood psychiatric diagnosis.

In order to understand how autism became the popular diagnosis it is today, we have to understand how it became a part of the *DSM-III*. But we cannot fully appreciate how autism became an official diagnosis without first appreciating the true provenance of the *DSM-III*. The two stories – of the *DSM-III* and of autism – may simultaneously shake your faith in psychiatry and give you hope.

EVEN AS A KID, I knew that something like the *DSM-III* would eventually appear. I knew it because my grandfather, Roy R. Grinker, Sr, told me so.

When I was in the fifth grade, my grandfather started to give me mini-seminars on psychiatry. It was 1972. He had just retired from being founding editor of the *Archives of General Psychiatry*, the leading psychiatric research journal. I remember him calling me at my uncle's photography store one Saturday morning, where I was working in the stockroom filling orders. He asked if I could come over after work to learn about how British and American psychiatrists confuse schizophrenia and manic-depressive illness (now usually called bipolar disorder). It would be the first of many Saturday talks about psychiatry.

During that meeting he told me that someone diagnosed with schizophrenia in the United States might be diagnosed with manic-depressive illness in the United Kingdom, and vice versa. Most of his colleagues, he said, didn't think diagnosis affected the way they treated their patients. It didn't bother them that two psychiatrists might diagnose the same patient with two different illnesses. But my grandfather believed that misdiagnosed patients were being treated incorrectly, and that to solve this problem, mental illnesses needed to be diagnosed by more scientific and less arbitrary methods. There needed to be a good diagnostic manual, one that provided a standardised group of criteria so that everyone could agree on what a particular illness was or was not.

Although two editions of the *DSM* had been published (the *DSM* in 1952 and the *DSM-II* in 1968), they were thin, cheaply made books that simply gave the broad outlines of about 100 psychiatric disorders. These editions were virtually ignored within the discipline. Indeed, the drive to create psychiatric classifications did not come from within the mental health professions; it came from the US Census Bureau. Beginning in 1840, the bureau wanted to count the number of 'idiots' in the United States. In 1918, the US government created the first *Statistical Manual for the Use of Institutions for the Insane*, a volume that contained 22 categories of mental illness, although mental health practitioners rarely used them.

Autism was not included in the *DSM-II* as a distinct disorder, and though doctors were beginning to make the diagnosis more often, no one seemed to object to its absence. Its only mention was in the form of an adjective in the description for 'Schizophrenia, Childhood Type': 'Autistic, atypical, and withdrawn behavior; failure to develop identity separate from the mother's, and general unevenness, gross immaturity and inadequacy in development'. The definition included further mention of mental retardation, which psychiatrists today know has no direct association with schizophrenia. What a difference twelve years can make. The *DSM-II* was barely 100 pages long. The *DSM-III*, published in 1980, was more than 500 pages long. The current edition, the *DSM IV-TR*, the bible of mental health, logs in at 943 pages and weighs nearly four pounds. It lists 297 distinct disorders, has been translated into more than a dozen different languages, and guides most of the psychiatric research and training in the world today.

How did this dramatic shift take place? For the answer, we must look to 1972, a watershed year in the history of American psychiatry. That was the year *Science* published Stanford University psychologist David Rosenhan's account of how he and several colleagues fooled psychiatrists into diagnosing them with schizophrenia, admitting them into mental hospitals, and keeping them there against their will. The so-called 'Rosenhan hoax' was devastating from a public relations perspective. The psychiatric establishment could do little to control the emerging popular consensus in America that psychiatrists were unscientific and violated human rights. At the same time, the emerging gay rights movement forced the American Psychiatric Association to finally state that homosexuality was not a mental illness. If that wasn't enough, the *Archives* published an important scientific article by R.E. Kendell and his colleagues about the differences between British and American psychiatrists that called into question the reliability of psychiatric diagnoses. In his study, Kendell showed British and American psychiatrists a video of a socially awkward man, described as a 30-year-old bachelor, and asked them to give a diagnosis based only on the video. 69 per cent of the American psychiatrists diagnosed the man with schizophrenia; only 2 per cent of British psychiatrists gave that diagnosis, most opting for a diagnosis of manic-depressive illness. (Even today, diagnostic differences abound. For example, it appears that PDD-NOS is a more common diagnosis in the US than it is the UK.)

Each of these events challenged 'reliability' in psychiatry – that is, how consistently two observers will come to the same conclusion. What was at stake was nothing less than the credibility of psychiatry as a science and as a legitimate field of medicine. The psychiatrists themselves had to wonder: Though they might disagree with public opinion, they had to admit that their discipline was often more subjective than objective. When we hear, even today, about this or that psychiatric diagnosis being made, especially a relatively new diagnosis like autism, we would do well to remember that psychiatry, even today, is interpretive and sometimes unreliable, just like all the other branches of medicine.

There had been rumblings about reliability before the publication of Kendell's article. In 1949, Philip Ash, an American psychologist, had shown that three psychiatrists evaluating the same patient with the same information agreed on the same diagnosis only 20 per cent of the time. Over the next 25 years, other psychiatrists gradually joined in to question diagnostic methods. 'One wondered,' says psychiatrist Mitchell Wilson, if 'there was little more than a random chance that two psychiatrists would agree on the diagnoses of a given patient.'

At the time the Kendell article was published, my grandfather was not very optimistic about the future of psychiatry. He thought the definitions of psychiatric terms were vague, the diagnoses too variable and confused by biases, the classifications too insecure, and the clinical interviews often made useless by the lack of methods. Epidemiological data on mental illnesses in adults were lacking, and data involving children were even more scarce. Government funding for psychiatric research was decreasing rapidly (by at least 5 per cent a year between 1965 and 1972), and insurance companies, vital to the health of the profession, viewed psychiatric care as a bottomless pit with inadequate methods of assessment and treatment. It's not surprising that my grandfather, who at one time had wanted to be a pathologist, sometimes became nostalgic about his early days doing autopsies. 'It is a wonderful thing,' he told me, 'to be in the presence of a disease you can see, touch, and feel.'

Yet, few psychiatrists were interested in diagnosis, or even the classification of symptoms. Instead, they wanted to discover the psychological or social reasons behind a symptom. Usually the reason they settled on was some developmental conflict, or even, more generally, the failure of the individual to adjust to his or her environment. The goal, at a time when psychiatry and psychoanalysis were so closely related that they were sometimes indistinguishable, was to comprehend the deep, underlying problem that gave rise to a symptom, and then treat the problem, not the symptom. In academic conferences during the 1960s, symposia on diagnosis were so unpopular that they would be scheduled for the final day, in the late afternoon, when no one would come.

My grandfather had predicted an impending crisis in psychiatry back in 1964, eight years before he had called to invite me to that first one-on-one Saturday seminar. He feared the psychoanalytic (and hence, also, the psychiatric) bubble was about to burst. Psychiatry had so dominated American thought during the 1960s that in 1961, the year I was born, the *Atlantic Monthly* published a special issue (28 July) called 'Psychiatry in American Life', with Freud on the cover. In the magazine, contributors spoke of how psychiatric thought – which really meant Freudian analysis, not the scientific method – pervaded nearly every aspect of American society in areas as diverse as education, religion, literature, and stand-up comedy. If psychiatry could explain everything, my grandfather feared, it would explain nothing.

In 1964, he published a short article entitled 'Psychiatry Rides Madly in All Directions'. In it he decried psychiatry's efforts to become the centre of all intellectual and scientific pursuits. He said the field seemed 'to suck partial ideas from many sciences as soon as they are announced as if it were a vacuum abhorring itself', warned of psychiatry's power, and predicted the antipsychiatry backlash that would soon take hold.

In his role as the director of a psychiatric training centre at the University of Chicago, my grandfather began to make quantitative measurements of the symptoms of depression, demanding that his students use specific protocols to interview patients and derive histories. He described behaviours using the language of an empiricist based on facts that could be documented almost identically by multiple observers. Instead of writing something like 'patient appeared hostile, aggressive, ambivalent about being admitted' in a hospital admission note, he would write, for example, 'patient threw a spoon at the nurse'. He wouldn't allow his students to make notes that were vague, such as 'often seems confused', because he thought they were meaningless. 'Often' could mean so many different things – Every hour? Every other day? Lasting several hours at a time, or only for a few minutes? And the words 'seems' and 'confused' were equally vague. Confused about what?

These changes might seem minor at first glance, but it was a shift away from subjective descriptions of internal states toward objective descriptions of observable behaviour. Knowing that no one could ever completely take the subjectivity out of psychiatric diagnosis, he tried anyway. He required his students to use a common set of words and concepts to characterise disorders. Never forgetting how appalled he had been that Freud took no notes during his sessions, he made sure his students took detailed notes.

Some psychiatrists, especially those who were also psychoanalysts, resisted both the medical model and the move to standardise the criteria used to make specific diagnoses. For them, diagnosis was actually a pejorative concept, at its worst linked to state-run asylums, since courts required diagnoses for commitments. But for my grandfather, diagnosis was paramount. It drove all research and treatment. He was confident that diagnosis would make psychiatry a science and, at least in part, return psychiatry to the pre-Freudian days, the days of the famous expert on mental disorders, Emil Kraepelin (born the same year as Freud), who in the late 19th century developed the first classification of mental disorders and made Germany the world leader in psychiatry.

With a debate brewing within the discipline about the future of psychiatry, sadly reducible to a battle between neo-Kraepelins and Freudians, the backlash my grandfather predicted began to take shape. Now called the 'antipsychiatry' movement, it grew out of the antiestablishment 1960s, just at the time when psychiatrists were really beginning to make progress treating patients with medications. Groups of ex-patients – always the fiercest critics of psychiatry – armed themselves with moral positions derived from a variety of scholars: the philosopher and historian Michel Foucault (who argued that the history of psychiatry and the construction of the abnormal/normal dichotomy was really a history of state control over bodies), the anthropologist Erving Goffman (who argued that the culture of asylums actually created the mentally ill), and Thomas Szasz (who called for the deinstitutionalisation of the mentally ill, people whom he believed were simply misfits – like the character Randle McMurphy from the book and film *One Flew Over the Cuckoo's Nest* – unlucky enough to live in a society that imposed illness categories on the marginal or undesirable).

For psychiatrists themselves, the antipsychiatry period was defined by two events: the Rosenhan hoax, and the gay rights movement's successful battle to eliminate 'homosexuality' from the *DSM*'s classification of mental illnesses. The Rosenhan hoax was especially devastating. It's not that psychiatry hadn't experienced resistance before, and from powerful foes, including the church and the courts. But this attack came from the inside – not from ex-patients but from mental health experts themselves.

The attack against the psychiatric establishment's view of homosexuality was actually a much broader attack against *reliability*, the extent to which two or more researchers will arrive at the same conclusion, and *construct validity*, the certainty that a disorder actually exists. Psychiatrists reliably diagnosed 'homosexuality', then classified as a mental disorder by the American Psychiatric Association, throughout the 1960s and 1970s. At certain times in any society's history, there may be political or religious pressures to identify certain kinds of behaviour as sickness. Political dissidents in the Soviet Union, for example, were often diagnosed with schizophrenia and committed to asylums. Homosexuality in the United States at that time was culturally unacceptable, something to be hidden, ostracised, and rejected as abnormal because it violated societal mores. Although homosexuality does exist, and therefore there was some factual basis to the diagnosis, few people,

even then, considered it to be a disease. The point the antipsychia-
trists made during the debate about homosexuality was that just
because psychiatrists called this illness 'homosexuality', and that
illness 'bipolar disorder' or 'schizophrenia', did not mean those illnesses actually existed. Conversely, of course, just because psychiatrists might not have a name for a particular group of symptoms
does not mean that no illness exists with those symptoms.

In 1973, the American Psychiatric Association removed homosexuality from its list of mental disorders and appointed an illustri-
ous and politically savvy psychiatrist and scientist, Robert Spitzer,
to chair a task force on the classification of mental diseases. This
task force would lead to the publication of the *DSM-III* and profoundly influence the evolution of psychiatric diagnoses, including, of course, the diagnosis of autism.

THE *DSM-III* WOULD TRANSFORM mental health, especially clinical
trials and psychiatric epidemiology. Researchers in disparate parts
of the world became more confident that they were measuring the
same illnesses, because all the researchers were, literally, on the same
page. Today, insurance companies will not reimburse any patient or
doctor for psychiatric care without a *DSM* diagnosis. Health–care
administration in the United States categorised as 'managed care'
has made sure that psychiatrists, psychologists, and other providers
of mental health services use the same diagnoses, with the same
criteria, and often the same treatments. Countries that do not use
the *DSM* have adopted the World Health Organisation's manual,
the *International Classification of Diseases* (*ICD*), with language and
classifications almost identical to those of the *DSM*.

Both the *DSM-III* and its successor, the *DSM-IV*, include carefully organised checklists. But the process of creating the *DSM-III*
was not so tidy. A little discussion about how it was created can

shed a lot of light on the imprecision of psychiatric diagnosis. In all the hoopla over skyrocketing rates of autism diagnoses, it is easy to forget how accidental, and just how messy, the production of diagnoses can be.

To make the *DSM-III*, top psychiatrists got together for brainstorming sessions. Robert Spitzer, the coordinator, frantically took notes while his colleagues presented their views and counterviews, interrupting each other continually. These discussions were punctuated by expressions of frustration about the mere idea of having to construct a document based on scientific knowledge that could serve as a guide for every situation. The participants were frustrated because there had, in fact, been little systematic, scientific work done in psychiatry, especially in comparison to the kind of data collected in the other sciences. The *DSM-III* was supposed to appear scientific even though the discipline did not yet have a solid scientific foundation.

Various mental disorders were nominated and then accepted or rejected. One that never made the cut, for example, was 'atypical child', because Spitzer's committee could never define it. 'Atypical child' might just as well have been called FLK (funny-looking kid), because it was one of those catchalls – like the suffix 'NOS' (not otherwise specified), which is used for some diagnoses in the new *DSM-IV*. 'Atypical child' had been used for all the children who had problems but didn't quite fit into any diagnostic category. The writer Alix Spiegel, in *The New Yorker*, noted that, for the most part, Spitzer wanted to be as inclusive as possible. In some cases, he took single disorders and divided them into two. 'Hysterical psychoses', for example, was divided into 'brief reactive psychosis' (short episodes of hallucinations and/or delusions) and 'factitious disorder' (this is when a person consciously feigns an illness).

Spitzer's greatest achievement was establishing checklists. Each disorder would have a checklist of symptoms that needed to be present in order to make a particular diagnosis (these were similar to the lists one uses to order from a menu at a Chinese restaurant – so many from category A, B, and C). And these checklists focused a psychiatrist's attention on symptoms rather than causes. This was a direct assault on psychoanalysis, which was, and is, largely about finding causes. Spitzer's committee wrote that the causes of an illness 'should be a classificatory principle only when it is clearly known … A diagnosis should be made if the criteria for that diagnosis are met.' The National Institute for Mental Health (NIMH) quickly sponsored large-scale reliability tests of the *DSM* in which 500 psychiatrists used the manual to diagnose more than 12,000 patients. The tests showed that the *DSM* was reliable, though this is not to say that the *DSM* was valid.

This standardisation would support scientific research. For example, before the *DSM-III* was published, multisite clinical trials of new medications often lacked scientific validity because it was unclear who exactly was being treated with them. One doctor's schizophrenic patient was another doctor's manic-depressive. Now, if a scientist wanted to test a medication on patients with a particular disorder, he needed to make sure that his diagnoses – that is, the identification of the patients for the drug trial – were made with criteria that were accepted and used by other scientists engaged in similar work. The problem would never be totally resolved, of course, in nonresearch, clinical settings. The same patient can still get a variety of different diagnoses if he goes to enough doctors, and Americans still diagnose schizophrenia more often than the British. But with the new checklists, drug trials at least could be carried out with more uniform populations than ever before, and scientists could test conclusions by replicating previous experiments. Psychiatrists increasingly relied on the *DSM* in clinical settings, too, and today they may know by heart the diagnostic code numbers needed by insurance companies (for example, Autistic Disorder is 299.00, Oppositional Defiant Disorder is 313.81) to manage customer claims.

The publication of the *DSM-III* signalled a major shift in power away from the clinician and his or her idiosyncrasies. Only twenty years earlier, psychoanalysis had reigned. A single book, designed to make psychiatry an empirical search for validity – not an interpretive search for unconscious meaning – had now become the bible of psychiatric diagnosis, research, training, and treatment. It had almost acquired a life of its own. There are many who argue about the diagnostic criteria, describing problems and needed modifications, and many continue to test the *DSM*'s reliability, but virtually no one challenges its right to exist and to guide psychiatry.

As a result, despite the proliferation of diagnoses psychiatry is a narrower field than it used to be. Psychiatric residents today learn to study what they can observe, not the structure of the human mind; they learn to provide synchronic pictures – snapshots – not the complex historical development of the person; and they learn to minimixe the role of the larger contexts within which the symptoms they study exist: culture, politics, the personal relationships between doctor and patient, religion, and kinship, among others.

Some psychiatrists envision a day when the *DSM* will move even further away from interpretation. It is their hope that the manual will contain not only descriptions of symptoms, but also the sites of the various genes involved in the illnesses. Ironically, that change would narrow the scope of psychiatry even more, drawing our attention more to genes than to the person. Geneticists are working hard to find the genes responsible for particular psychiatric disorders and even to devise genetic tests so that a diagnosis can be made by analysing someone's DNA. If that becomes possible, the diagnosis of a psychiatric illness would be universally valid. The psychiatric study and diagnosis of autism, bipolar disorder, depression, or any other mental disorder with a clear-cut genetic signature would then look much more like the other branches of medicine, which study 'real biological diseases'. Like coronary artery disease or breast cancer, a mental illness would be the same entity everywhere, whether the person who had it was South African, Japanese, Bolivian, Australian aborigine, or Native American.

This type of certainty is unlikely, however, for several reasons. The genes underlying diseases are generally just risk factors, not direct causes. Genetic predispositions interact with the lives we lead (the countries we live in, the families we form, the way we manage our bodies), and these interactions can affect illness expression. And even where there are genes that directly cause illnesses, like those involved with Alzheimer's, different mutations in these genes can produce different presentations of the same disease. Autism spectrum disorders are even more complicated, since abnormalities on almost every chromosome have been associated with some autism spectrum disorder. One study suggests that the most plausible genetic model for autism spectrum disorders involves at least fifteen different locations. Geraldine Dawson, an autism researcher at the University of Washington, says, 'There may be four to six major genes and twenty to 30 others that might contribute to autism to a lesser degree' and suggests that the susceptibility genes are different for boys than for girls, and for early onset and for late onset autism. Until the time that psychiatry becomes a fully genetic science – which most people doubt will ever happen – psychiatry will rely on the hard work and good judgment of caring doctors who analyse ideas and behaviour using the categories at their disposal.

The *DSM* is helping to launch psychiatry into the realm of science, but it's not producing any miracles. Even the disorders that have been researched the most by psychiatrists, neuroscientists, geneticists, and epidemiologists remain mysterious. For example, a recent review essay about the state of knowledge of schizophrenia cited 527 references, most of them published over the past ten years, and yet the disorder is so genetically complex that despite decades of research no genes have been shown to definitively put someone at risk for schizophrenia. Since the 1980s, psychiatrists have gained a better understanding of many aspects of schizophrenia: the genetics, the different manifestations of the illness, its course, the abnormalities in the structure and function of the brains of people with schizophrenia, and the chemistry of the neurotransmitter systems involved. They also have a better understanding of the way antipsychotic medicines work. But they still know little about the relationship between brain abnormalities and the actual appearance of the illness, or about which patients will respond to which treatments. The authors of that review wrote, 'In some ways we are not much further ahead than Kraepelin [who wrote about schizophrenia a century ago]; diagnosis is still based on the same clinical observations.'

These are disheartening words. Compared with schizophrenia, research on autism is in its infancy. And compared with adult psychiatry, child psychiatry is still in its adolescence. We don't even have good agreement among all researchers and clinicians about how to describe the phenotypes of autism – that is, the actual physical, behavioural manifestations of the disorder. So if child psychiatry and autism research seem imprecise and confused, it might be useful to think about these fields in developmental terms. Like a child going through puberty, they may have to get a little ugly before they get pretty.

Autism by the Book

WHEN I FIRST STARTED learning about autism, I assumed it would be easier to diagnose than almost any other mental disorder. Two of the leaders in autism research, Donald Cohen and Fred Volkmar, wrote of autism: 'There is no other developmental or psychiatric disorder of children (or, perhaps of any age) for which such well-grounded and internationally accepted diagnostic criteria exist.'

Then why is there still so much confusion about what is and is not autism?

IT IS NEVER EASY TO DIAGNOSE mental disorders – that's why my grandfather missed pathology and the simplicity of analysing a cadaver. It's especially hard to diagnose mental disorders in children, and even harder to diagnose across international boundaries. If psychiatrists in the United States and the United Kingdom can't agree about a diagnosis, speaking the same language and sharing a similar culture, imagine how difficult it might be to get agreement between American and Korean or Indian practitioners on the nuances and complications of the disorders on the autism spectrum. One of the goals of the *DSM-III* and the *DSM-IV* was to provide an international framework for psychiatry anywhere in the world and remove the subjectivity that comes from cultural differences, variations in training, or psychiatrists' personal idiosyncrasies.

But the fact is that diagnosis of any disease is, fundamentally, an *interpretation*, no matter what kind of doctor makes it. There are standardised tests in psychiatry that produce quantitative measures of symptoms, but such assessments often seem more objective than they really are. A patient measured by one scale might qualify for one disorder, while on another scale he might qualify for an entirely different disorder, or for none at all. Even using the same test on the same patient, two clinicians sometimes make two different diagnoses.

Words and behaviours provide the evidence of states of health or disease, but those words and behaviours have to be heard, seen, and interpreted. Diagnosis of psychiatric illnesses can only occur if people seek a diagnosis, which means they or others close to them have to perceive their symptoms *as symptoms*, as problems to be addressed. One person may believe that his or her emotional pain is due to a chemical imbalance in the brain, and may seek medical help for depression, while another believes his or her problem stems from poverty and may seek ways to make money. Culture often determines what is and is not considered evidence of a mental illness and what treatments should be sought.

Arthur Kleinman, a medical anthropologist and psychiatrist at Harvard University, posited a hypothetical experiment. He asked readers to suppose that ten North American psychiatrists, trained in a similar way and using the same diagnostic tools, were to interview an American Indian man who was mourning a spouse who had died within the past week and who had reported hearing his dead wife's voice calling out to him from the spirit world. Perhaps nine out of ten psychiatrists would concur that the patient reported hearing the voice of the dead spouse calling out to him from the spirit world. 90 per cent is reliable. But what do they make of the fact that he hears the voice of a dead person? It is likely that nine out of ten would decide that the patient is hallucinating and that the voices are evidence of a psychosis. Reliable again. If you were to bring in another ten psychiatrists, you would probably get a similar result. The diagnosis would be 90 per cent reliable.

But is it scientifically *valid* to call the voices evidence of psychosis? 'Psychosis' is a mental disorder. Yet, among many American Indians, it is normal to hear the voices of the dead as they pass into the spirit world, and some think it's abnormal *not* to hear them. The concept of 'psychosis', or even 'hallucination', in the context of bereavement would mean little to the American Indian patient, and he probably would never even seek treatment. In the American Indian example, there was reliability in the diagnosis without validity. It's unlikely that a diagnosis can be valid without reliability, but reliability, as this example shows, never ensures validity.

Reliability and validity are especially problematic when you're looking at mental illness in a culture vastly different from your own. Few societies around the world have categories corresponding to 'autism', 'borderline syndrome', 'bipolar disorder', or even 'depression'. And even if they did, they wouldn't necessarily define them the way they do in the United States.

Consider a specific group of American Indians, the Salish, who live in Montana. Terry O'Nell, an anthropologist at the University of Oregon, thought she knew the criteria for depression well when she began a two-year stay with the Salish Indians on the Flathead reservation. She also thought she knew the prevalence rates – that at any given time fewer than 5 per cent of people in the United States suffer from depression, and that even high estimates, such as the rates of depression among the elderly, do not exceed 15 per cent. But when she went to Montana, the Salish told her 'This is a good place to study depression. Almost everyone here is depressed.'

O'Nell found that not only were they depressed – perhaps 75 per cent of the community reported depression – but that they had incorporated depression into their self image. Only the depressed qualified as 'real Indians', since being an Indian meant that you had to have suffered great emotional pain. In other words, the Salish, O'Nell said, think of depression as a feature of their identity – not an illness.

The way to deal with the depression, the Salish believe, is by transforming one's sadness into compassion for others. It doesn't get rid of the depression, but it does make the depressed individuals more useful members of their families and communities. The Salish think that depressed people – that is, the most 'real Indians' – are the best guides and teachers for their community. It's not surprising that mental health workers on the reservation find that depressed people resist treatment. The symptoms of depression among the Salish are as bad as it gets – they experience severe weight loss, inability to work, feelings of worthlessness, and substance abuse, among other things – and in many cases they lead to suicide. Still, depression is not considered abnormal and is, in fact, highly valued.

The Salish case shows that we should not assume that a single set of symptoms will have the same meanings everywhere. Even in the same culture, the border between ordinary sadness and clinical depression isn't always easy to find. Culture – and bias and prejudice, too – thus plays a role in determining how mental illnesses get identified and classified. For example, many studies demonstrate that African American men with depression are more likely than any other group of people to be misdiagnosed with schizophrenia. How does this happen? Relative to the general population, African American men are more distrustful of the medical establishment, especially white doctors, and so they may appear unexpressive or silent. Lack of expressiveness can be a symptom of schizophrenia. In situations of diagnostic uncertainty, and when there are problems with communication, even the most well-meaning doctors may rely on assumptions and stereotypes. They see the silence as a symptom of schizophrenia rather than as a cultural barrier. Among the mentally ill, poor people are also overrepresented, perhaps a legacy to the day when insane asylums also served as poorhouses.

Like the Salish with depression, the Navajo Indians of the American Southwest do not fret too much about autism. Jeanne Connors, an anthropologist, and one of the few who have studied autism cross-culturally, wrote that the Navajo Indians of the American Southwest tolerate a high degree of intellectual and physical impairment in their children before seeking assistance from the Navajo Tribal Council or the US government. There is a Navajo word for autism (*nidiniil geesh*, literally 'state of unawareness'), but it's a new word that was devised by Western psychologists and Navajo translators in 1989 for the handbook of an Arizona school system.

There are about 230,000 Navajo, about 150,000 of whom live in the Navajo nation, a 25,000-square-mile area in Arizona, Colorado, Utah, and New Mexico. It's an impoverished part of the United States; half of the homes have no electricity or water. Two-thirds of the roads in the Navajo nation are not paved, so it can be difficult for a Navajo family to get to a medical centre, let alone one where someone might have a clue about how to treat autism. The unemployment rate is many times greater than that of the general population, and income is largely from welfare, wage labour, livestock, and crafts, although men are increasingly joining the military. Like many poor families in the United States and elsewhere, households tend to be female headed.

Female-headed households suit the Navajo just fine, however, because the Navajo are a matrilineal society. The Navajo reckon family identity through the mother, not through the father, and this means that no matter how disabled someone might be, he or she has the right to live with his or her mother or her family. A father is much more concerned with the development of his sister's children than with raising his own children, because the sister's children are considered his true kin. He's not even supposed to teach his own biological kids traditional ways.

Connors, and nearly every anthropologist to ever work with the Navajo, found that they treated disabled people with extraordinary compassion – a good thing, too, since so many Navajos are disabled. Alcoholism and depression occur at a much higher rate among Navajos than in the general population, as does deafness (possibly the result of chronic ear infections caused by poor sanitation). Spinal cord injuries from accidents are common, and diabetes is so rampant and untreated that many people suffer from blindness, amputations, kidney failure, and coronary artery disease. Not surprisingly, newborns are often born prematurely, and many children have cognitive impairments, including mental retardation.

Connors found that the Navajo feel no compulsion to treat impaired children until they attain the age of about six, when school begins. Only then will the mother, and the other main authority figure in a child's life, the mother's brother, start shaping and disciplining the child. Because those with autism or mental retardation – of any age – are seen as being in a perpetual state of becoming, it is thought that too many demands should not be placed on them.

Though the Navajo do not believe in trying to change young children directly, they may try to fix what they believe is the underlying problem. In a case that Connors followed closely, the mother's brother of a boy named Bill was convinced that a kind of spirit called a 'Skinwalker' had put a curse on both Bill and the entire family. Bill was almost blind from the repetitive self-injurious behaviours common to some people with autism. He pressed on his eyeballs so hard that he had destroyed his vision, and there was nothing the family could do to stop him. He was also mute, although the family said that Bill had spoken a few words before the age of two.

When Bill was still two, his mother's brother called on a medicine man to diagnose his nephew's problems. The medicine man found a lizard under the family's hogan, or traditional house, whose eyes and mouth were fused. As Bill became mute and blind, the family became convinced that the lizard was evidence of a curse on the family. Bill's parents believed that if they could find a strong enough medicine man they could heal him. But by the time Connors left the field, they had yet to find anyone capable of performing the healing.

Most Navajo families who have a relative with autism believe that autism is the manifestation of some kind of spiritual disharmony, and they are willing to pay for rituals to restore order. The most common ritual performed for this purpose is the 'Blessingway', a ritual designed to ensure beauty, success, and health at any stage of life. Once it is completed, the child may, in fact, not look changed at all, but since harmony and order are restored in the spirit world, the child is nonetheless considered to be cured.

Connors also found that often the most severely impaired people with autism were living at home, not in residential institutions. Only those children who became too aggressive, physically or sexually, or who habitually ran away were sent to institutions.

People generally avoided sending children to residential institutions because the children would then lose the ability to truly become Navajos. They would learn English only, if they were capable of speech, and no one would be able to teach them traditional customs and folklore.

Connors was once in a Navajo woman's house talking to her about her autistic daughter, named Clara, who had been sent to the Chinle School of Arizona for the mentally disabled. Clara was a 'runner' – a person with autism who tends to wander away and get lost – and her mother didn't know how to keep her from doing this. Someone offered to sever the tendons in her ankles, but the mother refused. She later told Connors that she continues to wonder if the surgery would have helped her daughter.

At one point in the conversation, Clara's mother said, 'You know, I have another one in the back room.' Connors was shocked. 'Another what?' she asked. There had been no mention of another child in the social welfare files Connor had in her possession. She followed Clara's mother to the back of the house and saw a young man, profoundly mentally retarded, but so docile that the mother could handle him. The government would have paid for his care at Chinle, but there was simply no need, and no desire, to send him away.

When Navajo parents do send their children away, they visit them religiously. One mother, 60 years old when her son left home for an institution, hitchhiked once a week from Winslow, Arizona, a distance of more than 70 miles, and then hitchhiked back the same day. The son had had many difficulties at home. He had bitten off half of his tongue, suffered broken bones from falls, and had been bitten by a rattlesnake. But she had kept him at home throughout most of his childhood because she feared that whites were going to take him away from her and the reservation forever.

There are more Navajo children with special needs living on the reservation today than at any time during the past 50 years. Mid-century, many Navajo children with special needs had been sent to a residential school in Phoenix called Valley of the Suns, located more than five hours by car from the Navajo nation. But with deinstitutionalisation throughout the United States in the early 1970s, large numbers of the autistic residents were sent home. The Navajo brought their children back to the reservation by the carload and got them ready for Blessingway ceremonies.

What these examples tell us is that the tools for diagnosis are embedded within culture. This general rule applies not only to the Navajo or to the Salish but to modern psychiatry as well. The history of the study of mental illnesses is replete with stories of how the most capable scientists of any given time period failed to identify groups of symptoms that we now see clearly, or to see a group of symptoms as a specific disease.

The culture of science makes us believe that medicine and psychology can tell us truths about our bodies, when in fact they can only tell us about the particular set of phenomena we're looking at, or more precisely, about what our time and culture tell us is meaningful to look at. In the 'facts and figures' culture we live in today, we falsely believe that everything can be quantified. Anyone who's ever had a lab test done knows how seductive quantitative measures can be. We're eager to find out the number of blood cells, or to see what the graph on the EKG says, because the data seem so real, and so true – so much so, they can fool you.

The Pygmies, with whom I lived in central Africa, made a similar point about the relationship between medicine and truth every time they came to me for some kind of medical assistance – malaria pills, antibiotics, sticking plasters, or anti-lice shampoo. They didn't believe that I was making a correct decision about their complaint unless I looked it up in a book, not because I lacked a medical degree but because of the magical power of the published word. If it's written in a manual, they said, it must be true. Even when I knew for sure how to treat someone, I had to point to a paragraph in a book to convince them I was right. If I didn't look in the book, they wouldn't accept the treatment.

THE *DSM* STANDARDISED the objects of psychiatric research. But what did it do for clinicians, the people who actually make the vast majority of diagnoses? Did the *DSM* help standardise *their* diagnoses?

It turns out that a host of experts can get together to publish the most explicit, coherent criteria possible, and there can still be tremendous variability, even confusion, in the doctor's offices over diagnosis. Part of the reason is that clinicians are more likely to give a child a diagnosis that he or she thinks will help the child receive the best services or school placement than a diagnosis that conforms to the *DSM* but will not facilitate the best possible form of intervention. In Maryland, for example, a diagnosis of autism gets your child better care and easier access to Medicaid from the state than a diagnosis of mental retardation.

Judy Rapoport, the chief of child psychiatry at the National Institute of Mental Health, is the most rigorous of research scientists. She is also devoted to the patients she sees in her small clinical practice. She told me, 'I am incredibly disciplined in the diagnostic classifications in my research, but in my private practice, I'll call a kid a zebra if it will get him the educational services I think he needs.'

The clinician-researcher is an increasingly uncommon combination these days. Most people are one or the other. But even people who are both, like Rapoport, will behave differently depending on which hat they are wearing. Clinicians, the ones who actually diagnose children, are generally better than researchers at figuring out what treatments will help individual patients. They make the diagnosis that they believe is the most helpful for the child, but are not slaves to the standardisation of *DSM* criteria. This is why you can take your child to four clinicians and conceivably get four different diagnoses. Researchers, however, are better than clinicians at understanding the complexity of developmental differences and more attentive to standardisation. You are much less likely to get four different diagnoses from four different researchers.

The differences between researchers and clinicians were made clear in 1988 in an important paper on the diagnosis of Attention Deficit Disorder and the question of why American clinicians reported hyperactivity much more often than British clinicians did. In the study, British and American child psychiatrists examined the reliability of diagnoses of hyperactivity using the *DSM-III* and the World Health Organisation manual, the *ICD-9*, which psychiatrists in England use. The authors wanted to find out if researchers and clinicians in the United States and England came to the same conclusions when faced with the same 36 cases of boys between the ages of six and eleven.

Half the cases were prepared by the Americans, the other half by the British, and most of them had received diagnoses of Attention Deficit Disorder (ADD) or the ICD equivalent, 'hyperkinetic syndrome', in their home countries from researchers using their respective manuals. The cases were evaluated by four separate groups – American and British researchers, and American and British clinicians. The psychiatrists came up with several different diagnoses (schizophrenia, childhood psychoses, personality disorder, and conduct disorder, among others). Still, the research teams agreed overall on three-quarters of the cases using the *ICD-9*, and two-thirds of the cases using the *DSM-III*. But if the researchers agreed most of the time, why were so many more children in the United States called hyperactive? The researchers weren't the problem. It was the clinicians, the people who actually make the diagnoses in everyday life. The clinicians agreed with each other only about 25 per cent of the time using either manual.

The reason researchers and clinicians differ so much is that researchers tend to work together, generally read each other's papers, and usually remain faithful to the *DSM*. They are experts on the particular illnesses in question, and are also much more rigorous in how they make diagnoses. They are rigorous because they need to make their studies comparable to other studies and replicable by other researchers. For example, if you conduct an experiment to find out whether a new drug alleviates the symptoms of a particular illness, you need to make certain that your diagnoses are all consistent so that you are sure you're using the drug on the same kinds of patients. Other scientists in other places and at other times need to be able to replicate your study in order to affirm, reject, or build on your findings, and this cannot happen if you have used your own criteria rather than a well-tested, standardised set. When Spitzer and the other psychiatrists worked so hard on the *DSM-III*, they did so because the stakes for research were so high.

In an effort to achieve scientific rigour and comparability, almost every country in the world uses either the *DSM* or the *ICD*, and it is why the two manuals use almost identical diagnostic criteria and classifications. Only a small number of countries – France and Greece, for example – use their own manuals, and this is perhaps why psychiatrists in those countries have contributed less to international psychiatric research than their counterparts elsewhere. This is also the reason why protocols for clinical trials, both in the private pharmaceutical industry and in the public sector, require stringent criteria for eligible patients. The researchers involved in the trials seek statistically significant differences between drugs and placebos in order to establish the efficacy of the drug for the FDA, and efficacy is, of course, determined by how well the symptoms, as defined by the manual, are treated.

Clinicians, however, are interested in treating individual patients, and effective treatment does not always depend on a precise classification of the mental illness. Clearly, it matters a great deal whether a child in the United States with autism is diagnosed with autism. If he's not diagnosed, he will likely not get the treatments and medical and educational services that we know help autistic people. But if a mentally retarded child without autism is incorrectly given an autism diagnosis, he or she might actually get better treatment than would be possible under the correct diagnosis.

CLINICIANS HAVE AN OBLIGATION to their patients, not to the *DSM* or a drug trial. Imagine a girl whose primary diagnosis is phenylketonuria (PKU), a genetic disorder that involves, among other things, delayed development and mental retardation. She lives in a school district that has a good autism programme, one that is more intellectually challenging than the programme for mentally retarded children. The doctor believes that she could benefit from a more advanced curriculum and begins to consider how to frame her disorder. He thinks, 'She makes poor eye contact and has trouble communicating. With the broad criteria psychiatrists now use, I can legitimately diagnose her with autism and get her into the more appropriate classroom.'

Financial incentives can also drive diagnoses. In Maryland, children with a diagnosis of mental retardation cannot receive a Medicaid waiver, but children diagnosed with autism can. The waiver permits a child to receive intensive supports and medical care even if his or her family is not near the poverty line. Similar autism waivers are available in numerous states, such as Colorado, Indiana, Maryland, Massachusetts, and Wisconsin, owing to the successful lobbying of parent advocate groups.

The psychiatrist or psychologist hired by the parent of an autistic child knows that diagnosis greatly influences placement in appropriate educational programmes. Psychiatrists occasionally have to ask parents to accept a certain diagnosis, even if the parents don't like it, in order to get a child into the most appropriate class. For example, in New York state, an autism diagnosis generally means that a child can be placed in a specialised autism programme, whereas a diagnosis of PDD-NOS or Asperger's Disorder may result in placement into a class for emotionally disordered (ED) children. According to Margaret Hertzig, a psychiatrist at New York Presbyterian Hospital, although many families prefer a PDD-NOS or Asperger diagnosis to autism because it 'sounds better or milder', in many cases their children with PDD-NOS or Asperger's Disorder will be better served in an autism class. Getting into that class usually requires that the child be coded as autistic. In other words, the psychiatrist will not say, 'Your child is autistic and thus he should go into an autism programme'; rather, he will say, 'Your child should be in an autism programme (or even a particular autism programme with which he's familiar), so let's give him a diagnosis of autism.'

Diagnosis also affects insurance reimbursement because certain diagnoses may be covered while others are not. We lost hundreds of dollars during the first few months after Isabel's diagnosis because we didn't know that our insurance company covered speech therapy services for children diagnosed with autism. The speech therapist had submitted the bills under the diagnosis of 'Mixed Receptive-Expressive Language Disorder', but they went unpaid. When the name was changed to autism, the insurance company suddenly started to reimburse us. Conversely, treatment possibilities can influence diagnosis. For example, if a doctor thinks that a certain medication will help a particular child – on the basis of some symptoms but not necessarily a full-fledged diagnosis – he or she may prescribe the medicine and then give a diagnosis consistent with the medicine. That way, the parents can be reimbursed by their insurance company, which requires this diagnosis before it will agree to reimbursement for that drug.

Dan Pine, an NIMH researcher who will be directing the child psychiatry revisions for the forthcoming *DSM-V* (expected to be published after 2010), gave the following hypothetical example.

> A mother and father bring their 12-year-old son to you because, as they report it, 'he is doing poorly' at an exclusive private school with a demanding curriculum. When you look at the boy's transcript you notice that the boy received mostly grades of B. Teachers report that he is somewhat fidgety, doesn't pay attention quite as often as other kids, and sometimes seems irritable, but they don't say he's disruptive, outside the norm, or in need of any kind of educational or cognitive assessment. He just isn't an A student and he is facing a tough middle school curriculum at a tough school.

Pine went on:

> Now you know this kid shouldn't really have a diagnosis of ADHD – as a researcher you'd never classify him as ADHD – but you ask yourself as a clinician: wouldn't a little Ritalin or some other stimulant actually help him? It might. He might do better at school. And the parents are pushing you to do something, and they even bring up the subject of medication by themselves, and they know all the criteria for ADHD, and they've read books and have been all over the internet on this thing. They've read some new article you haven't even seen. And so maybe you medicate him, and to medicate him and have insurance reimburse for it, you give a diagnosis of ADHD,

and suddenly you've got a kid with this label. See how easy it can happen?

Anyone who tells you that psychiatric diagnosis is a strictly scientific exercise is fooling you. In making a diagnosis, doctors consider the educational options, the treatments, the economics, even the sensitivities of the parents, who may prefer or dislike certain diagnoses. And to some extent, a clinician may feel, or sense, a diagnosis based on the experience of having seen hundreds of children in his or her practice, rather than on application of scientific methods. We should also face facts. In the United States, the vast majority of psychiatric drugs are not prescribed by scientists, or even by psychiatrists, but by paediatricians and primary care doctors, partly because of the small number of psychiatrists (especially child psychiatrists) practicing in the country and partly because many Americans still feel that seeking psychiatric care is stigmatising. These primary care doctors are on the front line, yet they have limited training in mental health, and limited time to get to know a patient the way a researcher or mental health professional would.

Epidemiologists are researchers who take special care to conform to *DSM* and *ICD* criteria and to make sure their findings are statistically significant. But even epidemiology has its problems with validity. The reality is that, for epidemiologists, every variable can make a difference. Rates for autism, for example, have been shown to be significantly affected by a host of factors: the country in which the study is conducted, the age of the population studied, whether the study uses historical records of diagnosis or new diagnoses made during the study, whether the population under study is clinic- or school-based, rural or urban, and the particular screening and diagnostic instruments used. A little tweaking here and there of the diagnostic criteria and the methods used to find cases in the population being studied can deliver very different rates of illness. One epidemiologist from New York, who preferred not to be named, told me that she could give me virtually any prevalence rate for Attention Deficit Hyperactivity Disorder I might ask for, and do it in a way that would pass peer review at many scientific journals.

How did the specific classifications and criteria in the *DSM* help make autism a more popular diagnosis?

In 1980, the *DSM-III* called autism a 'Pervasive Developmental Disorder' (PDD). It was no longer a psychosis. And it was no longer a unique illness separated from other disorders that involved similar impairments in social skills, language, attention, perception, and motor movements.

The PDDs included five categories. First was 'Infantile Autism' (or 'Kanner's syndrome'), the criteria for which were as follows:

A. Onset before 30 months of age
B. Pervasive lack of responsiveness to other people (autism)
C. Gross deficits in language development
D. If speech is present, peculiar speech patterns such as immediate and delayed echolalia, metaphorical language, pronominal reversal

The second category was 'Childhood Onset Pervasive Developmental Disorder' (to cover the small number of cases of autism that developed after the age of 30 months). The first and second diagnoses were then broken down further into two additional categories, 'Infantile Autism Residual State' and 'Childhood Onset PDD Residual State'. Residual state diagnoses were used when the features that fulfilled the criteria for that disorder in the patient had diminished significantly over time in either number or severity. Finally, there was an additional diagnostic category, the catchall, 'Atypical Pervasive Developmental Disorder', to describe the children who had problems and delays in multiple areas but not enough problems to warrant a specific diagnosis. Seven years later, in 1987, when the revision of the *DSM-III* was published as the *DSM-III-R*, that category would be changed to 'Pervasive Developmental Disorder Not Otherwise Specified (including Atypical Autism)'.

Many child psychiatrists were pleased with the *DSM-III* for the simple reason that the American Psychiatric Association had given a clear definition of autism distinguishing it from other conditions. If a child had hallucinations or delusions, under the new definitions he or she would automatically be excluded from a PDD diagnosis. This, it was hoped, would be the end of the confusion between childhood schizophrenia and autism.

But several problems remained. For example, the use of the word 'state' in 'Residual State' may have seemed logical to the *DSM* team at the time they created the autism definition, but it seems unusual today because autism never really goes away. The word 'state' suggests impermanence. The authors included the category because they wanted to recognise that people with autism can make a lot of progress, but it is ultimately misleading.

Using the *DSM-III*, there was also no way for physicians to note the difference between autism that appeared at around age two or three, as in Kanner's syndrome; autistic symptoms that appeared much earlier, as in congenital rubella or phenylketonuria; and autistic symptoms that appeared much later in a child's life as a consequence of a medical problem or trauma. In other words, a child like those in Kanner's first group of eleven patients, a child with congenital rubella, another with tuberous sclerosis (a rare neurological disorder with symptoms that include mental retardation, skin and eye lesions, and seizures), and another with PKU might all have the same diagnosis. Some psychiatrists found this problematic. They wanted a manual that would distinguish between the *causes* of a cluster of symptoms.

In the 1987 revision of the *DSM-III* (the *DSM-III-R*), autism became an even broader category. The bizarre 'Residual State' category was dropped. This meant a child could still have the autism diagnosis even if things changed considerably, and even if the child was now able to function at a high level. The requirement that the age of onset had to be before 30 months was also dropped, mostly because it began to seem arbitrary; there wasn't enough scientific evidence to give a date of onset. Many parents of children diagnosed with autism at age five or six told their clinicians that their child had seemed normal until the age of 36 months or more. What mattered, the American Psychiatric Association argued, was whether the person had the symptoms, not when or why they started to have them. And since children with autism grew up into adults with autism, the word 'infantile' was abandoned, and the disorder became simply 'autistic disorder'. Logically, the diagnosis 'Childhood Onset Pervasive Developmental Disorder' had to be dropped as well, since the age of onset now was considered insignificant. Nearly everything that didn't quite fit the criteria for autistic disorder became Pervasive Developmental Disorder, Not Otherwise Specified (PDD-NOS). Asperger's Disorder wasn't mentioned and wouldn't become an official diagnosis until 1994.

The result of the changes in the *DSM-III-R* was that more people were categorised as autistic than ever before. In one study of 194 children with a PDD, Lynn Waterhouse found that when clinicians used the *DSM-III-R*, they diagnosed 91 per cent of the 194 children with 'autistic disorder', as opposed to only 51 per cent when they used the *DSM-III*. Clinicians, isolated inside their offices, latched on to autism as a diagnosis and began to use the term more loosely. Rates of autism diagnoses really started to take off at this time, not only in the United States but in Scandinavia, England, and Japan, too.

The *DSM* was not intended to be a static document but rather one that could evolve over time as the science of psychiatry advanced. So almost immediately after the publication of the *DSM-III-R*, the APA started planning for the *DSM-IV*. Fearing that the current criteria for autism were too inclusive, leading to too many diagnoses, many mental health experts urged a major revision of the PDDs. The *DSM-IV* criteria for the PDDs were carefully planned. In addition to organising the normal working groups to review classification schemes, researchers set up a huge field trial of proposed *DSM-IV* criteria to be conducted in 21 different sites throughout the world (but only in places where clinical pro-grammes for autism were already in place). The researchers found that clinicians everywhere estimated that their patients developed autistic disorder even earlier than the 30-month age listed in the *DSM-III*, with an average age of onset of eighteen months. No one expected an age of onset this early. In fact, in stark contrast to what parents reported in the studies that led to the 1987 revisions, out of more than 300 cases of autism, clinicians reported only two people with an onset *after* 36 months. There was now no question that age of onset should be put back in the *DSM*.

But as to the breadth of the criteria, the working groups con-flicted. On the one hand, researchers wanted a narrower definition of autism so their study subjects would be more similar to each other; on the other, clinicians knew that a broader definition of autism would help ensure that many of their patients – on the border between autistic disorder and PDD-NOS – could get an autism diagnosis and become eligible for better medical and edu-cational services. Far more often than not, the services needed by a person with full-fledged autism are very similar, if not identical, to the services needed by a person with PDD-NOS.

In the end, some things did change when the *DSM-IV* was published in 1994. Vague language was rewritten to be more specific. For example, the *DSM-IV* eliminated the phrase 'markedly abnormal nonverbal communication', because it could mean almost anything. The phrase did not specify whether just one abnormal behaviour was enough to count as a symptom of autism; nor did it give any concrete examples for diagnosticians to consider. It was replaced with the phrase 'marked impairments in the use of multiple nonverbal behaviors such as eye-to-eye gaze, facial expression, body posture, and gestures to regulate social interaction'. To cite another example, 'No or impaired imitation' was changed to 'lack of varied, spontaneous make-believe play or social imitative play, appropriate to developmental level'.

The language that finally went to the printer provided a narrower definition of the PDDs than the *DSM-III-R*, but three things undercut that achievement. First, even though the *DSM-IV* criteria published in 1994 were more specific than the 1987 *DSM-III-R*, they were still more inclusive than the 1980 manual, the *DSM-III*. Whereas the *DSM-III* listed 'a pervasive lack of responsiveness to other people' as a criterion for autism, for example, the *DSM-IV* read, 'a lack of spontaneous seeking to share enjoyment, interests, or achievements with other people'. The old language described someone truly unresponsive, whereas the new language could describe a loner. The *DSM-III* phrase 'if speech is present, peculiar speech patterns such as immediate and delayed echolalia, metaphorical language, pronominal reversal', a phrase that provided examples of truly peculiar linguistic behaviours, was replaced by 'marked impairment in the ability to initiate or sustain a conversation with others', a phrase that, again, could describe a loner or an introvert. Many clinicians and researchers would agree that these *DSM-IV* revisions made the overall PDD criteria more inclusive than ever.

Second, even if one wanted to argue that the *DSM-IV* criteria were more restrictive for the category 'autistic disorder', there were now five different PDDs, including the increasingly common PDD–NOS and Asperger's Disorder. It would be difficult to be stringent about the autism spectrum when the range of symptoms had been expanded to this degree, and when new illness labels had been created for those with mild symptoms. The PDDs would, in a matter of just a few years, become popularly known as 'the autism spectrum'.

Third, there was an error in the final manuscript. It is not well known, even among experts, but in 1993, when the authors of the child psychiatry section of the *DSM* were editing the proofs of the new *DSM-IV*, which would be published in 1994, they missed a critical mistake. For PDD–NOS, the largest group of autism spectrum disorders, the authors had intended to write as the criteria, 'impairment in social interaction *and* in verbal or nonverbal communication skills'. A different text was accidentally published. It said, 'impairment of reciprocal social interaction *or* verbal and nonverbal communication skills, *or* when stereotyped behavior, interests, and activities are present'. The authors had wanted someone to qualify as autistic only if they had impairment in *more than one area*, but the criteria, as published, required impairment in *only one area* for a diagnosis of PDD–NOS.

The threshold for PDD–NOS was thus lowered considerably, without anyone realising it until it was too late. In a small study, the results of which were reported in a letter to the editor of the *Journal of the American Academy of Child and Adolescent Psychiatry*, the authors of the *DSM-IV* PDD criteria found that in 75 per cent of cases in which a clinician ruled out PDD–NOS, the *DSM* incorrectly identified the children as PDD–NOS. The editorial error, made in 1994, was corrected, of course, but not until a revised edition of the *DSM-IV* was published in 2000. By that time, psychiatrists, psychologists, and epidemiologists throughout the world had been following these extremely broad criteria for six years, during the period when the so-called 'epidemic' emerged. Although it is unknown whether those diagnostic criteria produced a large number of false positives, they certainly didn't reduce the number of cases. It is also unknown whether the corrections made in 2000 made a difference in the clinician's office, since by that time the 1994 criteria had already become a part of everyday diagnostic practice.

The foundation for 21st-century diagnostic ambiguity was now firmly set. Today, a child with autism is a child 'on the spectrum', a classification that tells us just how murky the diagnostic waters of autism have become. It is so imprecise that it tells us mainly that the person has deficits in communication and social interaction, has restricted interests and activities, and falls somewhere between profoundly mentally retarded and exceptionally intelligent.

WE HAVE COME A LONG WAY from the time of Kanner, when autism was unfamiliar, when diagnosis was guesswork, and when the symptoms of autism spectrum disorders could be accounted for by any number of other diagnoses. Now that we have traced the emergence of autism as a diagnosis, and how it became fixed in the repertoire of psychiatric disorders, it's time to look at the numbers and rates. Autism is a genetically based disorder, and there is no such thing as a genetic epidemic. Then how and why did rates of autism rise so sharply over the past two decades? Is there an autism epidemic?

Autism by the Numbers

Over the past several years, the print, radio, and television media have begun reporting higher prevalence rates for autism and related disorders. The rates come from scientific studies conducted by major university research centres and the Centers for Disease Control, but the media only began to take notice when advocates for autism research and awareness took the cause to the public. Through the media, epidemiological findings, however modest and focused on a few discrete populations, had outsized effects.

Parents and other relatives of children with autism, many of them influential politicians or public figures, such as Representative Dan Burton of Indiana, football quarterbacks Dan Marino and Doug Flutie, the Nobel Laureate James Watson, talk-show host Don Imus, and NBC president Bob Wright, all started to talk openly about autism and to raise funds for autism research and treatment. Some talked of an 'autism epidemic', a phrase that hit the airwaves in 1999 when the state of California reported a steep rise in the number of cases of autism between 1987 and 1998.

The reports have heightened fears that specific causal agents, such as vaccinations, mercury poisoning, or other environmental exposures, might be to blame for the rise in reported cases of autism. Led in large part by Representative Burton, who has a grandson with autism, members of Congress have begun asking scientists to investigate whether thiomersal, a mercury-containing preservative once used as an ingredient in some vaccines, may cause autism.

On 9 February 2005, in a speech before Congress, Burton said, 'Thiomersal is a preservative which contains 50% ethel mercury. And as children got more and more vaccinations, as many as 30 now before they start in the first grade, the incidence of neurological disorders, autism, and other childhood mental problems grew dramatically. It used to be 1 in 10,000 children were autistic according to the Center [*sic*] for Disease Control. Now it's 1 in 150. We have an absolute epidemic of autism.'

The debate about whether thiomersal is linked to autism has been fuelled by a recent book on the subject, David Kirby's *Evidence of Harm,* high-profile articles by Robert F. Kennedy, Jr, in *Salon* and *Rolling Stone,* and stories by Dan Olmsted of United Press International. In the anti-vaccine literature there is talk of a government and pharmaceutical industry conspiracy to hide the harm done by thiomersal in the United States and the rest of the world. Now, almost everyone I meet seems to think there's a relationship between vaccines and autism.

The passion behind this movement is reminiscent of anti-vaccine movements of the past. In the late 18th century, parents in England tried to protect their children from the first smallpox vaccine, which, given the state of medicine at the time, was indeed dangerous. The logic of the current movement is similar. Opponents of vaccination today, like those of the 18th century, argue that vaccines are unsafe, unproven, and evidence of government abuse of power. They question why a government should be able to infringe on civil rights by compelling people to inject their children with a foreign substance or a live virus. The difference between this and other anti-vaccine movements is how effectively the anti-vaccine message can be communicated today: It is being spread all over the world via the Internet and finding receptive ears, not among scientists or doctors, but among parents and families, the people most responsible for their children's welfare.

Indeed, in the summer of 2007, the US Vaccine Court began hearing nine test cases, representing the claims of nearly 5,000 families, on the question of whether thiomersal, the measles-mumps-rubella (MMR) vaccine, or both together caused autism in the plaintiffs' children. I attended the first case and heard some of the world's leading experts on autism, immunology, and vaccines testify that there is no biological model to account for an autism vaccine connection, no scientific evidence or credible studies linking the two. They argue, instead, that autism is largely genetic. And yet just before the hearing began, Robert F. Kennedy, Jr, wrote on the *Huffington Post* website that there are 'hundreds of research studies' from 'dozens of countries' providing 'undeniable' proof that vaccines cause autism. I could not find any basis for that claim in the scientific literature or even in media reports.

The widespread dissemination of information via the World Wide Web sometimes makes us ordinary parents believe we are experts, or at least paraprofessionals. To research topics relating to our children, the average parent can now explore a vast array of websites, including many that feature online scientific articles, Listservs, or chat rooms. The Informat on gap between scientists and the public is narrowing, much to the dismay of many doctors, who feel they are expected to know everything that their patients' families find on the Web (and more), including anecdotal reports about new therapies and possible causes of autism. Physicians sometimes find themselves arguing with families about the difference between scientific research, anecdotes, and conspiracy theories. Nowhere is this disjunction more salient than in the debate about the relationship between autism and vaccines. Parents insist that vaccines cause autism in children predisposed to mercury toxicity; scientists believe they do not.

It is important to note that while many Americans have embraced the hypothesis that thiomersal is related to autism and the change in prevalence of autism, the hypothesis has had less traction in the UK. Instead, many British embraced the hypothesis that the Measles Mumps Rubella vaccine (MMR) is to blame, a vaccine that never contained thiomersal (since the preservative would render that particular vaccine ineffective). Fears about the MMR began in 1998 when a doctor in England, Andrew J. Wakefield, published an article in the prestigious journal, the *Lancet*, in which he and twelve colleagues described twelve children, eight with autism and four with other neurological/developmental delays, who had a range of gastrointestinal symptoms and, the paper claimed, became autistic within a month after receiving the MMR vaccination. The symptoms of autism spectrum disorders are commonly identified during the same range of ages as the MMR shot is administered. Because of this, some people thought that Wakefield's conclusion was plausible. However, subsequent research has demonstrated that the apparent relationship between vaccines and autism is due to coincidence rather than cause-and-effect.

In 2004, several years after the paper was published, it was revealed that Wakefield had a number of conflicts of interest he had not disclosed. Moreover, the majority of co-authors, while agreeing that autism experts need to study the possibility of gastro-intestinal problems in autistic children, did not agree with the claim that there was a causal relationship between the MMR and autism. As a result, the authors retracted their support for the paper's conclusions, and the *Lancet* issued a partial retraction of the paper. The *Lancet* wrote, 'It seems obvious now that had we appreciated the full context in which the work reported in the 1998 *Lancet* paper by Wakefield and colleagues was done, publication would not have taken place in the way that it did.' As of this writing, Wakefield is defending himself against charges of scientific misconduct made by the General Medical Council, the body that regulates medical schools and medical licensure in the United Kingdom.

Many families, especially in the United Kingdom, have stopped getting their children immunised. They avoid, among others, the Measles, Mumps and Rubella (MMR) vaccine, and this is probably the main cause of the unusual rise in cases of mumps in England. The British Broadcasting System (BBC) reported that in 2003–2004, some 60 per cent of two-year-olds in parts of London were not immunised. In 1995, the British government reported 1,936 confirmed cases of mumps. In 2003, there were 4,265 confirmed cases, and in 2004, 15,503. Yet, the Centers for Disease Control in the United States has stated unequivocally that scientific studies do not link the MMR vaccine with autism, and they have assembled an elaborate website that describes these studies.

The most important piece of evidence provided by those who believe that thiomersal is related to autism is that rates for all the various autism spectrum disorders have risen dramatically over the past few decades. Indeed, every argument I've ever seen for that relationship is based largely on the assumption that the current epidemiological evidence suggests a true rise in the incidence of autism, a rise that began with the introduction of thiomersal in vaccines in the late 1930s (a few years before Kanner first described autism) and that intensified with the increase in the mercury concentration of thiomersal in the late 1980s (when autism rates skyrocketed).

But the increase in the rate of autism is more likely due to the result of new and improved science – more reliable definitions of autism and more awareness of autism among health-care professionals and educators. Maybe we are finally diagnosing and counting autism correctly. If this is the case, there may not be a true epidemic, even if the number of reported cases is higher than ever. We have to be extremely careful when dealing with epidemiology because high or dramatically increasing prevalence rates don't always mean the same thing as a true rise in the incidence of a disease. We should not discourage people from doing research on environmental toxins, since so many complex diseases involve the interaction between genes and the environment. But we also shouldn't look for needles in haystacks to find environmental causes for the increase in rates. After all, the most current and sophisticated epidemiological studies show a continual rise in rates of autism after thiomersal was removed from the vaccines. The scientific establishment has solidly refuted the hypothesis that vaccines or thiomersal are related to autism or changing prevalence rates of autism spectrum disorders. It makes sense to look for answers in the scientific practices that produced the reports of higher rates. Unfortunately, most anti-vaccine advocates do not want to look closely at the research that provides their ammunition, at times dismissing in depth analyses of the details of epidemiological studies as methodological quibbles. But in epidemiology, as we'll see, nothing is more important than methodology. If we do look at the methods, we'll find that we're finally, after all these years, getting the numbers right. And we'll also find that the high rates are in fact good news for the future of autism awareness, research, and treatment – with higher rates there will always be more research money and interest.

But first things first. How can we know for sure if autism is or is not an epidemic?

SCIENTISTS GENERALLY USE the term 'epidemic' to refer to a disease that occurs suddenly in a discrete population, an outbreak. An epidemic is not declared on the basis of high numbers but on the speed or rate that new cases pop up. In the 19th century, the word was used almost exclusively to describe a wave of infectious disease. In the typical graph of an epidemic, the number of cases is plotted against a measurement of time, such as days or weeks, to show how quickly the disease is spreading.

With the notable exception of AIDS, in modern times we've had less experience than previous generations with fast-moving infectious diseases, like polio or smallpox, that can affect entire populations. As a result, the time component of the definition of an epidemic has become less crucial. As one consequence, the definition of 'epidemic' has broadened. Now, we use the word with little reference to the speed at which new cases are occurring, which puts us one step away from the original usage. And when we talk about epidemics of conditions that are not contagious – such as skin cancer, autism, anorexia nervosa, and teen pregnancy – or conditions and situations that are not even real diseases – like alien abduction, or satanic child abuse – we're two steps away.

Politicians, journalists, philanthropic organisations, and advocates want to make an impact. They use the word so the echoes of that older meaning can be heard. 'Epidemic' arouses fear, a sense of danger – it is associated with a plague. It does have an impact on audiences and readers.

The simplest, most current definition of the term that I have found came from an epidemiologist at Harvard who told me, 'If there are more cases than you expect, it's an epidemic.' From this perspective, there is no doubt that autism is an epidemic, because there have been more cases of autism diagnosed over time than one might have expected, based on the numbers and rates of diagnosed cases in the past.

With the old sense of the term 'epidemic', clinicians distinguished between diseases that were contagious or posed a grave threat to large numbers of people and required an immediate intervention, and those that were relatively harmless. By comparison, the Harvard epidemiologist's definition of 'more cases than you expect' seems imprecise and raises more questions than it provides answers. Whose expectations are the rates to be compared with? Whose diagnoses are to be counted? What if the expectations were unrealistic or based on false premises? And if you find more cases than you expected, how many more do you need to find to claim an epidemic? There is no universal agreement about how widespread or fast an outbreak has to be before it can be called an epidemic.

Epidemiology is a complicated field of public health that combines basic science, survey work, and mathematics. The logistics alone are enough to make many epidemiologists wonder why they chose a career outside of a laboratory. But because the findings of epidemiologists are so important to society, they get reported in the media, where, by necessity, we hear about them in bite-sized and oversimplified chunks of information. So we need to be cautious, even suspicious, about claims of epidemics, even if they are useful fictions that raise awareness about a disorder.

Most of the news about the autism epidemic over the past several years has come from numbers derived from a particular kind of epidemiological research: *prevalence studies*. Prevalence studies produce rates that refer to the proportion of a population affected by a certain disease at a single point in time – for example, 1 in 300, or 4 in 10,000. Prevalence is the number of cases divided by the population screened. *Incidence*, which is *not* what we usually learn about in the news on autism, refers to the number of new cases of a certain disorder that occurs in a specific population in a defined period of time. Epidemics are usually defined by increases in incidence, not prevalence.

Compared to prevalence studies, incidence studies are rare. This is because incidence studies are very expensive to conduct and take a long time to complete. To conduct an incidence study, an epidemiologist first has to do a prevalence study to determine who in the study population already has the illness in question. Next, perhaps several years later, the researcher needs to follow up on the people who were well during the prevalence study, looking for new, 'first-ever' cases among this remaining, or so-called 'at-risk', group.

Incidence studies are vital to epidemiology because, by identifying the time and place that a disease appears, a scientist may locate variables that might cause that disease. For example, in one of the best-known epidemiological discoveries, the 19th-century scientist John Snow mapped new cases of cholera in Golden Square, London. He found numerous new cases of cholera – a highly contagious disease – appearing almost everywhere, but not among the inmates at the jail. It turned out that the jail used a different water supply from the rest of the square. Snow was therefore able to locate the source of the cholera in the infected well.

But in autism studies, there has been no clear geographical clustering, and no identifiable cause. Even more importantly, given that autism is not an infectious disease, and that it emerges very early in life, if researchers did conduct an incidence study few new cases would be diagnosed in the healthy population they screened in the earlier prevalence study. I'm aware of only a few English-language epidemiological studies published in peer-reviewed scientific journals that looked at diagnoses of autism in the same population over a period of time. Only one of these – a study conducted in Minnesota – produced any unexpected findings (I'll discuss that later). Assuming that there is no new environmental toxin or other catalyst to produce new cases of autism, the prevalence rate should remain stable. That is, unless there are major changes in the way autism is detected, diagnosed, and counted.

So how did epidemiologists count autism in the past? In the 1960s and 1970s, researchers mainly studied administrative records. They went to hospitals and clinics and looked at medical records to find the number of cases of autism, then considered a rare disease. This method yielded very low prevalence rates of autism because the diagnosis 'autism' was uncommon, even if the symptoms were not. With a disease like autism, you have to do research by, at a minimum, going to specialty clinics or looking through local or national special-education registries. Such a registry was established in the United States only in 1992 as a result of the Individuals with Disabilities Education Act (1991). Before that time, investigators consulted registries of people with a diagnosis of autism who sought educational, medical, or speech therapy services. But this method only counted cases that the clinics were already aware of, usually the more severely impaired people with autism.

Today, there is more awareness of the full continuum that we call the autism spectrum, and there are more services available and more people using those services. As a result, the registries give a better indication of the number of people with autism, ranging from the severely impaired to the high functioning. Investigators now generally use a three-stage approach to counting cases of autism, and it is capable of detecting more cases than ever before.

First, researchers ask school officials (in both mainstream and special education schools) or health-care practitioners to identify potential cases, and look for autism classifications in local or national registries, or in special-education 'child counts'. These counts, submitted to the Department of Education, report the number of children to whom the schools gave special-education services over the previous school year. Unfortunately, a few researchers, some journalists, and many advocates use these classifications as if they were the same thing as a diagnosis. As I mentioned earlier, autism wasn't even a legitimate code for the US Department of Education until the 1991–1992 school year, so there were rarely any children reported in the national special-education child counts with 'autism' before that time (instead they were classified under terms like 'mental retardation' or 'multiple disabilities'). But this doesn't mean that there were fewer children with autism before 1991.

In the second stage, and in the best of circumstances, parents and teachers fill out standardised questionnaires such as the ASQ (Autism Screening Questionnaire) or the ASSQ (Autism Spectrum Screening Questionnaire). These questionnaires, which have been studied extensively to make sure that independent researchers using them with the same case would come to the same conclusion, help epidemiologists identify potential cases. These are highly sensitive surveys that will capture even very mild cases of pervasive developmental disorders, as well as many cases that will prove to be negative.

In a third stage, epidemiologists use trained diagnosticians to interview and diagnose those who pass the screen, preferably with more than one structured, reliable protocol, such as the ADOS (Autism Diagnostic Observation Schedule) or the ADI (Autism Diagnostic Interview), tools that have been tested extensively in many locations. In most studies of mental illnesses, researchers use only one protocol, but in studying autism, a condition with a wide range of symptoms and severity, it's a good idea to use two or more tools. Some tools are sensitive for identifying autism in the higher-functioning cases, while others are more sensitive for autism in lower-functioning ones.

Ideally, the diagnoses are then validated by outside consultants using a group of randomly selected cases (some with and some without an autism diagnosis). When possible, videotapes are made of the diagnostic procedures. In addition, to determine how reliably multiple diagnosticians would come to the same conclusion about a subject, the researchers run a small test. Raters who do not know the diagnosis (that is, 'blinded' raters) of an individual case will watch the videotape and then offer a diagnosis. This last stage is especially important for validating the less clear-cut cases, the ones on the border between two different diagnoses or between a diagnosis and none at all.

This three-stage method, as used today – a period in American history in which autism awareness is at an all-time high, and in which the diagnosis of autism has broadened to include a wide range of different people along a spectrum – yields many more cases of autism than the older studies did.

'EPIDEMIC' LITERALLY MEANS 'of the people', so it's not surprising that the word is often used to refer to ideas or even fashions that are suddenly popular. Perhaps the most recent well-known book on epidemics is the bestseller *The Tipping Point* by Malcom Gladwell. Gladwell uses the word 'epidemic' to characterise anything that is contagious and spreads rapidly, including ideas and fashions – like the return of Hush Puppies and the uptide of teen smoking or teen pregnancy. 'Ideas and products and messages and behaviors,' he wrote, 'spread just like viruses do.' In fact, the 'tipping point' is a phrase that actually comes from the field of epidemiology. But Gladwell makes liberal use of it to refer to the moment 'when an idea, trend, or social behavior crosses a threshold, tips, and spreads like wildfire.' This more benign definition of 'epidemic' suits the study of autism (and most psychiatric diagnoses) better than the old one. Indeed, I would readily agree that we have reached a 'tipping point', a point at which autism became not just a terrible disability but an epidemic – not a real epidemic, in the old sense of the term, but an epidemic in Gladwell's world of rapidly prolif-erating ideas and beliefs.

Like fashion trends, diagnoses can spread, and there are more things spreading in society, according to the media, than you can count: alien abduction, restless legs syndrome, road rage disorder (also called Intermittent Explosive Disorder, or I.E.D.), and so on. These are just a few of the 'diagnoses' that have quickly become popular topics of discussion. There is no question that the people with these diagnoses have something wrong with them and that they are sick and suffering. What is open to question is whether these illnesses, some of them newly named, are 'epidemics'.

And just because we develop a new illness name doesn't mean that the illness is new. Rather, it means simply that we've gath-ered a group of symptoms together and made them into a distinct disorder. It also means that we're *treating* that disorder, since new illness names usually emerge because we're trying to do some-thing about the symptoms. Consider two brief examples of new illnesses.

The reported prevalence of Alzheimer's disease has doubled since 1980. It is said to afflict at least 4 million Americans. Although there is good evidence that Alzheimer's disease existed as far back as we have medical records, it was not formally described and named until the early 20th century. The vast majority of Alzheimer's researchers do not believe that there has been a genuine increase in incidence. But there is much more recognition of it, and the definition of the disease has broadened. Not until the 1980s, when reported prevalence rates rose dramatically, did researchers com-monly use the term to refer to late-onset senility. Before that time, the term was used primarily to refer to dementia in people under the age of 65.

Foetal alcohol syndrome, another example, is now estimated to occur in at least 2 in 1,000 people in the United States – a

high prevalence rate for such a serious disorder. Yet there is virtually nothing in the medical literature on foetal alcohol syndrome
before 1973.

Gladwell said that tipping points occur when three things happen. First, small changes are effected by a small number of people.
Second, a contagious message becomes memorable and 'sticks'.
Third, messages are communicated under just the right cultural
and historical conditions. The numerous changes in autism diagnosis and treatment over the past century that I have been describing
fit Gladwell's description. They together had big effects; messages
about the frequency, range, and causes of autism resonated with
large numbers of people, and they were communicated at a time
in history when child psychiatry, psychopharmacology, and the
special-education industry were beginning to prosper.

Elaine Showalter, a literary critic and historian of medicine,
noted two other ingredients necessary for medical epidemics: first,
physicians and enthusiastic writer/advocates who are interested
in popularising a diagnosis; and second, unhappy, vulnerable people who are anxious to understand and identify what is wrong
with them (or their children). Showalter believes that epidemics of
the relatively new and controversial psychiatric disorders, such as
multiple personality syndrome or even chronic fatigue syndrome
– controversial because some scientists think these disorders do
not actually exist – would never have become bona fide disease
categories, let alone epidemics, had it not been for the scientists
who helped make them visible, especially through the media and
the Internet, and the patients who were desperate to find the cause
of their troubling symptoms.

There can also be economic influences at work. In a book called
Pharmaceutical Reason, sociologist Andrew Lakoff tells the story of
how a French biotechnology company, in search of DNA from
people diagnosed with bipolar disorder, gave a psychiatric hospital

in Argentina $100,000 in return for DNA samples from 200 patients diagnosed with the disorder. The problem was that bipolar disorder is not a common diagnosis in Argentina, and much less common there than in the United States or Western Europe. The psychiatrists were under pressure to make more diagnoses of bipolar disorder so that they could provide the DNA and honour their end of the deal. We might conclude that if you get enough pharmaceutical companies involved with enough hospitals to make enough diagnoses of a particular disorder, soon you could have a significant increase in the diagnosis of a particular disease. And if those hospitals train enough psychiatrists, who then find employment in other hospitals, it might not be too long before someone claims an emerging 'epidemic'.

It remains to be seen whether there is sufficient economic incentive to fuel the autism epidemic, but we already know a few things. Medicaid waivers offered to families with autistic children allow children who would not otherwise qualify for government benefits to receive, for free or at low cost, a variety of treatments, including medications, respite care, and speech and occupational therapy. In the United States, pervasive developmental disorders constitute a large percentage of the clientele of speech therapy and child psychiatry practices; and numerous alternative therapies are beginning to emerge, ranging from house 'cleanings' that cost tens of thousands of dollars to remove all allergens, to the dangerous process of chelation, a therapy that removes mercury and other metals from the afflicted child's body.

MANY 'EPIDEMICS' WOULDN'T EXIST unless there were people willing to believe in them, with or without scientific evidence. But what do the *scientists* – especially the epidemiologists, who are the ones counting cases – say about the prevalence of autism?

Since 1966, about 50 epidemiological studies of autism have been carried out in fourteen different countries (Canada, Denmark, Finland, France, Germany, Iceland, Indonesia, Ireland, Israel, Japan, Norway, Sweden, the United Kingdom, and the United States), though most were conducted in North America or Western Europe. There are a few brief reports of autism in China, Ghana, Hong Kong, Nigeria, South Africa, Taiwan, Zambia, and Zimbabwe confirming that autism exists in these countries, in boys more often than in girls, but they describe very few cases and tell us little about the epidemiology of autism – so little that during the 1970s and 1980s some epidemiologists suggested autism was not a universal phenomenon but 'an illness of Western civilization'.

The psychiatrist and epidemiologist Eric Fombonne of McGill University in Montreal, Canada, recently analysed 43 English-language epidemiological studies of autism published between 1966 and 2001 (excluding those studies that did not conform to strict methods, were not published in peer-reviewed scientific journals, or were simply exploratory surveys). 21 of these studies, conducted in the fourteen countries mentioned above, were done between 1991 and 2001.

South Africa, South Korea, and India, three of the countries that I discuss in Part 2 of this book, are notably absent, despite the fact that they all have robust medical systems and sophisticated medical research infrastructures. Given the explicit criteria for autism, one might think that coming up with autism prevalence rates in these countries would be easy. But there have to be researchers and funding agencies interested in carrying out the studies, and governments to set autism research as a national priority. In these countries, interest in autism only started to take off over the past decade as their local media started to talk about the higher prevalence rates reported in the United States.

Only one large-scale epidemiological study of autism has been conducted in Australia, and it was confined to children already classified as intellectually disabled. We do not know what the rate would look like in Australia if children with autism who have average or above-average IQs were included. In Australia – and in other countries, such as India and South Africa – children with an intellectual disability tend to be diagnosed fairly late, by American and European standards, usually when they enter primary school at about age five or six. The prevalence rates derived from these older children thus exclude the two- to five-year-olds that are sometimes captured in the more inclusive epidemiological studies conducted in the United States.

These gaps in knowledge are not surprising, however, to people familiar with psychiatric research. Childhood mental disorders are especially hard to measure, for reasons described in the previous chapter. They are also especially hard to count. First, parents are more protective of their children than they are of themselves, so they tend to keep their children out of research studies. Second, you need to have multiple informants, such as parents and teachers – in contrast to epidemiological studies of adults, who can be interviewed directly. Single informants may supply inaccurate or biased information, because there is often little overlap reported between parent and teacher accounts of the child's mental disorder, and because, in cases where the child can supply an account of his or her own experiences, there is often little overlap between the child's account and those of his parents and teachers. Less is known about the prevalence of childhood mental disorders than is known about the prevalence of psychiatric disorders in adults. In fact, up until the early 1990s, when the National Institute of Mental Health began to increase funding for large scale, population-based child psychiatric epidemiology, most child studies were actually conducted with adolescents, and most surveyed fewer than 800 subjects.

The studies Fombonne analysed show a clear rise in prevalence rates for autism over time. For example, the median rate reported in studies conducted between 1966 and 1993 was 4.7 cases of autism per 10,000, while the median rate for the 1994–2004 studies was 12.7 per 10,000. The more recent the study, the higher the prevalence rate. And all studies that produced a rate of more than seven per 10,000 – a total of 22 studies – were conducted after 1987. By the mid-1990s, the rate rose to thirteen per 10,000, and was even higher when expanded to include children diagnosed with more mild autism spectrum disorders like PDD-NOS and Asperger's Disorder. What can account for these increases? There were at least seven major factors involved.

First, there is now better awareness and better diagnosis of autism in most countries in the world, but especially in North America and Western Europe. Teachers and the general public knew little about the signs and symptoms of autism before the 1990s. Most importantly, many paediatricians and psychiatrists in the United States and the United Kingdom did not know until recently how to recognise and diagnose autistic disorders.

Second, children are being diagnosed earlier than ever. In the past, as one consequence of the lack of awareness of the symptoms of autism, children who were diagnosed with autism tended to receive the diagnosis at a later age than they do today, often only after parents had taken their child to numerous doctors over a period of several years in search of an accurate diagnosis. Obviously, as the age of diagnosis decreases in any given population, the number of people diagnosed with autism will increase. If the studies previously counted children with autism who were age five and up, and now count children with autism age two and up, three extra years of children have been added to the total. By itself, the expansion of the age range wouldn't change the rate (the number divided by the population screened) unless more children in the younger age groups were being given a diagnosis of autism, which appears to be the case.

The change in awareness did not occur because governments made any decisions to increase knowledge about autism. Awareness increased because parents of autistic children advocated for special services for their children, and because some of the most influential parents, such as Bernard Rimland and Lorna Wing, happened to be mental health experts able to communicate to large audiences through scientific publications. The success of the movie *Rain Man*, which parents of autistic children in every corner of the world have seen, didn't hurt autism awareness either. Best-selling books also heightened awareness: books by people with autism, such as Temple Grandin and Donna Williams; memoirs of parents of children with autism, like the works of Clara Clairborne Park; and even novels that feature characters with autism – for example, Mark Haddon's *The Curious Incident of the Dog in the Nighttime*. The awareness of teachers was crucial to the rise in autism diagnoses. At the end of the 20th century, more children began attending preschools and daycare facilities, where teachers could compare these very young children to their peers and identify social and language deficits.

Third, autism and schizophrenia are no longer conflated. In fact, the distinction between childhood-onset schizophrenia and autism is one of the best-validated distinctions among the disorders seen in psychiatry today. Children with autism now tend to be diagnosed with autism. But if it could be documented that rates of childhood schizophrenia dramatically decreased as cases of autism rose, this would add supporting evidence to my theory that the increase in autism reflects a change in perception and definitions. Unfortunately, there are no epidemiological rates for childhood schizophrenia, because the illness was always classified under the general label 'schizophrenia' that combined rates for adults and children.

Fourth, the *concept* of autism has broadened. In the 1990s, largely as a result of the efforts of Lorna Wing in the United Kingdom, many epidemiological studies changed their focus. They began to count cases 'on the spectrum', the 'classic' autism described by Kanner plus the other PDDs. And now, PDD-NOS, at least in common usage, is subsumed under the category of 'autism spectrum disorders'. The rates grew as the concept of autism changed. Of eight studies conducted between 2000 and 2003, six found rates of between 52 per 10,000 and 67.5 per 10,000 (that is, as high as 1 in 155).

Even a small broadening can have a large effect on prevalence rates and IDEA school codes. That effect can be seen in the distribution of the cases that account for the increase in rates in epidemiological studies. A large percentage of the increase came at opposite ends of the spectrum: the severely impaired (who used to be called 'mentally retarded') and the very mildly impaired (who may have had no psychiatric diagnosis at all by earlier standards). In fact, in epidemiological studies of the spectrum, for every two children identified with classic autism there are three children who are on the spectrum but not impaired enough to meet all of the criteria for classic autism.

In 2000, three researchers working in northern Finland compared the narrow criteria first used by Leo Kanner in 1943 with the broader set included in the World Health Organisation's diagnostic manual, the *ICD-10*, which is similar to the *DSM-IV*. They found that when they used the older, more restrictive criteria to ascertain 'autistic disorder' (not autism plus the spectrum), they came up with a rate of autism of 5.6 per 10,000, but when they used the modern *ICD-10* criteria, they found 12.2 per 10,000.

Simply put, the newer criteria yield higher rates than Kanner's criteria – which is no surprise, since they allow inclusion of both less and more severely impaired children.

One example of the effect of the broadening of criteria on prevalence rates can be observed in statistics from California, where the number of people who received services between 1987 and 1998 under the category of autism rose by 273 per cent. Morton Ann Gernsbacher and colleagues, in a 2005 journal article, used an analogy to show how such an increase could happen in the absence of a true increase in incidence. They asked readers to suppose they had asked how many of the men who lived in McClennan County, Texas, were 'tall' at two different points in time – the mid-1980s and the mid-1990s, using two different definitions of tall. Suppose also that in the mid-1980s, 'tall' was defined as six feet, two and a half inches, but that in the mid-1990s, the criterion was loosened a little, to six feet. There would have been 2,778 tall men in the earlier group, but 10,360 men in the later group, reflecting a 273 per cent increase (the same size increase, incidentally, as the change in autism rates in California from the mid-1980s to the mid-1990s). Clearly, the hypothetical Texas study would be flawed – it shows a 273 per cent increase when there may not have been any real increase in height. Only the criterion for 'tall' had changed. Gernsbacher suggested the same thing had occurred with autism rates in California.

During the 1990s, new diagnoses emerged within the autism spectrum. These included a rare disorder called Childhood Disintegrative Disorder (CDD), sometimes called late-onset autism, and Rett's Disorder, an illness that afflicts primarily girls, and is typified by poor motor coordination and decreased head growth, along with the other common symptoms of the PDDs. And by 1994, in the *DSM-IV*, there would be yet another PDD, Asperger's Disorder, a group of socially impaired children without a language delay but with significant communication deficits. CDD and Rett's Disorder do not account for a large number of autism spectrum cases – they are rare disorders – but the presence of these disorders in the PDD category is yet another symptom of the broadening vision of what can count as PDD. It's PDD-NOS and Asperger's Disorder that make up a lot of the *new* cases in the spectrum – as many as 75 per cent of them, according to two well-respected researchers.

Fifth, in many cases 'autism' is replacing the label 'mental retardation' and a host of learning disabilities. Many children who might have been diagnosed with mental retardation – as my daughter might have been in the 1970s – are now diagnosed with autism. Given that at least 1 in 100 school-aged children is mentally retarded, it is likely that many of these children will be reclassified as the popularity of the autism diagnosis continues to grow. Indeed, in the United States as a whole, the number of children classified by special-education programmes as mentally retarded or learning disabled dropped in tandem with the increase in numbers of children classified as autistic (California is one of just a few exceptions to this trend). Moreover, there is plenty of anecdotal evidence of children with a previous diagnosis of ADHD or Borderline Personality Disorder being reclassified as having Asperger's Disorder. But to be fair, there are no published studies today that definitively confirm or disprove the hypothesis that higher rates are the result of diagnostic reclassifications.

In 2005, I interviewed paediatricians in Appalachia who told me that parents there have just begun to ask for autism diagnoses. Recently a woman walked into one of the paediatric clinics I visited in eastern Tennessee, where her mentally retarded ten-year-old son with cerebral palsy had been seen since birth. She said that her son was 'getting a little bit autistic'. The paediatrician asked her to explain, and the mother answered, 'He's having episodes of autism.' This mum did not have a very good understanding of autism, because the 'episodes' she recounted involved only problems with eye contact – namely, occasional movements of her son's left eye away from centre. It was good that she came to see the doctor, because the boy had a 'wandering eye', a *strabismus*, that needed to be repaired with eye surgery. But she seemed truly disappointed that her son wasn't autistic. She had been hoping for a change of diagnosis. Like other parents I've met, she believed a diagnosis of autism would mean that her child could improve someday. She fantasised that there was a normal child locked inside her son, waiting to be rescued when a new medicine or therapy came along to release him from his shell. However, the degree to which parents' interests in getting their child an autism diagnosis influences epidemiology is an open question. Certainly, the effect would depend on the methodology of a given study. A study that relies heavily on parent reports may find that parents' preferences for an autism label will influence the outcome of the study.

Sixth, epidemiological methods have changed. Administrative records proved to be poor resources for finding cases. For example, a Centers for Disease Control study in Atlanta, published in 2003, estimated that only 41 per cent of children validated by researchers as having a PDD had actually received a diagnosis of an autism spectrum disorder by their school system. The school system may have used a more restrictive set of criteria than the researchers, and school psychologists and educators may have used different criteria throughout the city. The new studies were able to find more cases because the researchers used different, more thorough, and more sensitive methods: intensive, multiple, repeated screening processes in clinics, schools, neighbourhood community centres, and so on. Researchers even used overlapping mechanisms that might locate the same child more than once – such as school administrative records, disability registries, school and teacher surveys, paediatrician surveys, and self-referrals (advertising on websites and newsletters) – just to make sure they captured all the cases. They practically went door to door.

Researchers conducting the more recent studies have also investigated smaller groups – populations in the tens of thousands rather than the hundreds of thousands – so they could be more efficient with their labour, resources, and diagnostic tools. Only two recent studies came up with relatively low rates (about 30 per 10,000 and 34 per 10,000, respectively), and these were huge studies of hundreds of thousands of people that relied primarily on information gleaned from administrative data.

Generally, the smaller the study, the more sensitive it will be to finding cases of autism. The larger the study, the less sensitive it will be and the lower the rates will be – in other words, the larger studies will tend to miss some cases of autism. The point is that different methods produce different rates. And, as Eric Fombonne has consistently pointed out, it is entirely possible to detect a higher prevalence rate over time, purely because of changes in method, when there is no true increase in the incidence of a disease.

Autism researchers in the United States and Europe have developed standardised instruments to measure the severity of autistic symptoms, screen potential cases of autism, and help make studies conducted throughout the world comparable to each other. Examples include: (1) the brief CARS (Child Autism Rating Scale) questionnaire developed by Eric Schopler and his colleagues in 1980; (2) the Asperger Syndrome Screening Questionnaire (ASSQ), published in 1999; (3) the Autism Diagnostic Interview (ADI), first published in 1989; and (4) the gold standard of contemporary autism diagnosis, the Autism Diagnostic Observation Schedule (ADOS), also published in 1989. While the *DSM* helps psychiatrists determine whether the patient has the disorder, these interviews and questionnaires produce a score that measures severity and numbers of symptoms. An instrument like the ADOS can be used not only to screen a subject in an epidemiology study but also to monitor his or her progress and treatment. The ADOS is especially useful for confirming diagnoses because it is not a questionnaire, but a lengthy, semi-structured process in which an examiner plays with the child and observes social communication and behaviour. The shorter, simpler instruments assist researchers and clinicians not so much in diagnosing as in flagging potential cases. Interview aids, like the ASSQ and the CARS, help ensure that they do not miss cases that could eventually be confirmed with more precise measures like the ADOS. And with better screening, more cases have been found and added to the reported prevalence.

Seventh, the term 'autism' began to be applied to people with clearly identifiable medical disorders, something not allowed in Kanner's day. In other words, conditions that caused autistic symptoms began to be counted as autism. It is often difficult for epidemiologists studying national or local disability registries to determine whose autistic symptoms were caused by a disease such as cerebral palsy, Down syndrome, congenital rubella, PKU (phenylketonuria), or some other chromosomal abnormality. Anywhere from 1 per cent to 4 per cent of children with autism also have an autosomal dominant disease called tuberous sclerosis (and 40 per cent of people with both tuberous sclerosis and mental retardation also have an autistic spectrum disorder). Up to 5 per cent of boys with autism also have fragile X syndrome, and as many as 25 per cent of boys with fragile X syndrome qualify for a diagnosis of an autism spectrum disorder (fragile X does occur in girls but more rarely and with milder symptoms).

Why are these people counted as having autism instead of being counted only in the other illness categories for which they qualify? Because, as noted earlier, the *DSM* is a descriptive document that lists symptoms, not causes. No matter how a patient got the symptoms, if he has them he can qualify for the diagnosis. Were the *DSM* to be based on genetics, causality would be crucial to diagnosis. A geneticist interested in how specific genes are related to specific presentations of autism would never want to include all the genetically different illnesses that cause autistic symptoms under the same category. But the *DSM*'s description has nothing to do with genetics, so the descriptive psychiatrists really don't care if all sorts of different illnesses are lumped together as autism.

TODAY, THE MOST WIDELY ACCEPTED *conservative* estimates, which is to say, the lower estimates, are as follows: Autistic Disorder (13/10,000), PDD-NOS (21/10,000), Asperger's Disorder (2.6/10,000), which gives a combined rate of 36.6/10,000, or about 1 in 300.

However, that estimate does not reflect the studies that show much higher rates, and it does not take into account the potentially large number of autistic individuals who are so high-functioning that they were never diagnosed or never came to the attention of the screeners. The less conservative and current best estimate for the whole range of autistic disorders, including cases of autism that may be diagnosed by clinicians and recorded in IDEA child counts, but which may not meet *DSM* criteria, is about 60 in 10,000, or 1 in 166. The most recent CDC estimate is slightly higher, at 1 in 150. In these less conservative estimates, Asperger cases account for between 14 and 19 per cent of the total autism spectrum population.

In a 2005 paper published in the *American Journal of Psychiatry*, Suniti Chakrabarti and Eric Fombonne confirmed the 1 in 166 rate by reporting on two studies they had conducted in Stafford, United Kingdom, one in the mid-1990s (with children born between 1991 and 1995) and another in 2002 (with children born between 1996 and 1998). They found the same rates in both cohorts, thus reaffirming the increased *prevalence*. But even more importantly, the study suggested that the *incidence* of the PDDs is stable.

The results were important but not surprising. When criteria broaden and detection becomes more sensitive, a rise in prevalence should be expected. But once the new criteria are in place and remain stable, as they were during the time between Chakrabarti and Fombonne's two studies, if there is no true increase in incidence the prevalence rate will also remain stable. In other words, although the reported prevalence of autism has increased in the societies in which epidemiologists have carried out their studies, the rate of increase has probably now levelled off. We may very well see the rate of new diagnoses drop, and we might even start to see prevalence rates go down a bit over the next few years (but not because there will be less autism).

What does all this mean? Reported prevalence rates rose in the early 1990s, but does this mean that more people are simply getting classified under the category 'autism', or that there is really more of the disease? Researchers hired by the state of California believed they had the answers to these questions.

IN 1999, THE STATE OF CALIFORNIA published the startling figures that I discussed earlier, the ones that Morton Ann Gernsbacher responded to in the hypothetical analogy about tall men in Texas. They showed that from 1970 to 1998 there had been a steady, steep increase in the number of people enrolled in state autism programmes. And between 1987 and 1998, the number of people served under the category 'autism' rose by 273 per cent.

California has an effective integrated system of regional agencies under contract with its Department of Developmental Services (DDS) to provide appropriate services as needed to children throughout the state. DDS was created in 1969, but autism, then considered exceptionally rare, was not formally added to the list of disabilities until two years later, in 1971. The 21 regional centres that are part of DDS code and record all cases referred to them, and so their data measure the numbers of children enrolled in the system. They do not record, however, where these people lie on the spectrum. Since the autism programmes do not recognise diagnoses of 'Asperger's Disorder' or 'PDD-NOS', anyone anywhere on the spectrum must enter the system under the general code of 'autism'. This means that the numbers California reported could represent people with a wide range of diagnoses, even if they received services under the same code.

When the state report was first released, the media started to mention the word 'epidemic', in large part because the report said 'the number of persons entering the system far exceeds the expected number determined by traditional incidence rates.' The state predicted a net growth in the number of children eligible to receive services for autism at the regional centres of at least 3 per cent each year, with significant growth in prevalence among children with mild forms of autism, including children with no or minimal mental retardation. Autism had increased a lot in comparison to the other major childhood disabilities, such as cerebral palsy, epilepsy, and mental retardation.

At first glance, it certainly looked like an epidemic. The state insisted it was only counting people served by the centres, not conducting an incidence study, but parents and the media paid little attention to the nuances and caveats. Of course, the figures the report supplied were *numbers* only, not rates, but the imprecise language in which they were delivered did not make that clear to most readers. For example, the authors said they had more cases of autism than the 'expected *number* determined by traditional *incidence rates*' (my emphasis). This is a vague sentence, if only because there *are* no traditional incidence rates. The authors should have said that they had done neither a prevalence nor an incidence study, and they should have defined what that meant.

The researchers reported only how many people were enrolled; they did not divide that number by the population. The population of California grew by more than 75 per cent between 1970 and 2002; and between 1987 and 1998, the crucial years in question for the 'epidemic', the population of the state increased from 27,777,158 to 33,145,121 persons, an increase of 19.3 per cent. The state's population of children from birth to fourteen years of age rose from 6,009,165 to 7,557,886, or 25.8 per cent. So part of the increase – though not all of it – was likely due to a simple increase in population.

Remember, too, that the figures were derived from enrolment in state services. California listed the enrolment beginning in 1970 and in a frightening graph showed a steep rise in prevalence from 4 in 10,000 in 1970 to 31 in 10,000 by 1997. Thousands more people are enrolled today than in the 1960s or 1970s. Why? Because in 1970 there were virtually no programmes in California in which autistic people could be enrolled; today, there are hundreds.

The California data probably wouldn't receive a passing grade in an Epidemiology 101 course at my university, and the California study was never published in any scientific journal. The report makes it appear that there was an epidemic when in fact all the researchers can really say, based on their data, is that there are more services available and that more people with the code 'autism' use them. Enrolment is not the same thing as incidence. It would be like arguing that the recent increase in the number of people who go to coffeehouses, like Starbucks, is by itself proof of an increase in coffee drinkers in the United States.

The California study also did not take into account how much diagnostic practices had changed over the period in question. Recall that people with the symptoms of autism who had mental retardation or epilepsy, or as the result of a medical or congenital condition, were often not diagnosed with autism during the 1970s and 1980s. Then the diagnostic criteria changed considerably between 1980 and 1994. With changing criteria, it's difficult to make a valid comparison over time. Many children now diagnosed with mild autism were previously called mentally retarded. Psychiatrist Stella Chess recalled, 'In my day, back in the early 60s, we often used the diagnosis "emotional block".' The children now diagnosed with PDD-NOS or Asperger's Disorders were previously considered unusual – they were bullied, called nerds, and often they performed well only in certain academic subjects. But many were still considered within the range of the normal. The paediatric neurologist Pauline Filipek, who graduated from medical school in 1980, fourteen years before Asperger's Disorder became part of the *DSM*, recalls referring many children with autism spectrum symptoms for psychiatric evaluations but with no expectation that autism was a possible diagnosis. She'd simply write on the referral note, 'There's something weird about this kid'. Another paediatrician, from Fairfield, Connecticut, told me she used to mark referrals with a code all the other doctors understood, 'FLK' (Funny Looking Kid). Their parents and their doctors wouldn't have imagined calling them autistic.

Furthermore, the California enrolment codes cannot serve as evidence of prevalence not only because enrolment numbers in general are not good epidemiological data but because the California figures are based on an outdated and simplistic evaluation report. The coding is determined by many different clinicians working in their respective regions using a diagnostic checklist written in 1986 that contains antiquated terms like 'full syndrome' and 'autism residual state' and that does not contain the categories of Asperger's or PDD. As a result, the clinicians must report on each case as either 'none', 'full syndrome', 'residual state', or 'suspected, not diagnosed'. In California's official reports, both full syndrome and residual state are grouped together under the term 'autism'. It is also likely that large numbers of children with a diagnosis of PDD-NOS or Asperger's are thus coded simply as autistic. Unfortunately, many journalists and bloggers have misinterpreted this coding system to mean that the enrolment figures do not include the full range of PDDs.

A 2002 report by the state of California, updating the 1999 report that precipitated all the talk about an epidemic, said that, as of December 2002, there were about 18,000 children from birth to age nineteen enrolled in autism programmes out of a total population of about 11 million children in the state. Eric Fombonne did the simple maths. Comparing this figure with a conservative estimate, 1 in 300 (or 30/10,000), one would expect to find almost twice as many children with an autism spectrum disorder in California – not the 18,000 the researchers found but 32,000. So the California figures are low! The true prevalence rate is probably much higher.

It is possible that there are many more children with autism in California – unfunded children in private schools, or those who are undiagnosed or do not get special-education services from the state; after all, the California data, like the IDEA data, only report children served by the state, and administrative prevalence numbers tend to be smaller than epidemiological estimates. In fact, the number of people counted as having autism in the California programmes is so small, relative to what the researchers should have expected, that their data undercut their claims of an epidemic.

We end up with a truly surprising situation, arguing for a higher rate of autism at the same time we argue against an epidemic: The California figures are not proof of an epidemic; rather, they are very low relative to the national averages and must underestimate the true rate of autism in the state.

JAMES G. GURNEY, who teaches paediatrics at the University of Minnesota medical school, used enrolment/registration figures, just as the state of California did, but to examine autism rates in Minnesota. He and his colleagues looked at the special-educational disability data from the Minnesota Department of Children, Families and Learning from the school years from 1981–1982 through 2001–2002 and examined each age cohort over time. The rate among seven-year-olds born in 1989 was 29/10,000; for those seven-year-olds born in 1991, just two years later, the rate was 55/10,000. This seems like a significant increase at first glance.

But there were more telling statistics as well, numbers that begin to reveal the source of the increase. One would expect that new autism diagnoses would plateau for children at about age five, because the condition would certainly have appeared by then. But Gurney found the number of diagnoses rising every year for the same cohorts up to age fifteen. In other words, fourteen- and fifteen-year-olds were being newly diagnosed with autism spectrum disorders and coded as autistic! For children born in 1989, for example, prevalence got higher with age: 13 in 10,000 at age six, 21 in 10,000 at age nine, and 33 in 10,000 at age eleven. Yet, remember, autism, when it exists, is in full bloom by about 30 months of age; in fact, the *DSM* does not permit the diagnosis of autism unless the onset was before three years of age. The only explanation for this dual finding – higher rates in the younger group and new cases being diagnosed in the teenage years – is that children were being diagnosed more often on both ends of the continuum: On the very low end, for example, there must have been children originally diagnosed as 'mentally retarded' who were being rediagnosed as autistic, and on the very high end, there must have been kids who could conceivably pass for normal or previously had diagnoses such as ADHD, Borderline Personality Disorder, or a learning disability. A decade ago, some of the very high functioning kids now called autistic would have been called weird or unusual. Some children in the Minnesota cohorts Gurney followed even lost the diagnosis of autism, despite the fact that autism is an incurable condition.

In another study, James Laidler from Portland State University examined US Department of Education (USED) data and found that there were 'as many children who are newly categorised as autistic at 15 years of age as there are at 8 years of age.' And, oddly, he found a decrease in diagnoses between the ages of eleven and twelve, when children are making the difficult transition to middle school and confronting greater academic and social challenges – just the time when you'd expect milder cases to be detected. He did not think there was anything unusual about eleven- and twelve-year-olds, but he did think that school coding tends to be highly subjective, inconsistent, and unreliable, and thus, in his words, 'unsuitable for tracking autism prevalence'.

There are variations, state by state and district by district, in how schools classify children with autism. One study in Texas found significantly more cases of autism in the administrative records of wealthier school districts than in poorer ones. Furthermore, rates derived from administrative records, as we saw in California, will always be different, and almost always lower, than rates derived by epidemiologists conducting thorough studies of entire populations in an effort to count every possible case, including people with autism who have never been diagnosed or recorded in administrative records.

Minnesota and Oregon provide good examples of how increasing awareness of autism, increasing services, increasing interest in using the services, and ever broader criteria can lead to higher prevalence rates over time. Autism does not suddenly emerge in fourteen-year-olds. However, awkward children struggling in school – academically and socially – can be given an autism diagnosis so that they can become eligible for special-education services. And with the establishment of whole classrooms devoted to autism, the number of children who were reclassified – from mental retardation to autism, for example – probably also increased. Moreover, given the fact that the US Office of Special Education Programs currently considers only twelve disability codes as valid under the IDEA, it is not surprising that so many schools choose 'autism' for children with impairments in social interaction.

In their analysis of the autism epidemic, Gernsbacher and her colleagues from the University of Wisconsin cited a 2003 e-mail from the Autism Society of America. The message, which the society sent to 20,000 of its members, said that 'autism in America's schools jumped an alarming 1,354% in the eight-year period from the school year 1991–2 to 2000–01.'

But it's common knowledge that there are huge increases in cases reported in a given category when that category is brand new. Both autism and traumatic brain injury were introduced as reporting categories in 1991–1992, and in that year autism was only an optional category. 'Traumatic brain injury' rose the same amount as autism, and in most years more than autism, but no one claimed there was an epidemic of traumatic brain injuries. Indeed, in 1996 US Department of Education officials wrote that the rise in reported cases of both autism and traumatic brain injury was due to the fact that these relatively new categories were being used for students who previously were reported under other disability categories. The school my daughter attended in 1996 was only just beginning to use the autism code; she was initially described as having 'multiple disabilities', since the school already had classrooms in operation for children with that code. The rise in autism cases as a result of the new reporting category was thus not unexpected. In the 1992–1993 school year, the total number of people with autism being served in public school systems in the United States was 12,222. Fast-forward to 2003: Maryland reported 3,536, Florida 5,915, New Jersey 5,146, California 19,034, Georgia 3,956, and Arizona 2,131, contributing to a national total of 140,920. And in May 2006, the Centers for Disease Control estimated that more than 300,000 school-aged children in the United States had at some point been diagnosed with autism.

The bottom line is that reported autism prevalence has increased, but the real prevalence has probably remained stable. Given how much more rigorous and sensitive the methods are today than just a decade or two ago, we should probably believe the newer, higher rates and question the older ones. But this does not mean that autism, as a disease, is more widespread. We see it differently. We see it more. And if we were to take our methods and go back to a time in the 1950s when autism was said to occur in only 3 in 10,000 live births, we'd find much more autism than anyone at the time thought existed. The registries and the child counts didn't exist, and there were virtually no services designed specifically for autistic children, even when it was diagnosed. Schools didn't have autism codes, autism wasn't listed as a diagnosis for insurance reimbursements for doctor visits or psychotropic medications, there were no autism Medicaid waivers, and there was so much more stigma associated with childhood mental disabilities that doctors made a diagnosis of autism for only the most obvious cases. But if we could somehow go back and count the cases like we can today, I would be surprised if we did not find similar prevalence rates.

We wouldn't have such high rates of autism if we weren't reaching out to the vast numbers of different kinds of people that make up this 'epidemic' population and giving them the interventions they deserve. That we now have an 'epidemic' of autism is an unexpectedly positive symptom of how far we've come. We could interpret the high prevalence rates as a medical emergency. But we could also conclude that if a child is diagnosed with autism today, he or she is not the victim of a dangerous toxin stalking our children, but rather the beneficiary of the growing sophistication of educators, speech therapists, psychiatrists, psychologists, and epidemiologists.

The same logic applies to diseases one can actually see under a microscope. Early detection in breast cancer, prostate cancer, or melanoma (the deadliest form of skin cancer), due largely to greater awareness, means that there are higher rates of people diagnosed with these conditions than in the past. So it's not surprising that in dermatology, for example, there is a debate raging about whether the increase in the incidence of melanoma (between 1986 and 2001, an increase of 240 per cent) constitutes an epidemic. But the good news is the increase occurred primarily in very early stage melanoma, when the cancer is more treatable, and not in later, more serious stages, when there is less chance of survival. With cancers, early detection means people can get help earlier, and the same is true for autism. Although there is no cure for autism, early detection enables children to receive educational and other services that lead to an improved quality of life.

My position should be clear by now. The prevalence of autism today is a virtue, maybe even a prize.

WHEN PEOPLE ASK ME TO EXPLAIN the high rates of autism, I begin by talking about the broadening of the diagnostic criteria over the years. They often respond that the changes in the criteria used by doctors couldn't possibly account for such a big increase. Then I mention the fact that children are being diagnosed at younger and younger ages, and that adults are being newly diagnosed, so that at any given point in time over the past several years, there have been more people with the diagnosis than ever before – not just children five years old and up along with a very small group of adults who were diagnosed as children, but babies of eighteen months and up, children of all ages, and both the formerly and newly diagnosed adults. But, they insist, the diagnostic criteria and the age of diagnosis couldn't account for the rise either. When I mention the fact that epidemiological methods are more aggressive today, leading scientists to find more cases than ever before, or tell them about how new the autism category is in the US Department of Education's child count, they have the same response.

I am not sure why people are so resistant to the idea that true autism rates may have remained stable over the years, and that there is no real epidemic. Perhaps they don't want to give up on the hope that, if only we could find the cause of the 'epidemic', we could help these children. We could eliminate the toxins, hold big corporations accountable, do something to reverse the trend. If there is no real epidemic, we might just have to admit that no one is to blame. Their desire is understandable. But we cannot find real solutions if we're basing our ideas on false premises and bad science.

I sympathise with these opinions, but I think they are wrong. Changes in clinical and diagnostic practices, administrative codes, and epidemiological methods can account for enormous shifts in numbers of cases diagnosed. The dramatic increases in the numbers are caused by several changes acting *in concert*, changes enacted by a series of key players who raised the visibility of autism and made it a cause worth fighting for.

Who are these key players? They include scientists, clinicians, parent advocates, philanthropists, educators, speech therapists, psychologists, and behavioural intervention specialists, among others. Not one of these groups has the power by itself to create or declare an epidemic. But together they have that power. And these key players operate in our culture – a culture that, for better or for worse, gives labels to people different from the norm, a culture in which new pathologies are continually discovered or invented, and in which new research hypotheses and data are diffused globally with a single keystroke, creating a force that is unstoppable. These are the conditions that led to the perfect storm of the autism epidemic.

PART TWO ～

Isabel in Monet's Garden

IN A CRISIS, I AM OFTEN completely stymied. When Isabel was first diagnosed with autism, I would have stood still, if Joyce had let me. Joyce likes to think a problem through, make a plan, and then act. She saved us all. She's shown me that no matter how hard it might be to raise a child with a serious, incurable disability, it's always better to try and *do something*. I'm convinced that our actions have helped Isabel develop more and suffer less.

I've subsequently encountered other parents in other parts of the world who understand the importance of decisive yet thoughtful action. Parents who waste little time to ponder their future or dwell on the 'whys' of their situation – Why autism? Why me? Why my child? Parents who, at least in the developed world, understand that they are not alone, and that there are things to be done. A medical team has to be assembled, an educational plan mapped out. Accurate diagnoses and cognitive assessments have to be made, inappropriate behaviours have to be corrected, medicines considered, teaching and speech therapy methods learned.

Joyce and I acted quickly, but in comparison to some parents I know, we've been conservative, relying mostly on what the experts say. There is now consensus in the scientific community that the earlier one begins therapies the better. This is why so many scientists in the United States are trying – apparently with some success – to find ways to diagnose autism in infants six months old and even younger. As diagnoses come earlier, and are more sophisticated, the question that arises is which form of treatment is most likely to be successful, or even possible, with such very young children. Scientists have shown that certain antipsychotic medications, such as risperidone (Risperdal), an atypical antipsychotic, and antidepressant medications, such as fluoxetine (Prozac), can help with specific symptoms of autism – anxiety, agitation, self-abuse behaviours, and sleep disturbances, for example – but these medications are not generally prescribed until the child reaches school age. Thus far, research has not managed to prove that any of the available nonpharmaceutical treatments or therapies help minimise autistic symptoms any more than time and love.

I've met parents and guardians who have tried almost every kind of therapy. This is understandable. Autism treatment is a process of trial and error, and there is no one treatment that is going to work for every child, so it makes sense to try different therapies. Unfortunately, the widespread diagnosis of autism has spawned legions of unproven claims of new and effective treatments. Many parents will try just about anything when they feel there is something wrong with their child. Whether you are a parent in a small village in Africa or a parent in suburban Maryland, you are not going to stand by if there is something you can do.

The autism lore is filled with anecdotes about this or that miracle drug or combination of vitamins, fish oils, and minerals. Some parents try gluten-free or casein-free diets because a few scientists have hypothesised that autism is in part an allergic reaction to certain foods, and the diets do help ameliorate the gastrointestinal problems that many people with autism experience. Increasing numbers of parents are placing their autistic children in hyperbaric oxygen chambers to repair what they believe is nerve damage linked to autism. Some who believe that mercury toxicity is linked to autism try the more radical and dangerous therapy called 'chelation', which removes metals from the body. In 2003, Terrance Cottrell, an eight-year-old boy from Milwaukee, was suffocated during a prayer service when church members tried to exorcise the evil spirits they believed were causing his autism.

Though the jury is still out on the effectiveness of treatments developed by psychiatrists and other mental health professionals, some hold promise. There are a number of behavioural therapies available these days for toddlers, most focused on improving social interaction and speech. The most commonly used therapy in the United States for children with severe autism is 'applied behavioural analysis', or ABA, a therapy usually identified with its founder, O. Ivar Lovaas. The intensive one-on-one therapy (sometimes provided for up to 40 hours per week) with a trained ABA therapist is basically a system of incentives and rewards for very young children. ABA is supposed to help extinguish negative behaviours and reinforce positive ones. It helps children learn simple or highly structured tasks like going to the bathroom by themselves, and more complicated behaviours involving academic skills and social interaction. Proponents of the method have long argued that it is the best nonmedical intervention for autism, and the only one whose efficacy has been measured in terms of improvements in IQ and behaviour in preschool children. Debates about ABA can get quite heated, however, especially when scientists argue that the results reported by researchers with a scientific or financial interest in ABA have not been replicated elsewhere.

Many parents also use the Picture Exchange Communication System (PECS), which draws on the visual strengths of children with autism. The goal is to have the nonverbal child use pictures to learn how to communicate with others (if they want juice, they show someone a picture of a glass of juice), and then later to convert that learned behaviour into verbal language. Joyce and I, as well as Isabel's daycare and early elementary school teachers, used aspects of the PECS system to help Isabel communicate, and it worked well.

We also used aspects of an approach called sensory integration therapy because there was clearly something wrong with Isabel's sensory system. She was hypersensitive to some sounds, but somewhat insensitive to pain. She might not laugh when tickled, even though she had been exquisitely ticklish as a baby. One of her favourite pastimes was cuddling, but it seemed to me that she liked it only because she would then be in a position to put our hands over her ears. She would press our hands hard against them, and she seemed to like it when I added my own strength too. I worried that it might hurt her. Only later would Joyce and I discover how common it is for people with autism to seek deep pressure stimulation; this is why Temple Grandin designed a hugging machine for herself. We also noticed that Isabel was more engaged with us – she used eye contact more and used more words – when she was in a swing or jumping on a trampoline. We wondered if she would be less anxious, and hence more social, if an occupational therapist trained in sensory integration could help her learn to tolerate the sensations that upset her so much. After two years of occupational therapy, Isabel did learn to manage those sensations, but we'll never know whether it was due to the occupational therapy, or just time and maturation of her sensory system.

We also tried 'Floortime', a method associated with the psychiatrist Stanley Greenspan. In Floortime, you sit with your child, follow his or her lead, and try to interact with him or her in increasingly long and complex turn taking. This is, in essence, the definition of social interaction: the continuous opening and closing of circles of communication. Joyce and I never felt we could do it as well or as often as our first psychiatrist thought we should, and our attempts at it made us feel inadequate. But we played with Isabel, teased her, tried to tickle her, asked her questions, and tried to get her interested in toys and games, assuming that we were, in effect, carrying out the method in spirit. Sometimes by simply using common sense and trying to communicate with their children, parents end up unknowingly applying many of the principles behind the established, named therapies.

Joyce and I concluded that ABA, Floortime, Rapid Prompting (a method of eliciting responses through intensive prompts, developed by Soma Mukhopadyhay), and many of the other named therapies that have been formulated in recent years shared a fundamental strategy that could be called simply 'in your child's face'. It means you don't let your child withdraw for very long, that you engage him as much as possible, pushing him to interact with you, however much he may resist. It also means that you follow your child's lead, playing with his toys when he plays with them, and even turning his face to yours to promote eye contact.

Isabel has so many social deficiencies that, left to her own devices, she'd spend her days repeating the scripts and soliloquies looping inside her head. She'd interact with someone only if he or she was an instrument to some personal goal, like reaching a drink in the refrigerator or a toy on a shelf. Sometimes I imagine her social difficulties are analogous to the difficulties that a left-handed person might experience if forced to use only her right hand. She'd avoid using her right hand, just as Isabel avoids social interaction. She would never be comfortable using that hand, and would never be very good with it. But with time, she could improve.

As we interacted with Isabel, we let her take us into a world that had meaning for her. This chapter is about how we tried to reach out to her, and how she reached back. With both hands.

JOYCE AND I QUICKLY REALISED that we couldn't endure the long hours of intense social interaction many experts recommended. Isabel would run away from us crying or simply wear us down. So we hired a speech therapist, who used sign language, play therapy, and incentives like M&M's and poker chips to get Isabel to speak. She also used social stories to help Isabel understand both how to behave in social situations and how other people *expect* others to act. The stories were designed to help Isabel learn 'theory of mind'. When we needed babysitters, I went to the student lounge in the Department of Speech and Hearing at George Washington University to find graduate students who were motivated to try using their newly learned speech therapy skills with a child with autism.

We kept her enrolled at her preschool in Chevy Chase, Maryland, where she had been before her diagnosis, so she could be around 'unimpaired' children who might serve as good social models. While we respect the ABA method, we both knew we wouldn't be able to handle the intensity of it by ourselves, or be able to afford an ABA therapist. ABA therapists may work with a child for up to 40 hours a week. Because there is a lot of pressure placed on the child to comply with the therapist, the whole experience can be emotionally difficult for both the child and the parents. More importantly for us, ABA is done at home, and our doctor wanted Isabel to be around other children in a mainstream preschool environment.

That's why we tried so hard to get Isabel into the Smithsonian Institution's Early Enrichment Center, described in chapter 1. By the time she left the programme, two years later, to start kindergarten in our local school system, Isabel had caused us and her teachers both great joy and consternation, showing how much a child can learn in the right environment, but also showing how persistent and pervasive the deficits of autism can be. From plucking a rare orchid at the orchid garden (I still break out in a sweat when I think about it, and so do her former teachers), to approaching the canvas of a Renoir, with fingers sticky from a peanut-butter-and-jelly sandwich, Isabel was a handful.

The philosophy behind the preschool curriculum was informed by a host of thinkers, such as Lev Vygotsky, who believed that social interaction was the key to cognitive and linguistic development, and Howard Gardner, who championed the idea that there are many different kinds of intelligences. Gardner believes that some people possess greater or lesser strengths in areas such as spatial intelligence, musical intelligence, bodily-kinesthetic intelligence, and interpersonal functioning, among others. By the time we learned about the Smithsonian, we already had a sense that Isabel's intelligence was different, with extraordinary deficits in speech and language as well as strengths in visual and spatial skills.

The Smithsonian curriculum was designed to achieve three things: to make education *concrete, sensory-based*, and *interactive*. Concrete education at the Smithsonian meant direct experience with a topic outside of class, through field trips such as visits to museums, art galleries, or greenhouses and sculpture gardens. These direct experiences involved sights, sounds, tastes, smells, and the physical sensation of actually travelling to a specific location outside of class. Additionally, the learning process required that the children not just look or listen but interact with their peers, teachers, and most importantly, the environment. The science of education shows that this kind of learning prepares young children well for the academic challenges of later childhood. Researchers have persuasively argued that one of the strongest indicators of how well a student will learn new information is how much they *already know* about the subject at hand. The Smithsonian wanted to produce more of the 'already known', or what is sometimes called 'background knowledge', by exposing children to as many academic experiences as possible, as early as possible.

For the field trips, the entire array of museums extending across the Washington Mall was available for exploration. It was perfect for Isabel – and for other children who were not so good at processing written or verbal information. Some children – not just ones who are autistic – think more concretely. They need to see something to learn about it – feel it, touch it, interact with it. So if the children were to learn about, say, dance, the teachers would bring in a ballet slipper for them to hold, then show them a photograph of one of Degas' famous sculptures of a young ballet dancer. They would then show them a print of Degas' pastel *At the Old Opera House*, which provides a glimpse of the dancer's legs and shoes during a performance on stage, and play classical music to accompany the image. Next they might show them a print of William Johnson's *Jitterbug*, African Americans in early 20th-century Harlem wearing broad-shouldered suits and dresses, and the children would begin to see that dance is a big category. And that's not all: They would see George Catlin's unromanticided view of a Native American ceremonial dance on the Missouri River, Gauguin's painting of three Breton girls dancing in clogs, and Matisses's vibrant *Danseuse Creole*, a colourful paper cut-out inspired by Josephine Baker. The Matisse is highly abstract, but whereas, just moments before, it might have been unintelligible to them, they could now understand it.

Obviously, a place like the Smithsonian can pull this off better than most places. But in principle, the curriculum could be adapted anywhere. All one needs is a teacher willing to make a collection of something – a bicycle perhaps, then a painting of a bicycle built for two, a photograph of Lance Armstrong racing, a photo of people using bicycles for commercial transportation in China. If the subject is more sophisticated, like the American Revolution, a teacher can still appeal to almost every sensory modality: The children can smell the same flowers, listen to the same music, and taste the same foods that 18th-century Americans did.

Isabel couldn't talk when she started at the Smithsonian – she was then four years old – but she quickly learned that museums were places to have fun, that you could go there to see one or two things and then leave, and that you had to respect the museum environment. Perhaps most importantly, museums, and the objects contained within them, were now part of her life. She could navigate through most of the museums; she knew the back staircases, the circuitous routes to specific exhibits; she knew all the security guards, and they knew her.

No parent, even those with a highly verbal child, can be sure of what his or her child has learned from a museum. But there were small marvels to be found. A quiet boy, Seth, whose mother was convinced he was oblivious to art, looked up at her one morning as she was putting on her earrings and said, 'Alexander Calder made jewellery like that.' Another boy, Diego, spilled some paint one day in the Smithsonian classroom and said, 'Jackson Pollock likes this kind of art.' And one Christmas season, Isabel decided to learn as much as she could about animals. The Smithsonian, in anticipation of a high volume of visitors at Christmastime, had built a large Gingerbread House, maybe three by four feet, with small models of animals in every room, and put it on display in the American History Museum. Isabel was drawn to the house so much that she became a topic of conversation among the security guards and staff. After New Year's, the curator in charge of the exhibit delivered the entire house, complete with animals, to Isabel's classroom with a note that said, 'To Isabel'. She loved the little models more than anything else, and this experience marked the start of a long fascination with biology and the classification of the animal world.

The Smithsonian created an educational world that engaged Isabel at a time when most preschools wouldn't have even accepted her as a student. The teachers introduced Isabel to stories, most of which had to be acted out in the classroom with props. They helped her learn how to calm her body so she could be with the other children at circle time – sometimes she sat in their laps – or take a nap during the rest period. They also taught Isabel how to see other people. Scientists know that people with autism don't see the same things a typical person does. While watching an emotionally charged scene in a movie, for example, the nonautistic person shifts his gaze from one actor's eyes to the next in an effort to interpret emotions and intentions, but the autistic person looks at a hand, a light switch, a mouth, a painting in the background. So how can he or she possibly comprehend states of mind or interact with others? At the Smithsonian, Isabel was forced to confront her mind-blindness. The teachers would gently move her head, saying, 'Isabel, use good eyes', and they would refuse to give her what she wanted until she did. They also prompted her to look into the eyes of people in portraits at the museums. They weren't teaching her to talk, but they were giving her an emotional vocabulary. They firmly believed that language would come only if Isabel had the desire, and the skills, to be social.

Throughout that first year at the Smithsonian programme and into the second, Isabel did begin to talk. But despite her advances in learning, we had no idea if she even knew the names of her classmates. On Valentine's Day, something amazing happened. She took all the cards and handed them out to the other students, one by one. Even if she couldn't read, she had seen the kids' names on their backpacks or lunchboxes and was able to match the letters in the name to the person. Several years later, she became the mail-delivery person at her elementary school because she was one of the only children in the school who knew the name of every single person, staff or student.

Sharon Shaffer and Jill Mankowitz, her teachers at the Smithsonian, both believed that Isabel's presence in the classroom positively affected the other children. 'It's not just that Isabel introduced diversity into the classroom,' Shaffer recalled. 'Isabel made the other children less selfish.' The children realised that Isabel needed some extra accommodations, and they learned to respect that. Mankowitz told me back then that when Isabel was absent from school for some reason, the other children seemed different. 'They were more competitive with each other, they snapped at each other. They didn't fall apart, but it was like they lost their center. Then when Isabel came back to the classroom, they got back to normal.' In years to come I'd hear an occasional comment from a parent or two about Isabel that echoed her Smithsonian teachers. Just last year, a woman came up to me at our local swimming centre. I had no idea who she was, but she seemed to know me. 'I just wanted to tell you that your daughter has made my son a better person,' she said. 'He's learned to care about other kids in a way I never expected. I think Isabel had a lot to do with that because he talks about her a lot – how smart she is.'

IN THE SUMMER OF 1996, when Isabel was almost five years old, she began to reenact stories with toy figures. She pored over *The Tub People*, a picture book about a family bathtub toy that falls down the drain. She rubbed the pages with her hands, and sometimes she smelled the pages, perhaps in the hope that she would glean new information through these senses. Unable to find any toys in our house that could represent all the characters, she arranged a Mr Potato Head family into one resembling the Tub family: father, mother, policeman, grandmother, doctor, child, and dog, careful to line them up as they appeared in the illustrations and then removed the protagonist. The story is like a concise poem expressing a concern with completeness, loss, and recovery. One curious tub child falls into the drain and sets the family into a crisis. A plumber rescues the toy, at which point all of the toys are moved from the tub to a new location in their owner's nursery. They are together again, the father, the mother, the grandmother, the doctor, the policeman, the child, and the dog.

By November, as the holiday season approached, she became preoccupied with the American Girl doll collection, and this entailed another set of toys to obtain (and maintain), unfortunately at a much higher price than the Tub family. The dolls came with pyjamas, shoes, and night caps, as well as elaborate day clothes, and she insisted that we change the dolls into pyjamas at her bedtime and then dress them again in the morning. This added fifteen minutes to her bedtime routine, and another fifteen minutes to the morning rituals. Within a matter of a few weeks, all the dolls had to come with us when we drove anywhere, buckled up in a row in the back seat.

We tried to join in when she played with the dolls, but when we entered her line of sight she'd walk away. If she let us stay with her while she played, she'd insist we sit next to but never across from her. With the Tub family and the dolls, she showed little or no creativity. She didn't talk to the dolls and rarely put them together into pretend social situations, like a tea party. But she did come up with brief exchanges between characters from *different* stories. For example, two of her American Girl dolls, Addie, the child of a mid-19th-century slave, and Kirsten, the 19th-century immigrant from Scandinavia, played out a short conversation she had seen take place between Woody and Buzz from the movie *Toy Story*. She did not generate new stories herself, though, and wouldn't allow toys from different domains to be near each other.

If you took an American Girl doll or any other toy and put it down with Mr Potato Head, Isabel would not abide it. Major category violation.

In the flow of everyday life, you simply cannot always act as a therapist. It would take too much out of you. So we complied. 'This is the grandfather,' she'd say, while I was making dinner and Joyce was paying bills. And then, looking at me, she'd say, 'This is the _____?' and wait until I said, 'grandfather'. Five seconds later, she'd ask again, and wanting her to stop bothering me, I'd say again, 'grandfather'. She was pulling us into her structured world, using us as props in her repetition. Joyce sometimes called it the 'Mad Libs' method of interaction.

The number of collections, like the Tub people and the American Girls, grew rapidly, and we struggled to find the source of anxiety behind her need for wholeness. I had all sorts of pop psychological explanations, easy for me to come up with, since I grew up with them. But in fact, little is known about the anxiety, rigidity, and routines so common in people with autism – sometimes called *perseveration* – whether it is the play of young children with autism, or the activities of teens and adults, such as studying bus routes or repeatedly doing a jigsaw puzzle. People with autism also frequently become attached to a small number of foods, to the exclusion of foods necessary for a good diet. In addition, once a child with autism starts a behaviour, and finds it pleasurable, it can be very hard to make the transition to a new behaviour. (Such rigidity seems to be much less common among people with both autism and mental retardation than it is among people with autism alone.)

Psychologist Uta Frith and others have hypothesised that if autism involves a fault in central thought processes, the repetition may reflect an inability for a central or high-level monitor to exert authority and change the behaviour. In other words, the need for coherence in a small, well-defined area – such as play with a group of toys – represents rigidity caused by the brain's failure to find coherence and exert control. Frith imagined the repetitions and rigidity in autism as a constantly running engine that cannot switch off because there is no central command. This theory may also account for some of the repetitive, self-stimulation behaviours common in people with autism, such as hand flapping, rocking, or head banging.

In the spring of 1997, during Isabel's second year at the Smithsonian, we bought her a group of toy miniature drummer boys, which she promptly named after all the children in her pre-school class. The naming meant she was using her imagination, but it also meant that she was connecting with a social world and play-ing without a rigid script. There was no story for her to imitate, no video associated with these drummers or with her classmates. She also began to use complete four- to five-word sentences and par-ticipate more in her preschool activities. And on 29 December, at the age of six, she made her first representational drawing, a crude picture of herself with the word 'Isabel' underneath. It seemed as if she was beginning to see herself, and perhaps this was a first step toward seeing herself in relationship to others, a milestone for which I give her early schooling full credit.

IN THE AUTUMN OF 1996, when Isabel had just turned five and was still almost completely nonverbal, she began refusing to go into the basement of our house where we had arranged a small play area. She had once loved it, but she now screamed if we even opened the door leading to it. Then, in early October, Joyce took her to a toy store at a local mall. Walking into the store, Isabel stopped dead in her tracks, frightened, a deer in headlights. She was looking straight at a book, *Klutz Face Painting*, the cover of which showed the face of a woman with a surprised look, painted as a mouse. Isabel was shaking. Joyce immediately recognised it as the book on the ledge of our basement steps, visible from the first floor. This is why she wouldn't go near the basement. Joyce removed the book as soon as she got home and threw it in the garbage (making sure Isabel saw her throw it away), and though it was hard to get Isabel to look at the ledge, we eventually got her to see that the book was no longer there.

The book, henceforth known in our house as the 'scary painted-face book', remains an object of terror. After a few weeks, Isabel began to go into the basement again. But every Halloween the book appears at bookstores. As a teenager, Isabel will not enter a toy store or book shop until Joyce or I have gone into the store ahead of her to make sure that the book is not on display. If it is, we hide it. If she sees a rack of Klutz books, she turns her head and places her palm over the eye closest to the display, so that if the book is there she will not see it in her peripheral vision.

She had never had a bad experience with face painting – or mice, for that matter. So this fear of the book was inexplicable, just like her fear of dogs. Although she has never been attacked or bitten by a dog, she was once so afraid of dogs that upon seeing one coming up the pavement – on a leash and well controlled by the owner – she might run out into the street screaming. We don't know what causes such extraordinary anxiety responses in children with autism, but we do know that they are not necessarily based on actual events, and they do not necessarily generalise to other objects that we might expect our children to fear. Though she was extraordinarily frightened of dogs between the ages of two and ten, she loved cats and other animals, and even took horseback-riding lessons for two years.

Isabel's anxieties reached their peak the next autumn, in 1997, when she entered the Montgomery County, Maryland, public school system as a kindergartner. She entered a special-education class that was 'contained'. That meant the children were main-streamed for only brief periods of a half-day kindergarten pro-gramme. At the time, she was, to my knowledge, the only member of the class with an autism diagnosis. The other children had dis-orders that included ADHD, an extremely rare form of dwarfism with associated neurological problems, and Riley-Day syndrome, a disorder that is known to afflict only about 600 people in the world, all Ashkenazi Jews. It was a class of wonderful children, for the most part, but the teacher, just graduated and green, was in over her head.

It's hard enough for a teacher to educate and manage the behav-iour problems of a group of children with a single disorder, let alone such a wide range, and there was little evidence that this teacher had the skills to do it. We observed the classroom, as did a psychologist we hired, and it was absolute chaos much of the time. During one observation, the teacher walked up to a fidg-ety boy who suffered from ADHD, and whose feet were held to the legs of the chair with rubber bands. He was scribbling on a piece of paper. The teacher lost her temper, crumpled the piece of paper up, and said, 'This is what I do to children who don't listen to me.' I thought, 'What does she do or say when there's no one observing?'

Autism may be a genetic, brain-based disorder, but children with autism can be very sensitive to their environments. Isabel began to have night terrors. She compulsively tapped her fingers and knuckles on walls, tables, or chairs, and she wouldn't walk without dragging her toes. Her child psychiatrist, after reading the psychologist's report on the classroom environment, said, 'She's stressed.' During the Christmas break, we all went to Florida, and over a period of about two weeks all of the symptoms of her anxi-ety abated: She no longer had nightmares, she stopped dragging her toes as frequently, she stopped tapping on things. We knew then that Isabel had been reacting to the extraordinary level of disorder and expressed emotion in the contained classroom. So when school resumed in January 1998, we refused to let Isabel return to that classroom and insisted that she be moved to the mainstream classroom with aide support so that she could have better social models around her, certainly better models than the classmates who were screaming, kicking, biting, and pulling hair.

Montgomery County, Maryland, has one of the best, and best-funded, public school systems in the country. Unlike many states, where the school districts are separate entities from county government, in Maryland the school districts correspond to county lines and are administered through the county budgets. The vast majority of parents of children with special needs in our county are pleased with the services their children receive. But I know from experience that they often have to work hard to get the services they believe their children need. The federal requirement of using individualised education plans (IEPs) for children with special needs does not require schools to do what is best for a child, only what is 'appropriate' and 'least restrictive' among the options. What we asked for would require the school system to treat Isabel more as an individual, perhaps with a one-on-one aide, at considerable cost to the county. The principal didn't answer our letters or phone calls. Her supervisor didn't answer our letters or phone calls. And when we finally talked with the principal, she was defensive and belligerent, and we realised we needed a lawyer. Indeed, the principal didn't even seem to know what autism was, and though she is a native English speaker she frequently said the word 'artistic' when she meant to say 'autistic'. She encouraged us to abandon the use of the term 'autism' because, as she put it, 'the word is rarely used in this county'. From that point on, we were in a constant struggle to be heard.

We needed evidence that Isabel deserved to be mainstreamed. Unfortunately, it is exceedingly difficult to test for intelligence in people with autism because the tests themselves require good communication skills. Isabel's intelligence tests, based so much on receptive and expressive language abilities, gave scores well below normal and within the upper range of mental retardation. Throughout much of Europe, definitions of mental retardation are based less on IQ scores than on the intensity of supports the child needs. In the United States, mental retardation is defined instead by IQ cutoff points. Based on her IQ, we knew we'd have a tough fight ahead.

In the 1960s, the prevailing educational philosophy was to put autistic and mentally retarded children in unstructured classrooms where they were taught little more than basic life skills. Only when scientists like Ivar Lovaas at UCLA (who designed ABA), or Eric Schopler at the University of North Carolina (who designed the well-known TEACCH programme), systematically studied and evaluated structured versus unstructured environments did it become clear that children with autism make the most progress in structured classrooms and that, for many children, inclusion in mainstream classrooms can be beneficial.

By the 1990s, the ideology of inclusion had become dominant, but Isabel was still segregated in a classroom with little structure. Some children are indeed better served by being educated in separate schools where they can be taught by experienced autism experts in small, structured classes. But Isabel's team — our psychiatrist, psychologist, and speech and occupational therapists — insisted that Isabel belonged in a mainstream classroom with aide support. To help us make the case for inclusion, a psychologist in Baltimore recommended Isabel take an intelligence test called the Leiter. It's not a new test — it's been around since 1927 — but what is new is that it is being given more frequently to children with autism to demonstrate their nonverbal strengths. The test was designed specifically to be nonverbal, suitable for foreign children who may have just arrived in the United States and for whom the appropriate educational environment needed to be ascertained. Some people believe the test exaggerates the intelligence of children with language impairment, and this may be one reason the psychologist thought the test might help us in our efforts to get Isabel mainstreamed.

The Leiter tests children ages two to eighteen for conceptual and problem-solving abilities but involves no language at all, and it uses only the minimal motor skills necessary to grasp and arrange small cardboard cut-outs into a frame or to connect puzzle pieces. Children match squares by their image or colour, solve small puzzles, sort a group of pictures that tell a story into a sequence, and the like, and the tasks get more difficult and abstract as the test proceeds. It looks for attention deficits, learning disabilities, and neuropsychological impairments, and it appears to have little or no cultural or language biases. The Leiter is scored much like an IQ test, with 100 as the mean. Isabel received a 146, a score that on a typical intelligence battery like the Wechsler Intelligence Scales for Children would put her in the range of near genius. Whether one believes the score or not – it *does* seem inflated – it affirmed our belief that she was bright, and it gave us some ammunition in our argument for inclusion. We would use the score every time the school system tried to pull Isabel down to a lower academic level.

Isabel was moved to the mainstream classroom. The struggle took a lot out of us, and it was only the beginning. We'd have to fight to get her more aide support in the mainstream classroom, fight to get the aide some training in autism, and fight to get the teacher and the aide to communicate with us about Isabel and the work she was supposed to do. But the fight was worth it. After four months, she was doing better than we, or the school, had expected. She was beginning to initiate social contacts, seemed to be learning how to sound out words and read, had begun to understand the basics of calendars, and could even do skip counting by odd and even numbers, a skill that in our county is a first-grade objective. Most importantly, she started to talk. When she came to school after spring break, she told her new teacher about her vacation. 'I went to Colorado. I went skiing. I ate a hamburger in Colorado.' At home, Joyce and I used Isabel's knowledge of numbers to help her speak. If she said, 'Juice,' we would say, 'Ask for juice using five words,' and she would say, 'Want juice please dad juice.' Over time, we raised the bar to seven or even ten words or more until she started to initiate some longer sentences by herself. In the year-end meeting to discuss Isabel's educational goals for the next year, her kindergarten teacher said, 'Isabel's academics are below age level but still within range of normal.'

AT THE END OF HER KINDERGARTEN YEAR, when Isabel was seven, still mainstreamed with aide support, we noticed some changes. She was again showing more signs of anxiety, like holding her ears and tapping her knuckles on the floor, a desk, or a wall. She was also more isolated in school, in large part, we thought, because her classmates were getting more socially sophisticated and couldn't figure out how to include her in their more verbal activities. Our new child psychiatrist, who took over when the doctor in Baltimore moved away, recommended we try a very small dose of the antidepressant medication fluoxetine (Prozac), not because Isabel had symptoms of depression but because Prozac had been shown to alleviate anxiety. Knowing that kids with autism are sensitive to medications – tiny doses can have big effects – he prescribed only a tenth of the dose that seemed appropriate for her height and weight. Isabel had never taken a psychotropic drug before, but we felt it was worth a try. Because she was so sensitive to unfamiliar tastes, we had the liquid form of the medication made into a chocolate syrup.

When adults take medications like Prozac, they may not notice a change in their target symptoms for weeks. This is particularly true in the treatment of depression or obsessive compulsive disorder. Although not well studied, children can respond much more rapidly, exhibiting less anxiety or fearfulness and fewer avoidance behaviours. Many physicians told me that when children with autism take Prozac, they may quickly become more energised and assertive. This was certainly true for Isabel, who after a week, started to talk more. Her eye contact improved. The improvement wasn't dramatic, but Joyce and I had to admit that it was real.

The older Isabel got, the more her teachers expected of her. When she was eight, and in the third grade, for the first time she had a teacher who wouldn't let her move around in class. She was supposed to remain in her chair, at her desk, for as long as an hour at a time. She was supposed to answer questions posed to her, and once she even had to come up to the front of the class and give a brief oral presentation. We wrote a script for her to memorise, and she managed to do it.

She started to read. We didn't know how much she understood, but she was able to sound out almost any word she encountered. In the winter of 1999–2000, she searched our local bookstore for a book she had first seen at the Smithsonian, a marvellous, beautifully illustrated book about Monet called *Linnea in Monet's Garden*. It tells the story of a Swedish girl named Linnea who travels with her elderly upstairs neighbour, Mr Bloom, to Paris and Monet's house and garden in Giverny, in the Seine Valley of Normandy. Mr Bloom, a retired gardener, is a gentle man with a passion for Monet's art. Bloom inspires Linnea to find the reality in the paintings she at first saw as sloppy, imprecise patches of colour. As Linnea looks at one of Monet's paintings of the Japanese bridge, Mr Bloom tells her that the bridge is real, that it is still there, and that they can go and stand on it.

Isabel wanted us to read the story to her often, and within a few days she had memorised it. Joyce bought an animated film version of the book, and Isabel became hooked on that too. She told us she wanted to stand on the Japanese bridge, and asked to go to the National Gallery of Art, which has a Monet painting of the water lily pond and the Japanese bridge. When we took her there, she would stare at the painting from around a corner, peering at it only briefly, then darting away, seeming to take in the entirety of the image in a split second.

Abstractions are never good enough for Isabel. If she becomes interested in a rare animal, like a Tasmanian devil, she wants to go to the zoo to see the actual specimen. She felt the same way about Linnea and Monet, whom she insisted on meeting, not minding at all the fact that Linnea was a fictional character and Monet was dead. She wanted to reenact the story. So she started to wear a black T-shirt, sundress, black shoes, and a hat, in an effort to look like Linnea. Joyce eventually found clothes that resembled Linnea's: black shoes, white socks, a gingham dress, and a straw hat. Isabel became Linnea as often as we would let her.

We have a shiny, circular marble coffee table in our living room. Sometimes she stood on it and said, 'Japanese bridge', clearly pretending that she was standing on the bright green bridge that curves over the pond of water lilies at Giverny. She would look up and down and say nothing. I wanted to believe that her mind was filled with the images of Giverny and wondered if, when she looked up, she was seeing a memorised image of the wisteria blossoms that form a canopy over the bridge. Though I asked her to look around her and tell me what she saw, she only looked up and down. But she was focused on the shiny surface, a mirror of sorts, Monet's double garden, the pool with its water lilies and the reflection of the sky and landscape. She spent a long time with her eyes fixed at an unusual angle looking at the table – the mirror – her head still, caught in the middle of an act, as if she'd stopped lifting a cup of juice she was bringing to her mouth because she saw something reflected in it. I can't remember how long she spent looking at the coffee table at any given time, but it seemed long to me, and she was uncharacteristically calm. I wouldn't see that sense of calm again until we took her to Paris and Giverny in 2000, to be, at least for a week in August, Linnea in Monet's Garden.

Our main strategy for helping Isabel to learn is to prevent her from staying too focused on a single idea or behaviour, so it might seem contradictory that we'd go to the trouble of continuing her obsession with Monet. What we really wanted, however, was to keep moving with the topic rather than allowing her to remain fixed in one text or viewpoint. We didn't want her to simply listen to the Linnea story over and over again. It's good for any child to be able to focus on a single thing, but people with autism do it to a degree that is pathological. Her obsession with Linnea was a good example of the common difficulty that people with autism have with moving forward beyond a repetitive behaviour, or per-severation, that inhibits learning more about a particular topic. Psychologists and speech therapists sometimes call this a problem with 'topic elaboration'. High-functioning people with autism may use a lot of words, but they have the same difficulty elaborat-ing, or making a transition from one topic to another. Timothy, a child I know with Asperger's Disorder, is, like many children, fas-cinated with dinosaurs and knows an extraordinary amount about them, but if you try to talk to him about other extinct animals, like mammoths, it's as if he can't hear you. In fact, he's so relentless that once he continued to talk to me about dinosaurs even after I had walked into the bathroom and closed the door. Other children like Timothy are preoccupied with odd topics like lawn sprinklers, ceiling fans, or light switches, to the exclusion of anything else.

So we went to Paris and Giverny to help Isabel make the leap from the restricted world of a book's finite words into a world of other subjects, like Monet's life and work, impressionism, and French language and culture. In the book, Linnea and Mr Bloom first go to Paris, where they stay at the tiny Hotel Esmeralda, on the Left Bank overlooking Notre Dame. The owner has a dog, Canelle, and two cats, Mona and Lisa. The hotel actually exists, and it looks just like the illustration in the book: an inviting and cosy grey stone house with sagging floors, a black and white print of Esmeralda, the heroine from Victor Hugo's *The Hunchback of Notre Dame*, hanging on the wall at the foot of the stairs. Unfortunately, no rooms were available during our stay, and sadly, the cats had died, but Isabel went to a window of the hotel, just as Linnea is pictured doing in the book, and seemed simultaneously stunned and overjoyed.

The trip went much more smoothly than we expected. Isabel tried new foods, started to say some words in French, and proved to be remarkably good at pronunciation. The hardest part of the trip, but eventually the most rewarding, was dealing with Isabel's fear of dogs. Dogs in France are like cows in India. They are everywhere, and sometimes treated better than humans. So Isabel's dog phobia intensified. At times, seeing a dog 100 yards away on the pavement, she'd tear off into the street, and Joyce and I had to grab her as she ran into traffic screaming. But we taught her how to duck into a doorway until the dog passed by.

Isabel made sure our entry into Giverny went by the book, buying a baguette and some goat cheese, as Linnea had done, and checking with the ticket booth to make sure that, as in the book, they would tell her that taking photographs in Monet's house was 'strictly forbidden'. Giverny was a marvel. We spent hours at the Japanese pond looking at the flowers and water lilies. In the late morning, after an early rain shower, the place was overwhelmingly green, Isabel's favourite colour. Like Monet's painting, the land and the water blurred together at the edge of the mirror Isabel knew so well. She raced toward the Japanese bridge and stood at its apex for an hour.

She was more serene than I had ever seen her – like Monet, I imagined, who must have watched the pond for hours waiting for just the right impression to inspire him. Did Isabel notice how the pond changed constantly, with every new wind or movement of the clouds or the sun? She was mesmerised, but by what, we'll never know. There were carpets of flowers, streaks of colour that she probably never noticed because Giverny was, for her, the repetition of a script. She was calm, but determined. She sat on the same steps Linnea did, picked up her right foot and stretched her arms above her head in joy the same way Linnea did, looked down at the water lilies, and above to the wisteria, and, like Linnea, took a small green leaf to press inside a book. She was getting her own impressions, but I think they were impressions of completeness: first the book, then the video, and now reality – she had been able to step inside of all three.

Call the trip extravagant and indulgent, but it made a difference. She was now more interested in art, much more interested in France, and no longer afraid of dogs. By the end of our stay, Isabel had learned how to say, 'Is your dog nice?' in French. She began asking the question, using the same words, with the identical intonation and emphasis, of every dog owner we encountered. She must have talked to at least 100 people and petted 50 dogs. When we got back home, we took Isabel to her familiar haunts at the Smithsonian, where she looked for more Monet paintings. She also let me show her other works of art. When she stood in front of a water lily painting, using what the Smithsonian teachers used to call 'museum hands' – hands behind the back when you get close to a painting – she showed glimpses of her Giverny calm.

Within a year she started taking early morning French classes at our local elementary school, and she surprised everyone. Although I had to sit next to her the entire time to keep her on task, she absorbed the new vocabulary and pronunciation and quickly became one of the top students in the class, often winning the occasional competitions, in which the teacher would show picture flash cards and allow the first child to announce the word for the picture in French to advance to the next round. It was a bit like speech therapy, since the children were being taught how to make simple conversation in pretend social settings, and I could see the changes taking place in Isabel. Few experts would ever suggest that a child with autism study a foreign language. But I recommend it. She applied the lessons learned in French class to new situations, at home and in public. The people she spoke to – the cashier at the grocery store or the man walking a dog on the street – didn't speak French, but it didn't matter to us. She was interacting with the world.

ISABEL HAS HER OWN DOG NOW, a French Bulldog. When we decided to get the puppy, some friends asked us if, given Isabel's longstanding fear of dogs, it would traumatise her. But within a day, Isabel had crawled inside the dog's crate, shut the door from the inside, and laid down next to her. Isabel's dog is small and gentle, brindle coloured with the hallmark bat-like ears, short snout, and loud nighttime snoring. Her name is Linnea, and she's registered with the American Kennel Club under the name 'Linnea of Monet's Garden'.

Igloos in India

MANY OF THE SCIENTISTS and fund-raisers who have helped advance knowledge around the world about autism are themselves parents of children with autism. Among them are Eric and Karen London, who founded the National Alliance for Autism Research, now merged with Autism Speaks, a foundation that works closely with the National Institutes of Health and the Centers for Disease Control and that has awarded millions of dollars for scientific research. Philanthropists Portia Iversen and Jon Shestack helped found Cure Autism Now, an organisation that has given millions of dollars for autism research and coordinated an Autism Genetic Resource Exchange to make sure that scientists aren't working alone, each reinventing the wheel. As the result of their efforts, autism has received extensive media coverage, and celebrities and philanthropists have joined the cause of autism advocacy.

The true leader in autism advocacy was the United Kingdom (despite the fact that special education in the UK has lagged behind the US). In 1962, before there was an autism society in the US, British parents of autistic children founded the National Autistic Society (NAS). In many ways, the UK is the 'home' of autism advocacy. It is the country in which parents founded the very first autism society and the first school devoted to educating children. It is the country which supported the first epidemiological study of autism (Lotter 1966) and where Lorna Wing, in large part responsible for developing the concept of the autism spectrum, was trained and works. Perhaps the most significant difference between the American and British autism advocacy organisations is representation. While American societies continue to be parent-directed and parent-focused, the National Autistic Society made a concerted effort to be family-directed and focused, and to include autistic adults in their strategic planning and outreach. This remains one of the most contentious issues in the US as autistic adults continue to feel marginalised from the centres of power in the autism advocacy and research communities. I suspect that Americans will follow the British example.

But beyond the advocacy groups, there are also countless parents in the US, the UK and elsewhere who are not scientists, experts, or philanthropists, and yet work to help advance autism awareness, research, and treatment. There are a few obvious heroes, of course, those who write books that inspire parents, who develop or promote new therapies, or who build schools. But for most of the ordinary people – parents and other relatives of children with autism – the heroism lies in the bits and pieces that few people ever see. It is in the poetry of our everyday lives, the special foods we cook for our picky eaters, the challenges we surmount to take our children to the dentist or a physician, the hugs we give even when our children do not hug back. Joyce and I shopped for weeks just to find a toilet whose flush sound wouldn't make Isabel cringe, and that is, in its own way, heroic. Change is forced upon us, and we embrace it, often without realising how much we're doing. Some parents' lives take such extraordinary turns that they cannot remember the kind of person they were before they had a child with autism.

Together, parents of children with autism are more responsible for the progress that has been made than any of them, individually, realises. They achieve greatness, in their own way, and they can be found in many places throughout the world. There is Lidija Penko in Croatia, whose husband is a fisherman and away from home much of the time, who takes care of her daughter Nina by herself, yet manages to run a local autism centre. She communicates regularly with autism experts in the United States and reads all the latest articles at an Internet cafe. There is Jill Stacey in South Africa, who, despite having to care for her autistic son, organised one of the largest international conferences on autism ever held. Monica Mburu, in Kenya, has single-handedly helped rescue autistic children from abusive treatment and started Kenya's first autism society. Most years, Teresina Sieunarine, in rural Trinidad, pieces together enough money to bring autism therapy experts from Minnesota to train local teachers and parents and to counsel parents that autism is neither their fault nor the curse of their ancestors. Lisa Matthews, from Thurmont, Maryland, raising three children profoundly affected by autism and struggling to make ends meet, is involved with nearly every autism project that will have her and donated her mildly autistic husband's brain to autism research within hours of his sudden death.

Autism shatters many lives, and it changes everyone. But many turn the hardship of raising a child with a disability into something positive, even if it means their futures are different from what they expected, or from what their families and cultures wanted.

ON MONDAY NIGHT, 10 September 2001, Maureen Fanning asked her husband, Jack, not to go to work. She needed help getting their two boys, thirteen-year-old Sean and five-year-old Patrick, onto their school bus.

Jack Fanning, director of hazardous materials for the New York City Fire Department, an office that was responsible for all five boroughs, said he couldn't stay home because he was already behind at work. After he left the house at 5:45 A.M. on the morning of September 11, Maureen would never see him again. He arrived at the World Trade Center soon after the hijackers' plane hit the first tower and died when Tower 2 collapsed. Like almost all the victims of the attack, Jack's body was never found. His charred white helmet was recovered, but not until March 2002.

Jack and Maureen, both of Irish descent, Roman Catholic, and raised in Queens, married in June 1986 when he was 39 and she was 30. He had already been a fireman, like his father, for more than two decades, and she was a registered nurse. When their first son, Sean, started preschool in 1991, he seemed to be developing normally. But the teacher soon told Maureen that Sean seemed 'out of touch with his environment'. Over the next few months, Maureen told me, Sean became less able to interact with others. Jack and Maureen went first to a paediatrician, who referred them to a neurologist. The neurologist refused to make a diagnosis, insisting that he had to wait until Sean was older and more developed. Three months later, suspecting autism, Maureen drove Sean to North Carolina, where, she was told, the TEACCH programme had the most experienced testing staff on the East Coast. After the testing, the staff at TEACCH was not encouraging. Maureen cannot remember the exact words that the clinicians used, but the meaning, she recalls, was 'Just enjoy your child'.

'They didn't talk about treatment. They said he had severe autism. It was as if he'd just never amount to anything.' She drove back to New York, dejected.

Jack and Maureen decided not to have any more children. But then, in April 1995, Jack was called to Oklahoma City to assist in the rescue efforts after the bombing of the Murrah Federal

Building. He had never seen so many children perish at one time. 'He didn't talk a lot about the devastation in Oklahoma,' Maureen said, 'but that's how he was – he wasn't a man of many words.' But Jack did start talking about having another baby. The Oklahoma bombing had put autism in a different light. The way he saw it, Maureen said, was that 'if it happens it happens. Life is what it is. Autism isn't the worst thing in the world.'

Patrick was born in 1996 and initially seemed to be different from Sean, less irritable, able to smile and coo. Yet Patrick never developed any speech beyond cooing, and in 2005, at the age of nine, he was still not toilet trained. With two autistic children, the household was now hard enough to manage, but then Sean became more aggressive. He started to run away, never for very long before the police found him, but often for long enough that he was expelled from the government-funded recreation group for children with special needs in their county. Then both children were diagnosed with immune disorders. Sean has Common Variable Immunodeficiency (which means he has insufficient immunoglobulins and white blood cells to fight infections), and Patrick has Selective IgA Deficiency (insufficiency of just one type of immunoglobulin). Every three weeks, they have to have infusions of gamma globulin. In 2005, Patrick had pneumonia four times. Maureen has to be especially vigilant about monitoring Sean's health. His immune system is so impaired that when he has an infection he can't mount a fever.

'All we were doing,' Maureen said, 'was working or taking care of kids, one-on-one. We were repairing all the things in the house Sean was destroying. We were cleaning and bandaging his self-inflicted wounds after he bit himself. Sometimes he tore large chunks of flesh off his hands.'

Patrick usually slept through the night, but Sean had suffered from a sleep disorder since he was a toddler and wouldn't stay in his bed. Sometimes Maureen and Jack would have to take him back to bed more than 100 times in a single night. They couldn't go out to dinner because the cost of hiring two babysitters with the maturity and strength to handle the boys was too great. Taking a vacation was very difficult. When Sean was seven, Maureen and Jack tried to take him to an expensive Disney show at the Nassau Coliseum. When they got there, the stimulation was too great. Sean screamed, held his hands over his ears, and wouldn't go in. Jack took Sean to the car while Maureen wept outside in the parking lot. 'It was complete desperation, twenty-four hours a day,' she said.

Sean was a large boy – as a teenager he grew to over six feet tall – and he rocked so vigorously back and forth in the family minivan that when it was stationary it moved from end to end. The rocking motion eventually confused the vehicle's speed sensor, causing it to malfunction. The car wouldn't go over 30 miles an hour, until it had several expensive repairs.

When Jack died at the World Trade Center, Maureen's sister wrote emails to New York Governor George Pataki and to Laura Bush, pleading with them to help find a group home for Sean, but not really expecting a reply. The First Lady's office never replied, but the governor did. In just a few weeks, Governor Pataki ordered the state's Office of Mental Retardation and Developmental Disabilities (OMRDD) to arrange for Sean to be admitted to the group home Maureen wanted most, the one that had rejected Sean only a few months earlier. Sean lives there today but comes home every Wednesday night to sleep at Maureen's house. She complained: 'My kids were invisible before the incident. Why did it take something like that for them to see what my kids needed?'

Maureen doesn't know if either Patrick or Sean understands what happened to their father. For years, Sean would get excited when he saw a car like his father's, a dark blue Crown Victoria, on the street, yelling 'Dad home!' For a while after September 11, Sean would look out the window all day long, watching for the car to pull up in front of the house. Maureen showed him photos of the World Trade Center in ruins, but Sean continued to look for the car. For Sean, its absence, perhaps more than Jack's, is the symbol of his father's death. He doesn't say that his father is dead, but he understands.

Not long before September 11, Jack asked Maureen what she'd do if she came into a lot of money. 'I'd pay off all my bills,' she said, 'and build a group home for autistic kids.' So Maureen Fanning now devotes herself to that project. Using money from Jack's estate and from numerous donations she received for the boys, Maureen founded the Jack Fanning Memorial Foundation, Angels for Autism. Its mission is to promote group-home development and to build recreational and vocational centres for teenagers and adults with autism. The foundation recently gave $100,000 to help start group homes in Long Island and gave smaller gifts for the purchase of equipment for the Hoboken, New Jersey, schools.

Maureen's main concern is the long-term future of Sean and Patrick and other children like them. What will happen, she wants to know, when children with autism grow up? Will there be a place for them after their parents are gone? In 1998, before September 11 and the establishment of the foundation, Maureen and several other parents had started meeting with members of OMRDD to try and get funding for one or more group homes. The state seemed more interested in intermediate care facilities – short-term residence – than in long-term housing for life. But these parents wanted homes for life. By 2002 they had secured approximately $300,000, or $25,000 per child, and by 2004 they had purchased two homes, which the state agreed to manage.

In 2003, Maureen traded in her useless minivan for a sport utility vehicle, a truck heavy enough to withstand Sean's rocking. She also repaired the exterior of the house. One weekend afternoon, a neighbour came up to her as she arrived home. 'You know what they call you now, Maureen? They call you Maureen Moneybags.'

She stared at him. She wanted to say, 'You want my life? You go ahead and try to live it.' But she held her words and turned back to the house. He called out for her, 'Hey Maureen! What's wrong?' But she kept on walking.

'Some people feel sorry for you. They say, "Oh, I see your son is retarded, I feel so sorry for you." I hate that,' she said. 'Other people are angry. They resent my getting money from Jack's death. I think I would have cared about this more in the past. Now I just want to make sure that my kids have the best I can give them.'

During one of our interviews, Maureen suddenly remembered a time in her childhood when she was perhaps eleven or twelve. She told me that she was a sensitive girl who prayed a lot. 'One day I saw a man with Down syndrome boarding a bus. I said to myself … '

She started to cry.

'I said to myself, "I hope that when he gets on the bus people are nice to him and don't say anything mean" … I wanted to protect that man so much. Now I want to protect my kids.'

DESPITE HIS NAME, six-year-old Big Boy in South Africa is small and slender. He enjoys drawing pictures of marbles, different colours but all the same size, so there are crayons scattered throughout the Khumalo's small apartment outside of Cape Town, as well as pictures taped onto the refrigerator and all the doors. Big Boy's father, Golden, is an artist, a painter and a sculptor, and he wonders if Big Boy takes after him. Golden and his wife, Suzanna, are Zulus who left their homeland to find help for their son. Suzanna told me that Cape Town feels like a different world. I joked that since they are so far from home and their own culture, perhaps they are like anthropologists, too.

When Big Boy stopped talking at the age of two, he began making strange movements with his hands and avoided all eye contact. Golden's parents took over, demanding that Big Boy go to a traditional Zulu healer, a *nyanga*. But Golden and Suzanna weren't interested in finding the cause of their son's strangeness. 'That is for the grandparents. They have to find the cause. That is *their* way. They want to find a cause so they can blame someone.' Golden said, 'I was not going to take Big Boy to a nyanga, where he might be frightened, or who knows what. I'm scared of them. How could I do that to my boy?'

Golden's parents were furious that Golden didn't want to treat his son in the way they thought was proper. 'My parents and I argued over words. I called Big Boy's problems a disability and they called it a disease. Or I called it bad luck and they called it a punishment from our ancestors.'

They eventually stopped listening to Golden's opinions and did what they felt was right for their grandson. If it had been an ear infection, or the flu, Golden's parents might have gone to a Western-style doctor. But for a child who appeared to be possessed by a spirit, possibly a demon, they felt they had no choice. Even at the risk of hurting their relationship with their son, they took matters into their own hands.

Golden told me, 'My parents called a diviner and did their own goat sacrifice to please the ancestors, and then that diviner brought in a nyanga to stay with us. I wouldn't talk to the man. He was angry and my parents were angry. Nothing happened for a while until a few months later.'

Eventually, Big Boy's symptoms worsened. He became more remote and unresponsive. 'The nyanga blamed me,' Golden said. 'He told my parents, "The boy's problems got worse because your son didn't come to the sacrifice.'"The whole process alienated Big Boy's parents and grandparents from each other. 'There is no way a nyanga will be supportive,' Golden told me. 'He will always find fault because that is his job.'

I asked Golden to explain the word 'supportive'. He said, 'It's this way. I want to know what to do for my son, who is a good boy. I don't want to punish someone else, someone the old people say is using spirit against our family.'

While Golden maintains that the nyanga are crooks, he also knows that there are both good and bad nyanga. The more dishonest, self-appointed nyanga, he said, tend to be found in the cities, while the nyanga in the rural areas are less likely to be opportunists. Perhaps that is because the rural villages – like the one where his parents live – are more stable, close-knit communities where the same nyanga have been well known for years. Nyanga do not claim to cure or treat every illness, only those thought to be caused by spiritual disturbances. Many nyanga advise some patients to seek Western medical care before trying their services. Finally, the reason a nyanga is so expensive is that the consultations can last days and can sometimes involve the nyanga staying at the home of the afflicted person or bringing the patient to his home to live for a time.

Families may also pay to bring a female diviner, or *isangoma*, to their homes to help them make a decision about which type of treatment to get for the illness in question. By the time a nyanga or an insangoma comes to a conclusion about the best course of action, he or she knows a lot about the patient – his living situation, his family life, his personal history – certainly much more than a Western doctor will ever know. But Golden dismissed the methods of the traditional healers. He claimed that these methods are the means by which traditional healers make their money, insinuating themselves into families and earning their trust.

The nyanga that Golden's parents hired claimed that Golden's ancestors were punishing the living for some unknown transgression, but that Golden had apparently exacerbated things. Big Boy, the nyanga said, was *idlozi*, which means that he was possessed by an ancestral spirit, but one that does not ordinarily do a great deal of damage. The ancestors made the possession much worse only *after* the initial possession when, in their anger, they gave Big Boy a white man's disease: autism.

Golden's wife, Suzanna, had a different theory. She is Golden's second wife, a fact that was not lost on a second nyanga consulted by *her* parents. That nyanga blamed Big Boy's illness on the ex-wife's anger and resentment. The illness had nothing to do with the ancestors, he said. Instead, the ex-wife, now a sorcerer, had gotten hold of some very powerful medicines. Both nyanga theorised that Big Boy was afflicted because of a moral problem, but one saw the problem in the evil actions of a spirit of the dead, while the other blamed a jealous sorcerer who was morally rotten through and through. 'She has no goodness,' Suzanna said, 'and the nyanga said she was jealous and her jealousy grew into hatred. She was so angry that she lost all of her goodness and did this to our son.'

'One Sunday,' she told me, 'we were at church in Diepmeadow [a township that is part of Soweto, just outside Johannesburg], and the choir was singing, and Big Boy had a fit [a seizure]. One child said, "this must be the devil," and started to pray. Big Boy got calm. But I know that the wife was near the church.' Golden's ex-wife did live in the same neighbourhood in Soweto – in fact, she lived just one street away from the Khumalos. Suzanna saw her one day and wanted to approach her to ask if she was angry at her and Golden, but she was afraid to go near her. The first wife spotted Suzanna, walked up to her, and said, 'So how is Big Boy?' 'Fine,' Suzanna answered, and walked on. 'Some days later,' Suzanna told me, 'the wife passed by our house in a car and she beeped the horn. Big Boy went into another fit.'

It was precisely because of the first wife that Suzanna and Golden decided to move to the other side of the country, from Soweto to Cape Town. Cape Town is about 950 miles away from their home – it is like the distance between New York City and Madison, Wisconsin – but even more than distance, it meant moving away from their extended family, and away from the vast majority of the other 10.5 million Zulu speakers in South Africa. Golden said they moved to escape the pressures from his parents, but that it hadn't been all bad. 'I'm making more money here painting houses and selling my art, and no one is telling me that Big Boy's autism is my fault. The teachers and the doctors tell me it's just an accident, something in his genes.' 'We could be okay with Golden's parents,' Suzanna said. 'We left to get away from the wife.' Golden now makes enough money to visit his parents and parents-in-law and pay for their airfare to visit Cape Town. 'I miss home,' Suzanna said, 'but I won't go back with Big Boy.'

Big Boy has a psychiatrist now and attends an excellent school for children with autism. But in getting psychiatric help, Suzanna and Golden have shown extraordinary courage. Psychiatry is well known in sub-Saharan Africa, but its history is brief and unfortunate. Nineteenth-century colonial physicians, most of them quite racist by today's standards, thought that Africans didn't have mental illnesses, either because they were too 'primitive' – so undeveloped intellectually that they could not experience emotional pain – or because they were too happy, living low-stress lives without the pressures of industrialised societies. European psychiatrists theorised that Africans were secure and healthy in the confines of their traditional social structures, but that outside those structures – in the cities, in the mines, or at the plantations – Africans could go insane. In early 20th-century colonial Africa, mentally ill

Europeans went to hospitals that were more like retreats for rest and recuperation, while mentally ill Africans were put in hospitals that were more like prisons. In the 19th century, Robben Island, where Nelson Mandela spent much of his life as a political prisoner, housed the destitute, the lepers, and the chronically mentally ill. Today there are 24 public psychiatric hospitals in South Africa, with about 14,000 beds. Still, community-based psychiatry is just emerging, and most hospitals are for acute and long-term patients.

Not surprisingly, many Africans, including Suzanna's parents and Golden's parents, remember the history of the psychiatric prisons, and they are suspicious about psychiatry in general. That makes Suzanna and Golden all the more remarkable, and that is why their parents know nothing of Big Boy's medical care.

IT'S 9 A.M. on a Monday morning in January 2005, south Delhi, India, and my taxi driver, having stopped three times to ask passersby for directions, looks as if he's about to give up. He's taken me to the right neighbourhood, Sheik Serai Phase 2, but it's a run-down area with few landmarks, and stray cows walking the streets. It's bigger than I thought it would be, and I don't have an actual address. 'The place is called "Action for Autism",' I tell him, 'just above Mahavira Chemist,' but he says he doesn't know this word 'autism' and suggests we go back to my hotel. Ten minutes later, I'm the one who finds it, a small white banner hanging from the third floor of a crumbling building in a Delhi slum, that said 'Action for Autism, Open Door'.

I'm carrying a large, heavy box from IKEA. Before I left the United States, I had asked the director, Merry Barua, if there was anything I could bring her, and she had sent back an enigmatic e-mail reply, 'igloos'. At first I thought it was a joke that I just didn't get, but I decided to e-mail back for clarification. There was no reply. Was it a cooler she wanted? Was this a sarcastic joke about refrigerator mothers? Maybe the igloo was a metaphor for India's failure to provide an appropriate place for autistic children, a symbol of autism's alien character. But then, knowing how much children with autism like to hide in tents and cupboards, Joyce suggested I go to IKEA in College Park, Maryland, where, to my utter surprise, they sold small, white, dome-shaped tents designed to look like igloos. When I got to Delhi, Merry would say flatly, as if she knew they were coming all along, 'Oh good, you found igloos.'

To get to the offices of Action for Autism, I go up three flights of dark stairs, past barely visible wall paintings of sea life, to a cold, crumbling group of dusty classrooms and a tiny central office where the director and her staff work cheek by jowl. One level higher, the teachers watch a dozen students play for a while before dividing them up into four small classrooms. Everyone is coughing and rubbing their eyes this morning, the result of a combination of the weekend's accumulation of dust and the fumes of masala being fried downstairs. This seems like an unlikely place to find the person who knows more about autism than anyone else in New Delhi, a city of 14 million people, and the capital of India (pop. 1.1 billion).

THE FOUNDER AND DIRECTOR of Action for Autism has no advanced degrees and no special training in child development. In a status-conscious country like India, she can't even get invited to speak at scientific conferences. But Merry Barua has arguably done more to increase autism awareness than anyone else in India. Small and thin, with black hair, cut short but tousled in a stylish way, Merry looks most comfortable with herself when she's wearing blue jeans and eating Domino's pizza. In her tiny office suite, she's totally in control, but she gives her assistants responsibility and decision-making powers. She darts from place to place but never seems intrusive. One moment she's caffeinated, multitasking, all at once on the phone, proofreading a hard copy of a grant proposal, and, if the electricity and phone lines are working, looking for something on the Internet; the next moment, she is sitting quietly with a distraught mother who wonders if there is any place on earth for her son, a mother who, at least for that moment, feels she is Merry's only concern.

On a crisp Sunday morning in January 2005, about twenty families gathered at the Bangladeshi embassy in Delhi to walk for autism awareness. A young boy with autism named Vishu and his mother came late, after all the other families had returned to the embassy grounds, but Vishu had been told it was a walk, and that's what he intended to do. Within a few minutes after his arrival, he was gone. His mother panicked. Had it been me, I would have screamed out with urgency: 'He's nine years old, wearing a striped shirt!' But Merry took the microphone, calmed the crowd, and packed all the vital information into a single sentence. She said, 'Vishu, like most little nine-year-old boys, loves cars and trucks, so let's just go check the parking lot, look inside and under the cars, and when you see his striped shirt, just give a yell.'

She had been through this before, like many parents of children with autism. Only three days earlier, in Bethesda, Maryland, my daughter's school bus had arrived at our bus stop without her. Isabel's bus had been delayed, so she had gotten on the wrong one. Once she recognised a landmark, she got off the bus and walked the two miles home. No matter how often it happens, the panic still comes, and you wonder, 'Is this the day that I'll really lose my child, the day she'll get hit by a car, or get abducted, or drown?"

I was still looking under a car when Vishu was found. No one had seen Merry call the police, but a patrol car had located Vishu about five minutes later. Delhi is a city teeming with street children and vagabonds, but not nicely dressed ones singing in the middle of a busy road, with arms flapping. The crisis hadn't lasted more than fifteen minutes.

Merry is a pragmatist, and she's all about action. Always her own boss, she's highly independent, strong-willed, and decisive. I've heard Merry talk to parents whose children had just been diagnosed. She doesn't ask them to think about their distant futures or invite self pity. Asking 'why me?' has little use, and besides, she knows that the families will ask that question without any encouragement from her. She talks about practical matters, like which experts to consult, what sorts of tests need to be done, what kinds of schools are available. She talks about sensitive issues like autism and sex, autism and head banging, faeces smearing, violence, and suicide with the insight of someone who has experienced all these behaviours first-hand, and wouldn't think of treating them as taboo subjects any more than a good doctor would. Once, when I told her about an animal sacrifice and exorcism described by a parent at the school she runs, she looked incredulous. 'Why do you seem so surprised?' I asked. She said, 'It's just so exotic, don't you think?' I quickly answered, 'But this is India!' She laughed and said, 'Sometimes I forget.'

Born to a middle-class Bengali family in Allahabad, Merry spent most of her childhood in Calcutta in the eastern part of the country, a deeply intellectual and largely secular city. Her father worked for Gramaphone Records printing the jacket sleeves and liner notes for LPs. When she married, in 1981, she left a career in journalism and started a family with her husband, Ratan. She welcomed and adored her son, Neeraj, when he was born, and saw no warning signs in his first two years.

Merry had seldom seen a disabled child, at least not a middle-class one (on the streets of Calcutta, poor, physically disabled children are hard to miss), let alone one who looked normal but had mental disabilities. She stayed at home with Neeraj for the most part, where she was relatively isolated and saw few children. In 1984, when Neeraj was two, Merry visited her husband's extended family and spent time with other children. 'My sister-in-law's daughter was just two weeks older than Neeraj and was talking about Walt Disney characters. I was amazed. Neeraj could barely say any words, and for the first time I thought, "What's wrong with my child?"'

If that didn't alarm her, the next month Neeraj's preschool teacher returned his school folders and notebooks, all of them blank, and told her he had been incapable of doing any of the things that the other children could do. So Merry took Neeraj to a paediatrician, who said, 'This is just a spoiled child who needs to be spanked.' Merry said, 'But I already spank him.' The doctor answered, 'Well obviously not hard enough.' A cousin commented, 'I raised five children and you can't even raise one.' Early photographs of Neeraj show him disengaged and flat. One, taken at Neeraj's fourth birthday party, suggests it was anyone's birthday but his own.

Finally, the mother of a neighbour whose child had Down syndrome referred Merry and Ratan to a psychiatrist, one of only a handful of mental health experts in Calcutta, who spent half the year practicing in Canada. He was, according to Merry, the only doctor in Calcutta making any autism diagnoses at all. With this diagnosis in hand, Merry went directly from the doctor's office to a library to take out all the books she could find on the subject. The few available, psychology textbooks, had perhaps one or two short paragraphs suggesting that autism was caused by mothers. The only full-length study was Bettelheim's *The Empty Fortress*, which she read quickly. 'It was devastating at first,' she said, 'I was wringing my hair [*sic*]. I couldn't believe it, but then I just put it down. I said to myself, "This book has nothing to do with me".'

I find it hard to put myself in Merry's shoes. When Isabel was a toddler, I had all the information in the world at my fingertips. Merry was told Neeraj would be disabled for life and that there was nothing anyone could do for him – no schools, no medicines, nothing. The Internet didn't exist. 'There was nothing to do or read – no Internet, no parent support groups, no one even knew the word. Imagine that someone tells you that you have a lifelong disorder but that nothing is known about it. What would you do? You'd suddenly be in a world all your own.' Merry had never felt so alone. Everyone around her, but herself most of all, seemed powerless.

Within a few weeks, she began writing letters and making telephone calls to the United States and the United Kingdom for information. She received many brochures and pamphlets from autism societies, but they didn't tell her much about how she should take care of her son from day to day. Despite Merry's best efforts, Neeraj was not improving, and he would get more difficult to care for as time went on.

In 1987, Ratan was transferred for a short period of time to Vellore in the south of India, and Merry took the opportunity to look for medical assistance for Neeraj. In Vellore, she happened upon the Christian Medical College, which had a small residential school for the mentally disabled that cost a few rupees a month. Mothers were required to live there with their children, in more austere conditions than she had ever experienced, but since she had no alternatives, she decided to stay. She and Neeraj moved into an eight-by-nine-foot concrete room with a small bed, one wooden window, and a wire frame door. 'I told my husband, "just get me a kerosene stove, a table and a chair, and I can survive here."' The residence was actually four adjacent rooms, one family per room, each of which opened to a large open courtyard, where there was a common bathroom with an Indian-style non-flush toilet and a large cement tub full of water for drinking and bathing. At one end of the row of rooms there was a shared kitchen.

Ratan was back in Calcutta within a few weeks, but Merry and Neeraj stayed on. Along with several other mother–child pairs, Merry and Neeraj learned how to engage each other in play. Neeraj learned the alphabet, numbers, and some words, and Merry began to feel that there was some hope for them after all. After six months, Merry returned home and decided to hire a special educator to teach Neeraj. But there were few takers. Friends and students in the neighbourhood volunteered, but no one lasted very long. When she finally did find a teacher, she was so grateful that she treated her like royalty. The teacher had close ties with principals and educators in the local school system. But one day, Merry was curious enough to spy on them and saw the teacher hitting Neeraj. For weeks she said nothing, too scared to jeopardise the relationship and the chance to one day get Neeraj into a proper school. Only after much agonising did she ask her to leave. Merry took over Neeraj's education herself, frustrated that she could find no school for him.

The vast majority of middle-class Indians send their children to private schools. Many are expensive, but most are affordable enough, the equivalent of a few dollars a month. In 1987, when Neeraj was five, Ratan's employer transferred him to New Delhi, but no private school would take Neeraj. Merry was sure that in a government school for the mentally retarded he would regress. Even today, with the Indian school system better funded than ever before, government schools serve only children of the poor. Some are so run-down that they hardly look like schools at all – just a carpet and, if you're lucky, four walls.

There are more than 300 million children in India today, perhaps 200 million of whom are of primary-school age. Yet the government's 2004 primary-school budget was only about $1.3 billion, or $6.50 per child. According to UNICEF, only one in six rural schools has a toilet. About 100 million children don't even go to school, many of them girls, as their parents depend on them to do household work, earn money, or work in the fields. There are estimates that about 2 million children are in some way mentally handicapped, and yet, as Merry found, there are few schools for the mentally retarded, even fewer for the mildly affected, and until she established her own school, Open Door, none specifically for autism.

Neeraj seldom slept through the night, often screamed incessantly, smeared himself with faeces, and destroyed much of what Merry owned: her jewellery, record player, and books. Wondering how long she could go on like that, she bought a book on assisted suicide, *Final Exit*, just in case she needed it. I asked her if she wanted to end her life, her son's life, or both. 'I never got far enough to make those distinctions,' she told me. She never sought professional counselling for her own well-being because that seemed to her to be illogical; she wasn't the one with autism. Her husband's main support to her was financial. Six days a week he left early for work, and he came home late at night. He isolated himself from both Merry and Neeraj, and they would soon separate.

Merry couldn't afford to send Neeraj to England, where educators had at least some experience with autism, but things were terrible at home. To prevent Neeraj from wandering off and getting lost, and from destroying everything in the house, Merry locked doors and windows, giving Neeraj a smaller, more contained space within which to live. That helped, but there were still problems that she had no idea how to handle. When he was ten, Neeraj resisted bathing, even when he was smeared with faeces, and Merry finally threw up her hands and decided not to react. Maybe ignoring it helped, or maybe it was the discomfort of the rash and the odour, but for whatever reason, he stopped within a few weeks.

Merry decided that if there was no school for Neeraj, she'd simply have to build one. Called 'Open Door', the school began in Merry's apartment with Neeraj as its only student. Within a few years, a girl with autism joined Neeraj, and the experiment seemed to be working. Both students were abandoning their most inappropriate behaviours. Within a few years, more students enrolled, and Open Door had become known in the Delhi psychiatric and paediatric community as the only place to educate an autistic child. The family of one of the parents donated a cosy, vacant apartment in a nice district of Delhi, called Vasantkunj, to house the school. There was a very small number of children, not because there are so few children with autism in India, but because so few had a diagnosis.

Today, Merry is the director of Action for Autism, the Open Door school, and the National Centre for Advocacy, Research, Rehabilitation, and Training. Open Door has approximately 60 students aged three through 21 and a teacher-student ratio of 2:3. It is still the only school for children with autism in all of Delhi. Before Open Door, children with autism were simply lumped together with children diagnosed with a variety of different disorders, such as Down syndrome and cerebral palsy. The centre offers counselling, diagnostic testing, and referral and sponsors a mother training programme. In that programme women come from Delhi and other cities in northern India for up to three months of training and supervision. They learn how to help plan their child's educational programmes, how to find information about autism, and how to participate in national and international networks with other parents and specialists. They also learn Applied Behavioural

Analysis and practical techniques for teaching their children both daily life skills and academics.

Since most children with autism in India are labelled mentally retarded, Merry mobilised parents to convince doctors, educators, and government officials that an autism diagnosis does matter, and that the educational and medical interventions for children with autism are different from those for children whose primary diagnosis is mental retardation. In 1999, they succeeded in getting the government to recognise autism as a disorder. Unfortunately, they did not succeed in their lobbying efforts in favour of an amendment to the Persons with Disabilities Act of 1995. But they did succeed in getting recognition of autism in a government document called 'the National Trust' that concerns the rules for guardianship.

Merry also successfully lobbied the Ministry of Social Justice to allow Action for Autism and other organisations to grant a Diploma in Special Education and to set the requirements for it. With an American psychologist, Tamara Daley, Merry designed a survey of paediatricians' awareness of autism that, while demonstrating how few doctors had ever made a diagnosis of autism, provided valuable information to physicians in poor and remote regions of the country.

She remembers well the time when Neeraj was first diagnosed. 'I was in a daze. It was like a tidal wave hitting you. That whole month I kept asking myself, "What do I do, what do I do?" I don't want other parents to feel that kind of impotence. It's a horrible feeling. But it changed my life, you see.'

Breaking the Rules

In India, most of the children who would be diagnosed with autism in the United States are called either mentally retarded (MR) or mad (in Hindi, *paagol*). So there is no 'epidemic' of autism diagnoses in India. The MR designation is usually made by a paediatrician. There are few psychiatrists there, and virtually no child psychiatrists. To my knowledge, autism researchers are also rare in India, and no one has ever conducted an epidemiological study there. So parents who suspect their children have autism usually have to get their information from the Internet. Like the South African parents I know, Indian parents usually assume that the numbers and rates derived from studies in North America and the United Kingdom are the same numbers that would be found in India if someone took the trouble to look for them.

The families of children who do get an autism diagnosis typically try some sort of medicine or vitamin regimen, but they often keep the diagnosis a secret, if possible, because the stigma is so great. Amit Sen, one of the two trained child psychiatrists in New Delhi, said that most of his patients' extended families have no idea that one of their relatives is getting psychiatric care. Sometimes he's happy about that because, as he put it, 'grandparents routinely subvert the therapeutic process'. Autism has become less of a secret over the past decade, as autism awareness in India has grown, and the diagnosis is becoming more common. 'Because of the Internet,' Amit Sen suggested, 'people know more about autism in India than ever before. It's wonderful, actually.' But rather than concluding that there is an epidemic, many Indians conclude that autism is a more accurate and useful diagnosis than mental retardation or madness.

As in the United States, in India psychiatrists and psychologists depend upon paediatricians for referrals, but often they don't trust the paediatricians to refer. They think paediatricians are either ignorant about autism or fear losing a paying patient to a specialist. Indeed, though paediatricians are the first to see a child with autism, few in India know much about autism, let alone its various manifestations. In January 2005, I went to a well-respected paediatrician who runs a large paediatric clinic in an upscale part of Delhi. 'Honestly, Professor,' he said, 'I wouldn't know if an abnormal child in my office had autism or not. I would just know he was abnormal. But I did see *Rain Man* with Dustin Hoffman, so I might be able to diagnose an adult.' Like doctors and laypeople throughout the country, he said that boys tend to talk later than girls, so a speech delay is nothing to worry about.

Tamara Daley, the American psychologist who worked with Merry Barua to increase autism awareness in India, has conducted research in several Indian cities. She believes that many doctors in India actually do know something about autism but are reluctant to give the diagnosis, either because they think there is nothing that can be done to help, or because they assume the families they see, many of whom are illiterate or poorly educated, will be unable to understand what autism means. Until 1999, the Indian government did not recognise autism as a disorder. A diagnosis of mental retardation, however, is common enough to be understood, since every village has at least some people who are mentally disabled. The tendency, she said, is to classify all mental capacity as either normal or retarded.

From the paediatrician's perspective, giving an autism diagnosis serves little purpose. Since there are no services, schools, or treatments available for children with autism, the diagnosis would bring only pain and stigma. Doctors delay any diagnosis of a developmental problem, even mental retardation, as long as they can.

Consider the case of a teenage boy I met in New Delhi named Rohit. Before he was two, Rohit's parents knew something was wrong. He didn't speak much, showed no interest in social interaction, had rigid, patterned behaviours, and walked with an odd gait. Rohit's parents tried religious healers, but when there was no improvement in his behaviour, they moved on to medical doctors, who diagnosed him with mental retardation.

By the age of five, he was interested mostly in memorising license plate numbers and showed great skill in identifying vehicle makes and models. By the age of eight, his speech, though still delayed, was articulate and fluent. But he had no friends. He still kissed and hugged his mother in public, which is considered inappropriate in India, and he used obscene words when talking to neighbours. Paediatricians said that Rohit needed a more lively social environment. No government elementary school would take him, so his parents paid $60 a month to place him in a good private school for a diverse array of children with special needs, many of whom were blind, deaf, mentally retarded, or had cerebral palsy. Rohit was enrolled under the diagnosis 'mental retardation'.

Six years later, when Rohit was fourteen, and as socially impaired as ever, a British-trained psychiatrist in Delhi came to the school to give a lecture to parents about developmental disorders, including autism, and urged the school to administer a particular autism rating scale, the CARS (Childhood Autism Rating Scale), to its students. The idea was to screen potential cases for further diagnostic assessment. Rohit's parents resisted. They had already seen dozens of doctors over the years, and each time they had been told that Rohit was mentally retarded. They'd already gotten comfortable with the diagnosis.

After the lecture, still knowing little about autism, they told the school director, 'Rohit cannot have autism because he looks fine physically'. Ten months later, the school prevailed over the parents' objections. Rohit was tested and then diagnosed with autism. Further examination showed no evidence of mental retardation. In fact, his IQ is above average. A psychiatrist promptly prescribed a small dose of Sertraline (Zoloft). Within three months, the family reported that Rohit's social relatedness had improved noticeably. It had taken them thirteen years to get proper treatment for Rohit.

There is emerging in India a disjunction between doctors, who often rely on outdated medical literature, and parents, who are increasingly well informed. The parents' source is the Internet, a central factor in nearly every autism story I've ever heard, no matter what country I was in. Many Indian parents have set up Google alerts to send them daily notices of every news article published on autism in any newspaper in the world.

Autism is slowly but surely becoming less exotic in India, and so also less shameful. Some of the positive spin comes from Merry's own website, an enormous store of articles and information. Enter the words 'India' and 'autism' in most search engines and your number one hit will be Action for Autism. However, many people consider the information on American websites to be more authoritative. Indian families with computers are just as likely to read the information posted by the Autism Society of America in Washington, DC, the National Alliance for Autism Research in Princeton, New Jersey, or the M.I.N.D. (Medical Investigation of

Neurodevelopmental Disorders) Institute in Davis, California, as they are to consult the Indian National Institute of Mental Health and Neuro Sciences in Bangalore or Merry's Action for Autism.

Indians also watch a lot of Western television. During one interview, a Bengali woman from Delhi told me that her husband watched *Baywatch* religiously. In one episode, a couple took their mentally disabled child to a public beach. After this, she told me, her husband agreed to stop hiding their son from friends and neighbours.

One day, as I talked to a group of three Bengali mothers waiting to pick up their children from Open Door, I noticed a remarkable similarity in their conversation to some of the positive discussions I'd heard in the United States. In the United States, parents often talk about whether Albert Einstein and Isaac Newton were high-functioning people with autism. Newton, for example, spoke little, had few friends, and was extremely awkward socially. In India, such comparisons involve religious figures. One of the Bengali women commented to me, 'You know, our god, Siva, was like an autistic person. He couldn't relate to others, and he walked around naked.' The other women lit up and joined in. 'He had no friends!' 'Yes, he was totally disconnected from the world.' 'He was abnormal.' Of course, they are right, and this is why Siva's parents-in-law- to-be were so outraged that their daughter might marry him.

'I heard that Ramakrishna was autistic too,' one woman said, but she could not say why. She was referring to the Bengali saint, Sri Ramakrishna Paramahansa, who was illiterate and bizarre, but revered in India. As a child, he wore girls' clothing and acted like a girl, sometimes pretending that he was a widow or an abandoned wife, and worshipped the Lord Krishna through *madhurya bhava*, a woman's deeply spiritual desire for her lover. He was thought to be *paagol* (mad) but also divinely inspired.

There is a long tradition of unusual saints and other holy men and women in India who had special powers but were incapable of having appropriate social relationships. Indeed, India has a role, often in cults or around shrines, for even the most peculiar people. There are ascetics, people who would be instantly diagnosed with psychoses in the United States, people with matted hair who ritually pierce their skin with hooks, with which they pull heavy carts. In this context, it's not that surprising to hear mothers describe their children with autism as untainted by the evils of civilisation; they use terms like 'pure' and 'close to God'. In fact, an important stage of the ideal Hindu life course is the eventual separation from the social world, the renunciation of society, with the greatest value given to the forest dweller who abrogates all social ties and family obligations.

Analogies can be found in other parts of the world. For example, in the 1990s, a particular group of ultra-orthodox Jews in Israel called Haredi began staging large public gatherings in which autistic children moved an adult facilitator's fingers to computer or typewriter keys in response to questions from rabbis. Few scientists believe that people with autism can communicate the sophisticated, abstract, and complex thoughts attributed to them through this method, known in the United States as 'facilitated communication', or FC. Researchers have found that the facilitator is the one actually communicating, although he may delude himself into thinking that the child is guiding his hand. But these ultra-orthodox Jews do not pretend the words are those of the child, but rather the words of the divine, messages from the spirit world channelled through him. Children with autism, they believe, are former sinners reincarnated as autistic people and sent back to the world to chastise the living for their transgressions and reassert community values. Young nonverbal children with autism have the facilitator type lucid sentences condemning people for having sex with menstruating women, or failing to study the Torah, and in one case a seven-year-old boy with severe autism even endorsed Benjamin Netanyahu's candidacy for prime minister in 1996. These mediums, the rabbis say, prove a point made in the Talmud, that after the destruction of the temple in Jerusalem, prophecy 'was taken from the prophets and given to the fools and children'.

DESPITE THE EXTRAORDINARY cultural variation of India – where there are close to 400 different languages in a country roughly one-third the size of the United States – Hindu child-rearing practices are remarkably consistent. Among all Hindu communities, the mother and child are nearly inseparable for the first two years of life, with mothers holding their children at the hip even when working around the house. Up until the age of two or two and a half, children are kings. They sleep with their mothers, and the breast is always accessible enough that they never have to cry for long. Weaning usually occurs between the ages of two and three, but in many cases, where there is no younger sibling, a child may breast-feed until the age of five or six.

In general, Hindu boys are tied to their mothers until about the age of five, when mothers no longer indulge them and they enter the world of the father and his extended family. Some Indian psychoanalysts have suggested that the tie between the child and the mother, especially between the son and the mother, is so close that it is almost pathological. A boy is so important to a mother's status in her family and society at large that her emotional attachment to him – or reverence – may be excessive from a Western perspective. The father, in contrast, is typically disengaged from his young children. While a child is enmeshed with his mother, however, the father and the extended family are always nearby. Gently, the mother weans the child not only from the breast but from his or her dependence on her, pushing the child into the bosom of the extended family: the father and, figuratively speaking, dozens of mothers.

The mother essentially renounces the son around the time he enters primary school. Mothers tease their children by suggesting that they will give them away. They discourage attention-getting behaviours, encourage self-restraint, and, if they do indulge them on occasion, they reject them afterward. For example, a mother might say, 'You had your milk, now get out of the house'. Other relatives push the child to voluntarily abandon the mother. They guide him to either the extended family, the joint family, or both, rather than to independence, promoting a familial rather than an individual identity. This structure is changing rapidly, especially in urban India and in the Indian diaspora, where men and women are entering competitive marketplaces that place a high value on individualism. Still, just as Americans idealise the nuclear family at a time when nearly half of all American children live in single-parent households, the ideals of the conventional Hindu family persist. For the women at Action for Autism, however, autism disrupted any hope of having their children merge with either an extended or a joint family.

Throughout the world, autism is commonly considered a disorder that is about being socially disconnected, and this is true in India as well. But in India autism takes a culturally specific form where the child is largely disconnected from his or her extended family and the maternal bonds remain unbroken. The Indian mother of a child with autism does not feel comfortable asking her in-laws to take a greater role in raising him. She does not entrust her child to anyone. The mother of a mute and mentally retarded autistic child would know her child was incapable of leaving her to spend more time with the extended family, even if the extended family was willing to welcome the child. She would most likely not even try a simple gesture of separation, such as asking the child to get permission from his or her grandparents to eat candy or play a game. Common acts that Hindu mothers use to foster separation, such as teasing the child, have no impact when the child cannot comprehend the meaning (for example, handing the child to a distant relative and saying, 'You take him! I don't want him anymore! I've cared for him enough!').

One couple I met, Shubrha and her husband, Rajiv, lived with their son, Gautam, in a joint family enclave until Rajiv was relocated to Delhi. 'It was a relief in many ways to be away from my in-laws,' Shubrha told me. She continued:

> They never blamed me for causing his mental problems and behaviors, but they did blame me for not doing the right things to help him. They said I was too overprotective, that I kept him home too much, that he didn't have an exciting environment to help him learn how to talk or be social. After a while the constant criticism gets to you and you think to yourself, 'Okay, if you know how to do it, *you* do it, you are *supposed* to do it anyway if you are his grandmother,' but then nothing ever happens. But that was okay for me because I knew I could take care of him better than anyone.

When Gautam was almost eleven, he started to go to a school for children with mental retardation not far from his home in Delhi. Though he had been toilet trained a year earlier, he now started to defecate in his pants on the way home from school, sometimes putting his hands into his pants and playing with his faeces. Once home, he refused to let anyone wash him, so Shubrha had to have someone physically restrain him while she cleaned him up. After a few weeks, Shubrha decided, just as Merry Barua had once done when her son resisted toilet training, that the only way to extinguish that behaviour was to let him sit and stink in his own faeces.

'It was horrible,' she said. 'The house smelled so bad. Gautam had rashes on his thighs and buttocks. I had to keep scented candles and incense burning most of the time but I held out because I knew the only way to stop the behaviour was to show no reaction to it. My husband kept saying, "How much longer can you take it?" I think it took the better part of a year, but it worked.'

Within a few years, Rajiv and Shubrha divorced. Shubrha now felt free to raise Gautam the way she thought best, often in ways that others might find shocking. When Gautam was about fifteen years old, he began to touch himself more frequently, arousing himself but not knowing what else to do once he had an erection. He became increasingly frustrated, irritable, and violent, and sometimes he scratched and hit himself. 'No one gives you advice about handling these sexual matters,' Shubrha said, 'especially in India where people have so many hang-ups about sex. I made sure not to use the word "masturbation" or any other sexual word around him because he'd repeat them in public. He once heard the word "scrotum", became fixated on it, and started saying it to strangers. But other than that, I couldn't figure out what to do.'

At a conference on special education in Delhi, Shubrha met a young American graduate student and asked for his thoughts. Gautam, he believed, needed to learn how to masturbate. He and Shubrha decided that Gautam should *see* someone masturbate, if possible on film, but it wasn't easy to figure out how to arrange that. Video recordings of any sexual act are a violation of Indian law, so pornography is difficult to find. It would be even harder to find depictions of men masturbating alone. So the graduate student set up his own video camera and filmed himself. When Gautam saw the film he showed no initial reaction, but after a few days, Shubrha said, it was obvious that he had learned what to do; Shubrha just had to make sure he learned to do it in private.

From the perspective of many parents, what Shubrha did might seem bizarre, but I thought it made perfect sense, given the situation, and that it was a deeply compassionate act. Parents of autistic children everywhere must improvise. They do what works. And they know their children learn *concretely*, through what is real, visible, and tangible rather than through abstract discussions, like lectures about the birds and the bees. True, it gives new meaning to the phrase 'hands-on education', but there is no denying that Shubrha improved Gautam's emotional health and taught him what is arguably an important life skill. And that is something she should be proud of.

Amla, another Bengali mother living near Delhi, considers that she has become a 'bohemian'. By this she means that she is ill-suited to the society in which she lives and that she dislikes convention, including materialism and her conservative parents-in-law. 'My husband Anil became a Bohemian too, which made him an unsuitable husband, or at least a poor provider,' she said. 'A couple of times he came home without a paycheck and a receipt showing he'd donated the whole thing to a shelter or a hospital.' When their autistic and only son, Sunil, was twelve, her husband died suddenly of a heart attack. Normally, the eldest son arranges the cremation and lights the fire by putting a flame to the lips of the deceased in a symbolic gesture to mark the spirit leaving the body.

'It was chaos in the house,' she recalled. 'People coming into the house, and the body was there – the typical Hindu thing – and Sunil was going crazy. He was unable to comprehend what was going on, why his father was lying dead in our house, and the crying visitors were too much. He stuck his fingers in his ears and screamed and screamed. I was devastated enough, but I couldn't do this to him.' So Amla did what few Hindu women are prepared to do. She took Anil to an electric crematorium and lit the cremation fire herself.

These days, one can find urban Hindu women arranging funerals and even cremating their husbands – all Hindus cremate, unlike Muslims, who bury – but it is still a clear violation of Hindu laws, and in a conservative family it is unforgivable. Traditionally, women are not allowed to step foot in the burning grounds – and this is true among all Hindus, regardless of linguistic or ethnic group. Amla's side of the family was appalled, and her husband's family vowed never to see her again.

MAMTA'S VILLAGE SITS at the foothills of the Himalayas, near the old British hill stations in northern India. She came to Action for Autism wearing jeans, T-shirt, and sandals one day, and then a traditional Indian sari the next. She told me that when her first child, Ohjyu, was eighteen months old, he didn't seem to behave like the other children did. 'I took him to a baby show. They have judges, and mothers exhibit the babies. The babies all did little tasks and won prizes. But my baby wouldn't do anything. I had no idea what was wrong and I didn't even know the word "autism",' she said.

On the way home from the baby show, she remembered having seen an article about developmental delays in an old issue of the Indian magazine *Outlook*. When she got home, she dug it out of the trash. The article listed the symptoms of autism, some of which Ohjyu had, such as poor eye contact, speech delay, and an inability to respond to his name. That killed me,' she said. 'It was so painful and I didn't share it with anyone, not even my husband. I knew he would be unwilling to believe that something was wrong. I didn't tell my own parents.'

Eventually, however, Mamta convinced her husband to take Ohjyu to a paediatrician. The doctor said that Ohjyu's speech was delayed because they lived in an isolated home in the mountains. He recommended taking him into a more stimulating environment, which she and her husband arranged by moving to the city of Gwalior. Although she contemplated terminating her second pregnancy for fear of having another disabled child, her husband refused to even consider it. In Gwalior, little changed for the better with Ohjyu; in fact, he looked worse. So they moved back to Nainital.

Unable to watch the progressive deterioration of her son, against the advice of her husband, and despite the outrage of her parents-in-law, she took the wide-eyed Ohjyu, along with his infant sister, on the seven-hour train ride to Delhi. There, a child psychologist diagnosed Ohjyu, then four years old, with autism. Armed with this diagnosis, Mamta decided that she was going to reach Ohjyu. She said:

> I belong to a people called the Kumaon, and we don't have many medical experts. I knew something was wrong, but, convincing my people? I cried nights. I was irritable, depressed. My husband avoided me and spent more time working. But now it's out. I spend most of my time with my mother-in-law, and we don't fight much. I respect her power. But I did disobey her. She didn't want me to go to Delhi or see the psychologist. Now when I see these other mothers here in Delhi, I say, 'You have to do what you have to do.'

Mamta's mother-in-law, seeking answers in her own way, left Mamta at home and travelled into the hills to see holy men and tantrics, some of whom said that Ohjyu was possessed by a demon. She eventually reached a conclusion and told Mamta: The mother-in-law believed that she herself and her husband had failed to please the god of the subcaste, and their grandchild was being punished for it.

It would be difficult to exaggerate the importance of boys in Hindu families. Sons carry on the family line and carry out the rituals that are crucial to success in this and subsequent worlds. So in Mamta's community, when a girl is born, goats must be sacrificed to please the unhappy village god; only then will they make it possible for boys to be born, and be born healthy. When Ohjyu was born, it had been thirteen years since Mamta's parents-in-law had made a sacrifice. 'They wanted to do the sacrifice earlier,' Mamta said, 'but something kept happening to prevent it. They'd get ready to kill the goats, and then someone would be born. But you can't do the sacrifice at that time without causing big problems. Then someone would die, and you can't do the sacrifice then either.' So Mamta's parents-in-law promised to sacrifice fourteen goats, at a cost of about 1,500 rupees (about $35 in US dollars) per goat, to the *devi*, or god, a form of Lord Shiva named Khandenagh. The god is represented by a small pile of stones in a temple in the mountains that is tended by priests, who perform a small worship ceremony for the devi twice a day.

When I asked Mamta if her parents-in-law blamed *her* for Ohjyu's condition, she seemed perplexed. 'They blame themselves for not making the sacrifices. But they do blame me for learning about autism, for leaving them, and for listening to the autism center instead of the priests.'

MERRY, SHUBRHA, MAMTA, and the many other women I met through Action for Autism weren't going to let stigma, or tradition, or even law, get in the way of helping their children. Though they feel connected to the world of autism, they are unsure about whether they should think about their children as part of a larger public health issue, such as an epidemic. Shubrha told me she values all the information available about autism, especially from the United States, but that she and other parents she knows do not sense a panic in India about autism — at least not yet. They are not concerned about vaccines or mercury. 'Maybe that will come,' Shubrha said, 'but we're keener to get educational services for our kids than we are about tallying up the numbers.' I was about to speak when she caught herself and, anticipating my response, said, 'I know they are related. If you have more of a disease in your country, maybe the government will give you more help. I just mean that each of us only has the time to worry about our own children right now. My son has autism. There is nothing that can take that away. I'm not going to go out and protest about something I don't know about. I will go out and protest about schools and awareness and stigma.'

No one can say if these strong, dedicated women were unusual to begin with — as if there were a single model for how a woman in any country should think and act. But we can say that autism changed them, possibly for the better, and certainly for good.

Half Past Winter in South Korea

As an anthropologist, I've learned that the best way to learn about the rules of any society is to see them broken. That's why sickness, when it makes people unable to live up to the rules of social behaviour, can teach us so much about ourselves. When everything goes smoothly and expectations are met, the rules fade into the background of social life and become almost invisible. We learn more when things go wrong. Just think about how much Shubrha, Amla, Mamta, and Merry's experiences taught us about the obstacles to mental health care in India, and the rules of Hindu society. For them, raising a child with autism was an act of resistance.

The disturbances they had to deal with were collective, as they felt the pressures of Hindu custom. But even if we could eliminate all the social stigma, they would still be left with personal and emotional turmoil. That's because diseases, however much we see them as biological or material in nature, are total life-changing experiences for parents, families, and communities. The writer Susan Sontag once argued that we'd all be better off if diseases were seen only as biological events. She protested the punitive uses of diseases as metaphors – the way tuberculosis was once the figure of death, or the way people talk about the evils of society as cancers – and argued that if we could rid ourselves of any non-material discussion of illness there would be less stigma and more social support for the ill, not only those suffering from the most stigmatising diseases like AIDS and leprosy, but also for people with more invisible afflictions like mental illnesses. Yet if we see a cancer, for example, simply as a tumour, we might easily ignore the complexity of human experience. If we see autism as just a brain disorder, we might miss the little victories that people experience each day with this illness.

The stories I've told of the various ways in which women struggle with their children's autism help us comprehend the difference between the words 'disease' and 'illness'. In the view of anthropologist Arthur Kleinman, a disease occurs when something is wrong with our bodily organs or systems, whereas an illness is the *experience* of negative or unwanted changes in our bodies or our ability to function in society. Autism is thus both a disease and an illness, and it cannot be otherwise.

The experiences of autism, even by women from the same country, can be vastly different. These experiences are shaped by the kind of community each woman lives in, her ancestry, the gender roles that are valued in her culture and how they are played out in her home, her culture's tolerance for diversity and difference, and even her own personality and personal will to care for her child in the face of harsh criticism from the people closest to her. For Seung-Mee, the mother of a nine-year-old girl with autism named Soo-Yong in South Korea, the illness of autism shines a light on the aspects of her culture that she disdains.

'YOU CAN'T ESCAPE BEING A VICTIM,' Seung-Mee told me with resignation as we sat in her apartment in Seoul. 'I inherited the resentment of my ancestors, my people's *han*.' 'Han' is a word that

can't be translated easily from Korean. It refers to one's conscious-
ness of ongoing trauma, the agony of injustices unresolved. Han
can grow and be passed on to successive generations, who look
to a utopian future when, in whatever manner – through revenge,
revolution, reconciliation, or generosity – they can overcome it.

For Seung-Mee, her autistic daughter, Soo-Yong, is yet another
manifestation of han, of the anguish she inherited from the wrongs
done over the past several centuries to her people in the underde-
veloped region called Cholla-do. But she wants to turn her resentment into something positive. She wants to see Soo-Yong not as a
symbol of what is wrong but of what she can do right. As Seung-
Mee put it, 'I don't like looking back to what could have been.
This is my life. It's like I'm always in the middle of winter. I can
go forward to spring or I can go backwards to when everything
started to go bad. It's not spring yet, but maybe I'll get there.'

Seung-Mee's positive attitude is reminiscent of the most
famous Korean folktale, a Cinderella-like story called 'The Tale of
Ch'unhyang', in which a beautiful but poor young woman successfully resists an evil governor's violent attempts to force her into
submission. When the governor is finally imprisoned, Ch'unhyang
begs the state to have mercy on him. Without him, she insists, she
would never have been given the chance to be a virtuous woman.
Similarly, Seung-Mee insists that she is grateful for autism. She is
convinced that having a child with autism has already made her a
better person, mother, aunt, and sister. There's a Korean word for
this – a type of han called *chonghan* – that refers to the ability to
use positive feelings to overcome negative ones.

At times, Seung-Mee, like many of the mothers of autistic children I've met, seems like any devoted mother anywhere. She worries about her children, wants only the best for them, has little time
for herself, and shoulders the extra burden of being a woman in a
male dominated society. But look more closely, and it's a different

world. Her worries are different, her choices fewer, and the different futures she imagines for her daughter more limited. Seung-Mee's everyday life, much more so than mine, reminds her that autism is not just a group of diagnostic categories, but a window into the strict rules and expectations of her society.

SOMETIMES SEUNG-MEE LONGS for the countryside because she thinks Soo-Yong might be better off there. Two children with autism, one on a rural farm, the other in a downtown high rise, may have the same disease, with similar symptoms, similar language delays, stereotyped movements, and social deficits. But as an *illness*, autism in the countryside is different from autism in the city. Her yearning to give her daughter this other experience reflects deep cultural beliefs – beliefs about place, about illness, about motherhood. But it also reflects her sensitivity to differences that often do exist between urban and rural areas, not just in Korea but in other parts of the world.

In Seung-Mee's hometown in the mountains of Cholla-do in southwestern Korea, elementary schools are boarded up for lack of children, and there are few young adults to be seen anywhere. In one village where I stayed for a few days, there were 100 households occupied by only 126 people, almost all of them widows. Cholla-do is like many other rural areas in Korea: Everyone has left to find their fortunes in the big cities, especially Seoul. Only a small number of men remain behind in the villages, usually sons or eldest children, to take care of their children, parents, and the land. With few young women to choose from in the villages, many of these men marry Southeast Asian women by arrangement through the mail or over the Internet. Once married, they live together in a place where, only a decade ago, the idea of international marriages would have seemed laughable. Korea is an ethnically homogeneous country with few foreign workers and virtually no immigration.

An agricultural area often belittled by Koreans and long neglected by the government, Cholla-do remains the most under-developed region in one of the richest countries in the world. Cholla residents are familiar with discrimination and adversity and find it hard to improve their class and social status. They consider it a great success to make one's career in Seoul, where more than 25 per cent of South Korea's 44 million people now live.

There can be absurd incongruities. Young adults there may have personal computers and Internet access, but many do not have indoor plumbing. One of the most common household accidents is losing your mobile phone by dropping it in the outhouse.

Still, after asking a few questions here and there (Are there any children who don't speak well? Are there children here with brain disorders?), I found a sixteen-year-old boy and a nine-year-old girl in a mountainous county. Everyone seemed to know about them. And when I talked to the barber and the local grocery-store owner about them, there was no hint of discomfort or pity. Peter, as his mother wanted him to be called, was good with bicycles and served as a messenger for two villages, delivering letters and pack-ages with a broad smile. He saw a doctor once every two months and was medicated with a small dose of an antipsychotic drug that calmed his anxiety and some of his repetitive movements. The girl, Soo-Rin, was in the village with her single mother only on weekends because she attended a special school for children with Down syndrome, cerebral palsy, and mental retardation. But eve-ryone knew her too. Her room at home was lovely, pink with lace curtains, stuffed animals, and Disney characters. Her mother said she takes a medication at school to help her pay attention, but she didn't know what it was called. In these villages, you can find proof of something the World Health Organisation has been arguing for years: People with mental disorders do better over time in remote, nonindustrial societies than in urban, industrial ones.

In Seoul, a city of 11 million people, the story is different. There is invisibility in numbers. Posed to an adult, the question 'Do you know any children who don't speak well?' usually goes unanswered, partly because people are reluctant to talk about such things for fear of shaming the child's family. Equally, people with autism are sometimes hidden away, often go untreated, and are seldom integrated into community life. Some children with autism go to mainstream schools, but they do not last long there. There are few special-education classes or classroom aides. By the last year of middle school, all but the high-functioning children with autism are home-schooled or enrolled in schools designed for both physically and mentally disabled children. As of this writing, there are no special-education services in Korean public high schools.

This is not to say that life for the disabled is easy in the villages – even someone with a mild speech impediment, who is otherwise normal, will have just as much difficulty finding a spouse as an urban dweller with the same problem. And parents can be just as devastated. One man confessed to me that in his despair he once took his young autistic son high up in the mountains, intending to slit his throat, but couldn't bring himself to do it. But for most parents of disabled children, life in the rich city of Seoul is more stressful than in the more humble village. One of the paradoxes of rural life is that people in the villages tend to be relatively accepting of diversity. Little remains secret, and there seems to be a place for everyone. In the rural areas, people assume that things would be much better for their children in the city. But in the city, in the sprawling, indistinguishable apartment complexes of Seoul, most people do not know their neighbours, even though they watch them as closely as they can. The pressures to measure up can seem overwhelming, and families try to keep anything that might reflect badly on their status hidden from public view. The moment you bring your disabled child outside in this densely populated city is the moment you are confronted by strangers, people who will watch and judge you.

By any measure, Seoul is a difficult city in which to live. The traffic alone is worse than anything I've experienced in the United States. But life in Seoul is especially difficult if you are coming from Cholla-do, with a Cholla-do accent and Cholla-do manners. Seung-Mee struggled with poverty, discrimination, and loneliness in Seoul, and partly because of her unpopular ancestry, it took a long time to find a stable job and a husband. Seung-Mee knew she'd make it in Seoul one day, but she didn't expect that with a full-time job as a middle school teacher and as a mother and wife in one of the largest cities in the world, she'd be so isolated. When you are from Cholla-do *and* you have a child with a serious disability, the loneliness can be overwhelming.

SITTING AT HER DINING ROOM TABLE in her small apartment, toys and clothing scattered about, Seung-Mee looked tired. She had recently gotten a new hairstyle, streaked in the orange colour popular these days among Koreans. During our visit, she was trying to keep it neat, but she was unsuccessful. Soo-Yong kept running behind her to mess it up. As we were talking, Soo-Yong came over and slugged me hard in the chest. I admire Seung-Mee's strength, and yet she looked fragile under her forced smile. Sometimes her focus on the positive appeared defensive.

Soo-Yong is Seung-Mee's first child, so Seung-Mee will forever be known as *Soo-Yong omma* (Soo-Yong's mother), since Koreans do not normally refer to Korean mothers by their proper names. Having your identity defined by your child, and your role as a mother, can be immensely pleasurable for many women. But Soo-

Yong has not brought much joy to Seung-Mee. She was a slow child from the start – slow to learn to turn over, slow to sit up, slow to walk. At ten months, Seung-Mee took her to see a doctor, but given that she had a fairly low birthweight, the doctor suggested that Soo-Yong was perhaps a bit premature at birth and would eventually develop appropriately.

Seung-Mee was careful never to mention her concerns among her friends and family because, she told me, a problem with your child's development is a very sensitive subject in Korea. Unlike some parents of autistic children, Seung-Mee decided to have another child, primarily to give her husband (and her husband's family) a son; few men (or women) consider themselves successful if they have failed to produce a son. Fortunately she was successful, and the boy, she says, now nine years old, is definitely not autistic. 'I look after Soo-Yong, but I cannot look after everybody,' she said. Soo-Yong routinely hits her brother, and he refuses to bring friends to his home for fear of being embarrassed and teased. He does not want to reveal his sister's disorder to his friend's families. The relatives do not visit, either.

'My sister-in-law is so disappointed in me,' Seung-Mee said. 'She expected – she was right to have expected – that I would help out more in the family, especially helping her mother and father, but Soo-Yong takes so much time. I just cannot do it.'

Last year, at Chusok, the Korean Thanksgiving Day, Soo-Yong had a tantrum at home and the family was so delayed that by the time they arrived at her brother-in-law's house the food was ready to eat and her relatives were furious that she had done nothing to help them prepare. The situation only got worse. Soo-Yong ran around the house and was so heavy-footed that the downstairs neighbours complained.

'We had a big fight that day and it really saddened me,' she said. 'My sister-in-law ordered me to control Soo-Yong. I don't want [my husband's family] to hate her. At least they don't ask me to stop working. They know we need the money.'

Seung-Mee's day starts at 6 A.M. She looks outside her bedroom window to check on the day's weather. Through twisted blinds she sees a small playground, several rows of shops, and beyond them the elementary school that all of the children in the neighbour-hood, except Soo-Yong, attend.

By 7 a.m., she drops Soo-Yong off at Angel's Place, a daycare centre for children with special needs. If she did not have a full-time job, she would not be able to bring Soo-Yong to Angel's Place, not only because she would be unable to afford it but because it would be unseemly. A Korean housewife should be able to take care of her children by herself.

Soo-Yong's father is a stockbroker with an annual income that is equivalent to about $50,000 in US dollars. He is lucky to be able to finish work earlier than many Korean men, about 7 P.M., but nearly half of his income goes to the daycare facility and Soo-Yong's brother's daily private tutors. Tutors are standard for the vast majority of Korean children these days. As a whole, Koreans spend only 4 per cent of the gross national product (GNP) on in-school education, which is less than what most European countries, the United States, and Japan spend. Yet if you include out-of-school education, Koreans spend a higher proportion of their GNP (12 per cent) than any other country in the world. And this is just for kindergarten through high school. In addition, Soo-Yong has language therapy, music therapy, art therapy, and sports therapy at least once a week through Angel's House, and this costs about a million won, or the equivalent of $1,000 (US) per month. It is a major point of contention in the household, since Soo-Yong's father does not think the therapies are effective. He notices that other families with autistic children don't give their children so many treatments, and he wonders if he's just wasting his money.

'My husband says Soo-Yong never changes, so why do we spend so much money?' Seung-Mee said. 'He puts his work first and I feel sorry for that, especially for Soo-Yong because we argued so much when I was pregnant. Maybe that stress hurt her and caused her autism. Or maybe it made her autism worse.'

This feeling that her husband does not support her led Seung-Mee to join a Methodist church, despite being agnostic. Though she has been totally honest with the pastor and the congregation that she is 'not really religious', the church has embraced her. They've embraced Soo-Yong too. They tell her that Soo-Yong is a spiritual child, perfect in her own way, pure like the body of God.

Seung-Mee said, 'They talk to me without making me feel guilty or inadequate. They seem to like Soo-Yong. When I show up for church or even other church activities the mums rush to Soo-Yong and take care of her. I can get some time to relax and talk to an adult and not watch Soo-Yong constantly. It is sad to think about. Going to the church is what I think going to visit my own family should be like.'

Soo-Yong is a challenging child, in part because she has so many phobias. She is terrified of balloons. She will not sleep alone. But her brother was so frightened of sleeping in the same room with her, behind closed doors, for fear that she might hurt him in his sleep, that Soo-Yong's father had to remove the door. Soo-Yong cannot stand to be in the same room with fish or seafood, and she is able to detect even small amounts of seafood in a room when no one else can smell it. She has sleep disturbances, and when she wakes up in the middle of the night, she seeks attention or wants to take a long bath, perhaps because it soothes her. But this means that nearly every night Seung-Mee is awake with her at some point, and she often is sleep deprived. Soo-Yong likes to destroy books and rip paper, so the family's important documents remain in a small, locked refrigerator. The doors and windows have to be locked as well, as Soo-Yong's parents do not trust her to stay inside. On several occasions, she has left the apartment and gone off into the neighbourhood, mostly to wander around a small grocery store around the corner, where, fortunately, the owner recognised her and brought her home.

But Seung-Mee, like many other parents I have met, is thankful for one thing: Her child is affectionate. The idea that autistic people are unaffectionate is a myth that was started by mid-20th-century psychiatrists. The Korean word for autism, *chapae*, exacerbates the misconception. Like the English word 'autism', it means, literally, being closed in on one's self. Soo-Yong is not mildly autistic; she is a classic case of autistic disorder according to the *DSM* criteria, and yet she loves cuddling and being cuddled.

'We get our word for autism from the Chinese character *Za* meaning "by oneself", and *pae* meaning "closed",' Seung-Mee said. 'Shouldn't there be a word that says something like "lack of social understanding"? Or maybe "sensation problem"? People think the closing must be closing something that was opened and then got closed, that it wasn't closed to begin with. They think there must have been a sudden shock that makes the person close themselves to hide the trauma. This is why we mothers get blamed. We must have done something wrong to make our children close themselves.'

Seung-Mee said that several doctors, believing that Soo-Yong's condition was caused by neglect, made two diagnoses. They diagnosed Soo-Yong with Reactive Attachment Disorder (RAD), and Seung-Mee with depression. The doctor ordered Seung-Mee to quit her job, but no doctor has ever recommended any medical treatment for either of them. As for Soo-Yong's condition, Seung-Mee doubts any medication or behavioural therapy will help her. I found it peculiar that the two poor children I met in the mountains of supposedly 'backward' Cholla-do took psychotropic medications, but the middle-class children in a cosmopolitan city like Seoul seldom took them. Many women I interviewed in Seoul said that doctors recommended this or that medication, but most believed the medications would drain their children of their energy and make them glassy eyed. This is a widespread belief. I heard it in nearly every interview I conducted in Seoul. It is one of the reasons that few parents give their autistic children prescription medicines.

When I asked Soo-Yong's parents, or any parents of an autistic child, for that matter, for the names of the drugs that can be prescribed to help autistic symptoms, I usually got a blank stare. Only in the past few years have doctors and pharmacists in Korea begun to put the names on bottles of medication. Patients may follow the doctor's orders, but they almost never know what medicines they are taking – such is the strength of the Korean medical establishment, in which doctors are largely beyond reproach. In fact, talking about medicines with Seung-Mee made me feel as if I was pushing them. This was our conversation.

'Do you want to try any medicines?' I asked.

'There aren't any, I thought.'

'If there was a medicine that could help, would you give it to Soo-Yong?'

'Nothing cures autism so why should I risk hurting my daughter?'

'Would you think it was worth a try?'

'If something bad happened, I don't know. I would just ...'

'You could always stop the medicine if you didn't like the effects.'

'But you can't cure autism.'

'What if a doctor could give a medicine that might help her sleep through the night?'

'It's okay. I don't mind getting up with her.'

SEUNG-MEE CONSIDERS her decision to go to church to be an alternative to both mainstreaming and medicines. 'Why not go to church?' she asked. 'My husband does little for me, Buddhists are too hard to approach, whereas so many people in the church really wanted to pray for me ... I thought about going to a shaman, but they scare me. I feared the shaman might bring another ghost into my life and the ghost (*kuishin*) would hurt my family through the shaman's prayer. I did try a fortune teller, but he refused to talk about the future! And there is only so much I can afford.'

'In the church,' she added, 'they tell me that my daughter is a child of God. So what they're saying is that we are all the same, none of us are different. Or, if we are different, we're all different in the same way. We are all just different images of God.'

The great burden of urban Korean parents of emotionally or learning disabled children is that they live in a society that places such a high value on sameness and seeks blame for difference. One of the most remarkable features of American society today is that the concept of 'diversity' has been extended beyond race and ethnicity to include disability. This is possible because the English word 'diversity' has a positive connotation.

In Korea, autism confronts a different cultural framework. *Ijil*, the word for 'difference', either individual or cultural, has a negative connotation. Ijil is something to be overcome, like the differences between the North and South Korean people. I've written elsewhere that one of the reasons that the two countries are still technically at war 60 years after they were divided by the superpowers is that they continue to hold on to a mythic view of Koreans as homogeneous, awaiting their unification. In fact, unification is often phrased as 'the recovery of homogeneity' (*tongjilsong hoebok*). The dream of unification is so sacred, and so idealised, that they cannot begin to take the practical, uncomfortable, muddy steps necessary to unify the nation. One of these steps would be accepting that the North and South Korean people may be culturally different after all these years apart and that cultural differences can be acceptable. The principle that lies behind this terrible conflict also lies behind attitudes toward people with disabilities. For Koreans, difference is unnatural and unwanted.

EVEN THOUGH SOME PARENTS have read everything they can on the Internet or in books or articles, most South Korean parents feel that they know very little about autism. Either they think nothing can be done, or they want to know what I know. It doesn't matter that I'm not a physician or even a psychologist. As a professor and as a father of a child with autism in the United States, they think I should be able to help them, yet their focus is not on what symptoms my daughter has or whether she takes medicine, or advice about how to cope with the emotional strains and stresses of raising a child with a developmental disorder. Instead, they want to know how their child can be cured or educated. Psychiatrists, they insist, don't have any answers, yet they need the answers, not only for themselves, but for the schools.

They ask me, 'Things must be better in America, right?' The answer, of course, is that things are better in the United States because we have more child psychiatrists, psychologists, teachers, speech therapists, play therapists, and others who understand what autism is and is not. Most importantly, we *treat* children with autism much more often than Koreans do. In the course of my research in Korea, I met many parents of children with autism, and many elementary school teachers. They do not think that autism is a common disorder in Korea. Parents are reluctant to accept any diagnostic label for their children, or even to seek medical treatment if it does not promise a cure, and teachers are frightened enough of parents that they will only complain about a child's behaviour in the most serious cases.

In the nearly two dozen Korean elementary schools in which I've done research, teachers say privately that they have students who range from the profoundly mentally retarded to the mildly autistic, but that there is little they can do for them. They rarely consult with the parents, despite the fact that the children do not appear to be learning and merely exist in the school. As a result, my own epidemiological research on autism in Korea has been fraught with difficulties. Many teachers and parents refuse to cooperate with me because both groups are fearful of potential diagnoses. The government health-care sector certainly hasn't helped the situation. Until 2005, when I launched a prevalence study of autism in Korea with a colleague at Yale, no one had attempted to assess the prevalence of autism in Korea using rigorous, scientific methods. This absence of research is due largely to the fact that Korean scientists and Korean government funding agencies do not think autism is a serious medical problem, and there is little money in the United States for Korean health research. American public research agencies like the National Institutes of Health award grants primarily to research projects that are conducted in the United States or are directly relevant to American health concerns.

The only study I know of that looked at the severity of symptoms of autism in Korea made an interesting observation: that the absence of treatment has a significant effect – for the worse. In 1991, Gyeong Hee Seo, a psychologist at the University of Texas, found that although Korean children with autism were less impaired than American children between the ages of four and six, by the time the children reached the ages of thirteen to twenty, the

Korean children were more severely impaired than their American counterparts.

In Korea, children with autism are often diagnosed with Reactive Attachment Disorder. RAD is sometimes described pejoratively as 'lack of love' (*aejong kyolpip*), a term that, for Koreans, conjures images of orphans craving affection and care. In Korea, RAD is thought to be a condition mimicking autism that is caused by a mother's absence of attachment to her son. But in the rest of the world, psychiatrists give the RAD diagnosis to those orphans or children adopted after infancy who have pronounced problems with social relatedness, or to children who have similar social problems due to some kind of pathological care. In fact, the *DSM* does not allow a diagnosis of RAD unless there is evidence that the child has been in an abusive, adverse, or 'grossly pathological' environment.

I've heard of only a few instances in the United States where a child with autism was misdiagnosed with RAD. Autism, unlike RAD, involves repetitive and stereotyped movements and interests, and children with autism usually come from supportive environments, not the neglectful environments seen in children with RAD. In Korea, however, the diagnosis of RAD is common, and it places blame squarely on the mother – a Korean version of the 'refrigerator mother'. In fact, some clinicians in Korea even prefer to drop the word 'reactive', because that word identifies the pathology in the child rather than the parent. By calling RAD simply 'attachment disorder' (*aechak changae*), the blame can be more clearly placed on the mother.

Oddly, RAD is a diagnosis that many parents prefer, even though it directly indicts the mother as a pathological caretaker. It's a popular diagnosis for three reasons. First, they think that unlike autism, RAD, or lack of love, can be ameliorated by giving love; it's not a permanent condition. An autism diagnosis is seen as a statement that the child has no future. Autism, at least in Korea, is widely considered to be untreatable, and many parents who try various therapies, such as speech therapy, vitamin regimens, or herbal medicines, give up after a while if their child is not cured. The Seoul-based psychiatrist Dong-Ho Song, one of the busiest child psychiatrists in Seoul, had a patient with autism who had been diagnosed with RAD first at the age of eighteen months and then subsequently by several other doctors throughout his early childhood. He was almost eleven years old when he came to Dr Song and received his first diagnosis of autism.

Second, RAD is not a genetic condition so it doesn't impugn the family and harm family members' marriage prospects in the same way a genetic disease might. This fear of autism as a genetic disorder is found in India and other countries as well, where parents fear that they will be marginalised from the social networks they feel they are entitled to. Thus, though RAD may stigmatise the mother, autism stigmatises the whole family, past, present, and future.

Third, and perhaps most importantly, the diagnosis makes sense to Koreans. Korea has been undergoing rapid social change for the past 50 years, emerging from the devastation of the Korean War to become one of the richest countries in the world. Conservatism and resistance always accompany social change, and women make easy targets. Mothers are entering the workforce in unparalleled numbers, and Korean sociologists and child-health experts are responding. They argue that women no longer know how to care for children. They leave their children with grandmothers or nannies and thus cannot bond with their children. Korean psychologists and psychiatrists thus ask: 'Is it any wonder, then, that the children of working mothers have language and social deficits?'

The backlash against working mothers is picking up steam. I know full-time working mothers whose normal children are blocked from participating in parent-run English, maths, science, or Korean-language study groups. The nonworking mothers argue that children of working mothers will be delayed in their intellectual growth and drag the other children down.

There are programmes popping up throughout the Seoul area, some of them based in university hospitals, to help mothers learn how to bond with their RAD children and help their children learn language and social skills. A mother with time and money may shuttle her child around the city several days a week for speech therapy, play therapy, art therapy, occupational therapy, and classes to promote mother–child attachment. But she would be less likely to make this effort if her child had a diagnosis of autism. Mental health experts encourage working mothers to quit their jobs. If, after the mother begins to devote herself full-time to her child, he improves, the clinician may conclude that the diagnosis of RAD was correct. If the mother refuses to quit, but enrols her child in play or speech therapy, and the child improves, the diagnosis is also confirmed; the assumption is that the therapist is providing the love the mother could not give. If the child does not improve, or worsens, the clinician may conclude that the mother's pathology is worse than he originally thought, or he may conclude that the child has autism.

It's important to understand that, in Korea, what happens to the child happens also to the mother, and therein lies her stigma. If he is socially disabled, she is as well. The mother of an autistic child cannot wait outside the *hakwon*, the after-school educational programmes, with the other mothers and bond with them. She cannot brag about the results of her child's exams, or his extracurricular successes. She becomes marginalised.

And when she takes her child out in public, people stare, much more so, it seems to me, than they would in the United States. 'I saw a seven-year-old boy in a stroller [in Florida] at Disney World,' a Korean mother of an autistic girl told me, 'and no one seemed to care. They'd never let you do that in Korea. A total stranger would come right up to you and say "Why is your son in a stroller? Can't he walk? You're treating him like a baby!"' A Korean teacher I know recently took her autistic son to her community E-Mart, the Korean equivalent of Wal-Mart, and her son had a temper tantrum. She carried him, against his wishes, out of the store and into the parking lot, where she was met by angry customers and a policeman. They had followed her – not because they feared she was abducting the boy but because they believed she was abusing her own son.

As an illness (as opposed to a disease), the identification and treatment of autism is also affected by the Korean medical establishment. There are only about 1,500 psychiatrists in the country (that is, 3 psychiatrists for every 100,000 Koreans, compared to more than 40,000 psychiatrists in the United States, or more than 13 psychiatrists for every 100,000 Americans), and only 70 board-certified child psychiatrists (compared to approximately 7,000 in the United States), almost all of them in Seoul. Most parents take their children to psychologists or other nonmedical professionals, who treat autism more as an emotional problem than a neurobiological one.

The experience of autism in Korea is also shaped by the nature of the Korean educational system. The term 'inclusion' was put into the government's special-education laws in 1994. In 2000, the government ordered 56 districts in the country to designate at least one school to serve as an inclusion model. The result of the legal change was that parents, especially those who were more educated and wealthy, began to feel entitled to enrol their young children – even profoundly mentally retarded ones – in mainstream settings. Schools felt powerless against the parents because the institutional framework for the educational system as a whole is so weak.

Of course, a private school could turn away such a child, but there are not many private schools in Korea. With only a few exceptions, such as international schools for diplomats' children, or highly focused performing arts schools, Korean schools for grades K–12 are run by the government. National education policy also limits the licensing of private schools that admit students on the basis of merit. Because mainstream schools traditionally did not allow disabled children to enrol, many lower-income parents have yet to be emboldened by the laws and continue to home-school their children.

Parents and teachers reach a crisis point only when children with autism get older, their deficits become more pronounced, and they fail one exam after another. By secondary school and high school, the students have been expelled because of behavioural problems, have dropped out, or have transferred into one of the few special-education classes or schools. Some parents in Seoul, dissatisfied with the government services, have banded together to start cooperative preschools or 'alternative' elementary, middle, and high schools that are friendly to children with developmental delays. The mission of such schools is to resist the cutthroat educational environment so prevalent in Korean society. The schools are governed by what their advocates term a 'slow-teaching, nature-friendly' philosophy. Unfortunately, the government has not sanctioned them, and they are inaccessible to lower-income families.

What does inclusion mean in Korea? It often means placing a child in a mainstream classroom – a physical inclusion – but not really an effort at educational integration. At a school I visited in Suwon, a town just south of Seoul, a mentally retarded girl sat alone and unengaged at the side of her third-grade classroom, and the children told me that when they misbehave they have to sit next to her as a punishment. Children with disabilities are marginalised and mistreated in the United States too, but it's not done so explicitly.

The Korean government offers few supports to the teachers who have special-needs children in their classrooms, but the teachers put the blame on the parents. They told me that parents are unwilling to acknowledge their children's disability. A teacher I know from the town of Pusan, in the south of the country, lamented that there was no special assistance for a severely autistic child in her third-grade class. 'The parents,' she told me, 'insist there is nothing wrong with him so I shouldn't ask for help. They are wealthy, really well-educated and strong people. We even have a special-education classroom in our school but they won't let us put him there.' The child, she said, is learning little in the mainstream environment: 'His mother and father are so concerned with the appearance of a normal education that they are getting in the way of real education and treatment.' The parents of the other children are complaining loudly, but the school says it is bound by national laws that oblige them to provide an education for all children, though not necessarily an appropriate one.

For their part, parents tend to blame the teachers for ignoring children's needs. Indeed, when my research collaborators in Korea administered screening surveys to parents and their children's teachers in the autumn of 2005, they quickly found several cases in which mothers reported profound social or language deficits in their children but the teachers reported few. In the first five months of our work, we found two mentally retarded elementary school children with IQ scores between 40 and 50 who were being taught exclusively in a mainstream classroom. Such low scores are most often found in children who have a recognisable syndrome, like Down syndrome, who often require extensive classroom supports and will likely never live independently. The teacher told us that they had only mild cognitive deficits.

To UNDERSTAND THE PREDICAMENT of the autistic child and his or her family in Korea – to truly appreciate the reasons why the child with special needs receives so few services and supports – one must understand the intense pressures of the Korean educational system. There is a long cultural history related to what has come to be called 'education fever' in Korea. Premodern, pre-20th-century Korean values made education, prestige, and moral virtue equivalent. The scholar had a moral authority to guide both village and government and often did so by assuming high-status government positions. These jobs were awarded only to those who passed competitive exams, and only elites (*yangban*) were eligible to take them. When the Japanese colonised Korea between 1910 and 1945, they effectively destroyed Korean education, mostly because they did not think it necessary for their Korean colonial subjects to receive any kind of higher education. Koreans were forced to take Japanese names and were prohibited from speaking Korean in public, and only a small number of Koreans were permitted to attend any level of schooling beyond middle school. So both precolonial Korea and Japanese-controlled Korea had denied education to most Koreans.

Low-status Koreans had to wait until independence in 1945 to have any serious chance at either higher education or class mobility. The new post-Second World War ideology was a response to both that old hierarchical order, now largely defunct, and the repression of the Japanese regime. It was an ideology of democratisation and equality, the conviction that everyone was entitled to an education. Until public education blossomed in the 1940s and 1950s, the stereotype of the good parent was the poor farmer who sold his oxen or his best plot of land to provide tuition for his son. Self-sacrifice and an obsession with education helped reduce some of the disparities between educational levels in rural and urban areas. By 1961, classrooms were standing-room only with a teacher-to-student ratio of about 1:58 in the primary schools. Only countries like India and Indonesia had a worse ratio. In 1945, there were only 8,000 Korean students enrolled in four-year colleges or universities; by 1960, there were 93,000. By 1995, that number would grow to 1.2 million.

Yet hierarchy remains integral to Korean society, and experts on Korea believe that the obsession with education over the past half-century reflects the desire of the huge Korean middle-class to achieve rank and status through the successes of their children. Even though there are now more than 200 institutions of higher learning (colleges, universities, junior colleges, and graduate schools) in South Korea, only a few schools, all in Seoul, have the status to truly enhance one's family reputation and ensure a student's social and economic future. Seoul National University stands alone, with Yonsei University and Korea University in the second tier. In the United States, this would be equivalent to having to go to Harvard to assure a high-status career. Parents dream that their children will go to Seoul National University, which has more power to establish reputation than all the American Ivy Leagues combined. Parents, especially those who are poor, hold out faith that their children can help the family's status through academic achievement, only to find that not everyone can go to college. There simply are not enough spaces. So class mobility often proves elusive. One of the fathers in my study had just quit his job at the Samsung Corporation to work elsewhere because he realised that, as a graduate of a second-tier school, he had little chance of rising to middle management or an executive position.

How do you fit a child with a disability into such a system of values?

To make matters worse, over the past two decades the South Korean government has transferred the burden of financing education to parents. There is still free education in the schools, but there are high costs related to all the additional tutors and after school activities, expensive (and expected) gifts for teachers, exam fees, and enormous Parent-Teacher Association (PTA) dues. Sending your children to school during the day has become almost a formality, something you do because you have to, but not because you think your child will really learn much there. The real education starts after school. It's private, and it's reserved for unimpaired children.

Almost all children from middle- and upper-income families attend group tutoring sessions ($160/month) or private sessions ($300/month) in as many as four or five after-school programmes, or *hakwon* (academies), which can total more than $1,500 per month. A typical family provides group English lessons to each child about eight times a month. Private English classes cost exactly twice as much as the group lessons, or about $320 per month. Music lessons are another cost. Gifts for teachers and tutors run at least $100 a year (and sometimes involve extravagant items like stereos, computers, and plasma TVs). The minimum PTA fee is about the same. Parents also frequently subscribe to services that mail the children extra homework materials to enhance the school-based education. I have yet to meet a Seoul family with school-age children that did not have one of these subscriptions. All of these extra expenses were illegal during the early and mid-1980s, under the regime of President Chun Doo-Hwan, because the government didn't want the wealthy to have such a clear advantage over the poor. Parents still hired college students to tutor their children, but it was all done under the table. These days, the afternoon traffic is dotted with the hundreds of small yellow hakwon buses, like New York taxis, taking children to their after-school programmes.

Most children go to the hakwon directly from school, and some don't get home until after midnight. In the wealthy suburb of Pundang, just south of Seoul, tour buses line up on the major roads to bring children home, and they operate until 1 A.M. No one likes this brutal system – 'we rarely get to spend time with our own children,' a Korean businessman told me – but parents feel they have no choice but to have their children attend all these programmes; it's a necessity in the competitive modern world, and the children will have to sink or swim. A mother and father I interviewed in Pundang told me that they do not know a single family that doesn't send their children to the hakwon. This father of two daughters, ages fourteen and ten, said, 'If a family decided not to pay for hakwon, it would be weird, and even disgraceful. They would be purposefully destroying their child's opportunities to be successful.'

One mother, who is moving with her daughter to Canada to escape the competitive educational system in Korea, told me, 'Education in Korea is a war'. 'In Canada,' she said, 'I will actually be able to spend time with my daughter.' It used to be that Koreans in the countryside moved to Seoul to escape the dead end life in the villages. Now they're starting to leave Seoul for the United States and other countries to escape this stressful, competitive atmosphere.

There has been a rise in the number of Korean children in American elementary, middle, and high schools as thousands of parents separate for the sake of their children, some as young as six. It's usually the mother who leaves, taking her children with her, and the father who stays. Such fathers are popularly known as *kirogi apa* (wild geese fathers). Koreans tell me they use this term because, like the parent and child who leave Korea, wild geese are migratory. I asked Isabel if she knew anything about wild geese. As usual, she answered by asking a question, and had she known the context, it would have been profound. 'Do they call for their young?' she asked. It seems that's exactly what Koreans are doing.

This is the context in which parents of children with special needs see their dreams collapse. Being a good parent in Korea means that your child is successful by the standards of society as a whole. It means you fight for everything, make your children study almost constantly – even if they have to stay up until 1 a.m. every night to finish the work assigned by their after-school tutors – and pay fees for your children to attend special libraries, English classes, private tutoring sessions, music lessons, and more.

Given these pressures, it is understandable that parents of children with special needs children often feel that their efforts to educate them mean nothing. What does it matter, if they cannot be totally cured? And for those with one or more other children, every bit of time, energy, and money they give the disabled child takes away from the ones who might be able to succeed. If the normal child fails to make it to the university, the parents will be criticised for having exerted so much effort on the child who never even had a chance to begin with.

Becoming Visible

O<small>N A WINTER MORNING IN</small> 2002, an eight-year-old boy stood alone on the shoulder of a modern highway outside Cape Town, South Africa, flapping his arms. Four hundred yards further on, another boy stood on the shoulder. And 400 yards from him, another. The line of children continued for two miles. Commuters, making the 40-kilometre journey from the townships to Cape Town, sped by them, unheeding. Two miles away from the first boy, the panicked driver of the school van and his aide, who were supposed to be transporting these children, ran as fast as they could toward the nearest police station. As they ran, they talked on their mobile phones, pleading with the police to search for the eight boys and girls. All of them had autism, and all of them had little or no capacity to speak or communicate.

The van was the property of one of the six small schools in South Africa (pop. 45 million) that specialise in educating children with autism. The children they pick up live in Langa, Khailetsha, and Gugulethu, the sprawling, predominantly black townships that lie outside Cape Town. They are among the most violent communities in the world, with high rates of homicide and rape, gang violence, vigilantism, and 'taxi wars' (turf battles between rival taxi companies), nurtured over the years by the racist 20th-century system of segregation and discrimination in South Africa known as *apartheid* (separateness).

Many in the townships live in small shelters walled with cardboard, corrugated iron, and paper, and they are impoverished and often malnourished. The unemployment rate of the townships has been estimated to be as high as 70 per cent. But this doesn't mean that 70 per cent of the people don't work. Virtually everyone works in the informal, unofficial economy – whether this means selling baked goods to their neighbours or trading auto parts, the most common job. A fourteen-seat van on the township's dirt roads is like gold.

On this morning in Gugulethu, two gunmen had hijacked the van, ordering the driver, Peter, and his assistant, George, out of the car. They probably planned to repaint the van, turn it into a private, unlicensed taxi, and pack the fourteen seats with 24 or more paying customers en route to jobs in the city. Because they didn't want to waste any time getting out of Gugulethu, they took off with the autistic kids still inside. They turned onto the N2, the main highway that runs southeast of the city centre, and stopped every quarter-mile to put one child out of the van. It took the police about an hour to find and collect the children, but each one was standing quietly on the side of the road. No one had stopped to help them, and no one called the police to report the odd sight.

In fact, none of the eight children looked in need of assistance. They had no crutches or wheelchairs, and most were neatly dressed in school uniforms. Those commuters who did note their presence on the side of the road no doubt concluded that they were simply waiting for a ride to school.

The invisibility of autism poses a dilemma. A child who seems physically normal and causes no fuss may not even be noticed. A child who seems physically normal but behaves abnormally may

be thought to be undisciplined, or, among some black populations in South Africa, possessed by an evil spirit. But such children
are not often seen as simply disabled. The South African parents I
know, like parents elsewhere, complained about this to me. One
Afrikaner man wore a T-shirt when he came to meet with me at
a school outside Durban, on the east coast of South Africa. It said,
'I'm autistic. What's wrong with you?' The goal, he said, was to
make people refrain from judgment. A Zulu mother laughed at
the shirt but said that she didn't know many people who had even
heard the word 'autism'. 'That would *never* work in the townships,'
she said.

The families I met in South Africa – in the small city of
Pietermaritzburg, in the medium-sized city of Durban, and in
the major urban area, Cape Town – consistently called autism 'the
invisible illness', invisible because people know so little about it,
invisible because parents of autistic children know so few other
people with autistic relatives, invisible because the families claimed
to have never seen an adult with autism. One after another, parents
asked me, 'What does an adult with autism look like?' They might
have also asked another question – 'What do the *families* of people
with autism look like?' – because, as hard as it is to believe, many
had never had a conversation with another parent of a child with
autism.

I asked the headmaster of Brown's, a private special-education
school outside Durban, to arrange for several families to meet with
me one evening, and when they showed up I quickly realised that
this was something new. There were nine couples – three Xhosa
families, one Afrikaner, two English, and three Indian. Two of the
Indian couples knew each other, but the others were meeting for
the first time. Identity is a sensitive issue in South Africa these days
– it's politically incorrect to even ask someone what ethnic group
they come from. But it was obvious that these couples were from

quite different communities and wouldn't normally socialise with each other. And since the school provided transportation for all their children, they wouldn't have come to school often enough to bump into each other. It became clear that these couples had never spent more than a few minutes with an autistic child other than their own.

IN SUWON, A SUBURB OF SEOUL, I interviewed Sung-Hee Kim and her husband, Kyung-Soo. They live with their three children in one of the hundreds of modern apartment buildings that look like hundreds of others in and around Seoul. But to the outside world, they have only two children. Hyung-Bu is only five years old, but they already know his condition is permanent. Psychiatrists at one of the finest medical schools in Korea had just changed the diagnosis. He had been thought to suffer from Reactive Attachment Disorder, but he's now diagnosed with autism. Hyung-Bu doesn't go to school or day care, and Sung-Hee doesn't know any other parents who have children with autism or RAD.

Sung-Hee's two other children, who are older then Hyung-Bu, do not like to have friends to the house, which is fine by her, since she doesn't want anyone to know about Hyung-Bu. The moment a diagnosis of a developmental disability is made public is the moment the price of her apartment, and possibly her neighbours', drops a few per cent. The marriage prospects for her other children would be diminished, for who would want to marry into a family with autism? If Sung-Hee needs to take Hyung-Bu out of the house, she rushes him out of the building, and she locks him in his room when visitors arrive. She barely speaks to her mother-in-law anymore, the person who blames her most for Hyung-Bu's condition. But she still wonders if the new diagnosis could change things.

In mid-July 2003, six mothers and a special-education teacher sat with me for tea and rice cakes after a special Sunday worship service for families with handicapped children in the Seoul neighbourhood of Dunchondong. Soo-Yong's mother, Seung-Mee, was among them. Indeed, this was the church she had told me about where she had found so many understanding people in the congregation. An aide volunteering for the church watched the children, who were playing outside in a small playground. I was impressed by how much the women shared as they jumped back and forth between the positive and the negative. They found good in their children and in their experience raising them. Perhaps this was because they were sitting with others and were concerned that if they complained too much they might come off as too negative, or perhaps it was because they were on church grounds, counting their blessings. None of them had been regular churchgoers, and two didn't even identify themselves as Christians, before their children were diagnosed. They decided to approach the church because of a lack of both emotional and practical support from their families. The church, they said, had given them an inner strength they did not know they had, and the staff and members of the church had helped them to make decisions about their children's education and health. When they were at the church, they did not feel stigmatised.

With the exception of one mother who has twin autistic boys, most had at least one other child who was unimpaired. All of the mothers worried that their normal children would find it difficult to get married, that no worthy person would ever want to marry the sibling of someone with a mental disability. Families with divorce, alcoholism, suicide, or unemployment are disadvantaged enough in the Korean marriage marketplace, but evidence of an actual biological or genetic abnormality is enough to frighten most families away.

The mothers complained most about their in-laws. 'My son's [paternal] grandparents will not let us take him to their house or permit him to spend any time with his cousins anywhere.' Most of these women do not celebrate holidays with their in-laws. Another mother's comment summed up the gist of all of these conversations: 'When my child became autistic, our family's peace was broken.' And then, finally, there is the least discussed subject, and yet the one that is the most troubling to these women: husbands.

I do not want to give Korean men a worse reputation than they already have as husbands and fathers – even in families without disabled children, husbands in Korea generally spend little time at home and know little about their children's day-to-day lives or schedules. But when these women opened up to me, it became clear that they frequently felt like single mothers. One woman did not speak at all during the conversation but agreed to talk with me alone afterward. She said, 'My husband hates my [autistic] daughter.' Her eyes welled up as she said, 'He hates her.' She continued:

He wants us to send her away. Where [would she go]? He thinks she is horrible and that he is being punished by God. But she's actually very smart. She graduated from the sixth grade. He avoids her at home and says, 'She's not my daughter'. He insists that the property value of our apartment has gone down because no one will want to buy an apartment in which there was a disease like autism. He wanted to get a divorce but the church intervened and we are still together. But he will not pay for any education or speech or art therapy because he says that a mother should be able to do everything and that extra money for education is only for high-class Koreans. We don't have enough money, and insurance doesn't pay for all the therapies.

Another woman's autistic son is now sixteen years old, has a severe sleep disturbance, and sometimes needs attention throughout the night, but the boy's father rarely gets up to help because, he claims, he needs to get a good night's sleep before work. The mother also works full-time, but she gets home in the late afternoon. Her husband, like most Korean businessmen, frequently has to attend dinners and go to room salons (private rooms with drinking, karaoke, and a range of activities extending from simply eating fresh fruit to having sex with hostesses). When he comes home, often after midnight, he wakes her up to make him a snack of soup with noodles or leftovers.

Since men earn the bulk of the household income in most families, they have a lot of power in deciding how much to help with their children – or whether to help at all. Talking about these issues seemed to embolden these women – not only to be an advocate for their children, but to think about their own situation. Listening to them, I imagined that it was like witnessing the early stages of a revolution, when the resistance begins to take shape. In January 2005, they were given a powerful new weapon.

THAT MONTH A LOW-BUDGET Korean film entitled *Malaton* (spelled the way the main character pronounces the English word 'marathon') was released. The film was based loosely on the real-life story of a young runner named Bae Hyong-Jin. Bae worked part-time on an assembly line in a tool factory when, at the age of seventeen, he ran a marathon in Chuncheon, Korea, in 2 hours 57 minutes. While not anywhere near elite runner times, which are under 2 hours 8 minutes, Bae's time was enough to earn him national recognition. Why? Because Bae Hyong-Jin has autism.

But the film is not about running. It's about the complexity of autism as a disorder and the problems people with autism confront in their family and social lives. It is one of the most realistic and compelling cinematic representations of autism that I've ever seen. The film was made after the Korean media began to publish stories about people with autism. The media had begun to publish the stories because parents, informed by the Internet and the international media, started to talk about autism in public.

Within one month after its release, more than 10 per cent of the Korean population had seen the movie, and it was the second-largest moneymaker in the Korean film industry in 2005. Largely as a consequence of the film, millions of Koreans have at least a basic understanding of autism. On website chat boards, disability rights advocates, parents, and educators in Korea are claiming that more diagnoses are being made, that people are more willing to bring their children with autism out in public, and that educators are more willing to accommodate children with autism in their classrooms. No one knows whether these changes will last, but optimism is sweeping the country. Parents of children with developmental problems think that their children may have a brighter future than they previously imagined.

In *Malaton*, a middle-aged woman (played by Kim Mi-Sook) is obsessed with making her son a runner. Twenty-year-old Cho-Won (played by Cho Seung-Woo) has had fast legs since he was first diagnosed with autism at the age of five, and his mother believes that, through running, he can find a place in the society that has shunned him. As she puts it, she doesn't want him to be 'special' or 'different'. She pushes him hard, promising him Choco-pai's (a chocolate treat, Korea's equivalent to the American Twinkie) if he runs farther and faster. She hires an alcoholic former track star, who has been sentenced by the courts to do community service, to coach Cho-Won. In the process, she neglects both her husband, who has never been tolerant of Cho-Won's disorder, and her younger son. As Cho Won progresses with his running, she becomes even more obsessed. Her unimpaired son leaves home for a time, and her husband leaves her too.

Cho-Won does what his mother tells him to do, but he seems motivated less by the prospect of running a marathon than by his love of cheetahs and other African mammals. (Throughout the movie he repeats sentences from a book about the Serengeti.) Then, too, he's motivated by a desire to give the right answer to the question, 'Are you tired?' and reflexively replies the way she has taught him to: 'No, I want to run.' When the coach suggests that Cho-Won stop running because he is suffering from the rigorous workouts, the mother reacts aggressively, as if her own identity is being threatened. We begin to see that Cho-Won is not the only one in the movie who depends on someone else.

Cho-Won can be difficult. He has tantrums. He eats only a few foods – like his favourite, noodles with black bean paste, called *chajangmyun* – and is interested in African animals to the exclusion of all other topics. His emotional expression is flat. He cannot use honorifics correctly; he thanks an elderly man by saying the English equivalent of 'Thanks, dude', and speaks to his younger brother with the verb suffixes one should use with an elder brother. He wanders off. In a flashback, Cho-Won is lost at a zoo and becomes fixated on the stripes of a zebra.

My heart pounded as I watched the movie. Isabel's favourite food is chajangmyun. She's obsessed with animals, especially African ones, and repeats sentences about animals just like Cho-Won. And Isabel's sister, Olivia, like Cho-Won's brother, has many of the qualities one sees in only children: She is often more comfortable socialising with adults than with her peers, and sometimes seems hyper-responsible and independent for her age.

Much of the film revolves around the different expectations that Cho-Won's mother and coach have for him. She insists that Cho-Won is no different from anyone else, while the coach, reluctant to complete his community service, and initially uninterested in Cho-Won, insists he is too different to participate in a mainstream activity like a marathon. But they reverse positions later. When Cho-Won's mother is hospitalised for a bleeding ulcer, she realises in the midst of the crisis that she has been as single-minded as Cho-Won, having pushed him to run for her own purposes. The English subtitles have her saying, 'I am a bad mother', though a more accurate translation of the Korean she uses is, 'I'm a bitch and will go to hell'. The coach finally acknowledges Cho-Won's dedication to running and decides that he must run. He tells Cho-Won's mother, 'He's not different.' She answers, 'No, he is different. He has a disability.'

The coach has registered Cho-Won for the Chuncheon marathon, but when the T-shirt and number arrive in the mail, the mother throws them away. Cho-Won finds the materials. He's so determined to run that he secretly leaves the house and takes a bus to the site of the marathon. By the time his mother realises where he has gone, and takes off to Chuncheon, the race has almost started. She tries to stop him from running, but he refuses. 'I'm not going to collapse,' he tells her, and it is the first time in the movie he's said something that is not an echo of someone else's language. During the race, a spectator offers him a Choco-pai, and he throws it to the side of the road, a symbolic act of independence.

But perhaps the most moving scene takes place much earlier in a subway station. Some weeks before the race in Chuncheon, as Cho-Won and his mother eat a snack before boarding their train, there is an announcement on a loudspeaker that a five-year-old girl is missing in the station. The words resonate with Cho-Won, who remembers his own experience getting lost at the zoo so many years earlier. While his mother is buying something at a pharmacy in the station, he walks away, perhaps to look for the girl. On the platform, a woman is wearing a skirt in a zebra pattern, and he fixes his eyes on it. The woman's boyfriend orders him to look away, but Cho-Won continues staring and reaches out his hand to touch the back of her skirt. The boyfriend punches Cho-Won in the face just as his mother comes to the platform looking for him. Now collapsed on the ground, Cho-Won, bloodied and in pain, screams repeatedly, 'I'm a disabled child! I'm a disabled child!' It's a phrase that in the Korean language is blunt; it's like he is calling himself defective, which is very different from the politically correct English subtitle the filmmakers decided to use ('I'm a special child').

Later, Cho-Won's mother shudders when he tells her, 'You left me at the zoo,' and for the first time she admits to herself, and to her husband, that she let go of Cho-Won's hand on purpose, that she had actually wanted him to get lost. For me, as a parent of a child with autism, such bold honesty is startling. It is an expression of the ambivalence that must exist somewhere in the mind of any parent whose child has a serious disability. For it must be more common than we generally think for parents to have fantasies, consciously acknowledged or not, about freeing themselves from a burdensome child.

The same year *Malaton* was released, the Korean Broadcasting System began airing a popular prime-time drama in Korea, *Letters to My Parents,* in which the central character is a woman who has a young son with autism. In addition, the Korean media drew attention to the swimmer Kim Jin-Ho, who in 2005, at the age of nineteen, set a world record for the 200-metre backstroke at a world championship event in the Czech Republic for athletes with intellectual disabilities. Kim's mother, Yu Hyon-Kyong, made public her struggle to find a school for her son — he was expelled from his first elementary school despite the fact that his mother did what she could to help by attending classes with him. And she admitted that, when her son was younger, she seriously contemplated killing herself — and him.

Some parents I know complain that Koreans now wrongly assume that all people with autism are exactly like Cho-Won, but most applaud the awareness. They are starting to bring their children to shopping malls and swimming pools, using the Korean word for autism, *chapae*, to describe them. They're joining Internet chat lines and support groups where they can meet other parents of children with autism. 'The biggest change,' one mother told me, 'is in the schools, because it seems like, suddenly, they understand something about my son and are more comfortable with him.'

By the end of 2005, universities in Korea had begun training psychologists, psychiatrists, and other clinicians to use lengthy diagnostic tools to identify children on the autism spectrum. The government has also responded. The Korean Ministry of Science and Technology has been meeting to discuss plans for a study of the genetic causes of autism, and linguists, anthropologists, and sociologists, among other academics, have announced new research programmes. The Ministry of Education is planning to increase significantly the number of special-education classes in regular schools. The Ministry of Justice is beginning to allow lawsuits brought by parents who allege that their children have received inadequate educational services. The Ministry of Culture and Tourism has begun airing documentaries, several from the United States, about inclusion of children with special needs, and the Ministry of Defence has just announced that men can fulfil their required two-year military service by working in a school as a 'shadow' aide for a child with special needs.

As RECENTLY AS 1995, the residents of a quiet and wealthy neighbourhood south of the Kangnam River in Seoul had picketed the site where a school called Milal, for children with autism, was to be built. Angry protesters cut the school's phone lines, physically assaulted school administrators, and filed a lawsuit to halt construction, ostensibly because they believed that the presence in the neighbourhood of children with disabilities would lower property values. The school opened in 1997, but only with a compromise. It was required to alter its architecture so that the children were completely hidden from public view. Some of the protesters were brutally honest. They said they didn't want their children to see or meet a child with autism.

A decade later, the Milal school is a jewel in the Ilwon-dong neighbourhood. Hundreds of neighbours volunteer to help out there. The architect was given an award for the building. And the gym is used for community events, such as concerts and church services. In the afternoon when school lets out, families come by to pick up their children and sometimes take a leisurely walk in the neighbourhood, for all to see.

13

Getting in Tune

IN NEARLY ALL THE STORIES I'VE TOLD in this book, it is a mother's eyes that are the first to truly see her child and accept her child's difference. But simply to see a child with autism is not the same thing as integrating him into a social world. Those doors have to be worked open. Visibility is also more than just legislation ensuring a child's rights to an education. The Korean child with autism from Suwon who was given a place in a classroom, but treated only as an object of disgust, was neither seen nor understood. Parents all over the world work hard to make sure that their children are not shunned by society, especially when they feel so alone in being confident of their potential. The world's blindness is understandable. In order to make something visible you first have to notice its invisibility.

The school system in my community took years to finally 'see' Isabel. They dismissed our claims that, given the right curriculum and educational environment, she would be more capable academically than anyone expected. It doesn't matter if you are the leading expert on autism in the world. In the conference room of an elementary school you are just a parent saying what parents so often say: My child can do more if he or she is challenged. Advocating for your child can feel like a full-time job: It requires writing letters, making calls, attending meetings, and gathering data from your child's doctors or therapists to make a case for what you believe your child needs.

People who do not advocate often find that their children are given fewer services than those whose parents do advocate; it's the principle of the squeaky wheel getting the grease. School systems, even rich ones, have limited funding, and they are constantly trying to save here and there. As a result, some children will simply not be given the more expensive accommodations, like having aide support in a mainstream classroom.

When Isabel was in first grade, Joyce and I, and our doctors, were confident that Isabel needed to be mainstreamed in school, with all the kids from the neighbourhood, but we didn't think she could participate in a mainstream environment without aide support. The school system would have to hire someone to be with Isabel for most of the day, a costly proposition. The school balked. There were plenty of special-education classes that already had staffing; putting her in one of those would have cost them virtually nothing. We had been unsuccessful getting our school system to pay for psychological and educational tests for Isabel and we paid almost $1,500 to have it done privately. So why would they hire an aide for Isabel at perhaps $20,000 a year?

We had to go to the school system administrators for a special meeting. We knew that we had a lot of rights. The Individuals with Disabilities Education Act (IDEA) guarantees Isabel and other disabled children a free and appropriate education in what is called the 'least restrictive environment' (which means giving her an appropriate education while maximising the amount of time she spends with nondisabled peers in a regular educational environment). Still, I was amazed at what I saw in the conference room on the day of that meeting. There were fifteen people in that stuffy, windowless room: administrators, lawyers, and the special-education coordinators to represent the county; the principal, Isabel's teacher, an occupational therapist, and a speech therapist from the school; and our own doctors and lawyer. It was intimidating. All the men (except me) were wearing suits, and the chief lawyer for the county's special-education office, the person who would be our main adversary, was introduced as Mr Law.

I remember the first thing that went through my mind. What if I wasn't a professor used to speaking to large numbers of people in conference rooms? What if English wasn't my first language? What if I wasn't educated in, and emboldened by, my legal rights? I wouldn't stand a chance. Not a day has gone by that I don't appreciate the fact that many of the excellent services Isabel has received in Montgomery County, Maryland, were given to her because we had the wherewithal to fight, and the money to hire the very best attorney. And what about the fact that we prevailed? I'd be lying if I said I didn't feel guilty. I often wonder if our successes deprived another child of the services he or she needed.

We were asking our county government to provide a one-to-one aide for Isabel so that she could participate in a mainstream classroom. Isabel needed the aide to help her stay on track, listen to directions, and make the transition from one activity to another. Without the aide, Isabel was lost, simply staring off into space, reciting some lines from a video, or wandering around the classroom.

At the time, Isabel had received assistance only sporadically whenever an aide had time to pop in to her classroom. The principal had told us simply that she hadn't been given any money for an aide. If we didn't want to go to an established special-education class somewhere else in the county, far from our neighbourhood, we'd have to petition the administration. She didn't offer to help us; she just bumped us upstairs to her superiors.

At the county meeting, the school staff agreed that Isabel had a delightfully gentle and humorous personality. Her first-grade teacher stressed that, with assistance, Isabel made good, and sometimes amazing, progress in developing both social and academic skills. Isabel's eye contact had improved, and she seemed more interested in the other children, running up to them to say a word or two and then running away. She added that for Isabel to participate in the mainstream, 'what is really needed is adult one-to-one assistance'. The principal shifted in her chair and sighed, because this is not what the teacher was supposed to say.

The meeting became testy the moment anyone from 'our side' spoke up. We brought photographs of Isabel, as we did for every meeting, so that the administrators could see her as a real person, not just as a statistic in their budget. Everyone from the county administration looked uncomfortable. When we said that Isabel skis, ice skates, and swims, the principal replied tersely, 'We know that.' When our psychiatrist stressed that a first-grade class in our school system was largely auditory and didn't cater to Isabel's visual or spatial skills, the principal stopped him: 'We are all familiar with what a first-grade class is like.' And when our psychiatrist insisted that Isabel needed to be given aide support, Mr Law said, 'That is for us to decide.'

I looked at him.

I said, 'Who are you?' and there followed an awkward silence.

I said, 'Have you ever met my daughter? This is a doctor who has seen thousands of kids with autism and has been my daughter's doctor now for a long time, and you are suggesting he has no voice here?'

Our lawyer stepped in and said,

You know, you're lucky you have two reasonable parents who are willing to pay for the outside for services you don't provide, like bringing in these experts. But if you don't want to listen to us, then listen to Isabel's own teacher. She said she is doing well with aide support, so there is no justification to put her in a more restrictive environment. Be grateful you've got an expert here, an M.D. who is board certified as a pediatrician and a psychiatrist. You all know how long I've been doing this. I cannot recall one case in which you guys had an M.D. or a Ph.D. so involved with an autism coding.

When I left that meeting, it occurred to me that someone looking in from the outside would have thought that the county officials weren't interested in Isabel's welfare. But the reality is that nearly every one of these people is committed to special education. Many have children or relatives with special needs. It's just that somewhere along the line, the system became so adversarial and bureaucratic that it pulled a curtain over their compassion.

A SPECIAL-EDUCATION ATTORNEY I interviewed for this book remarked that almost every case in his practice is about inclusion, and about half of his cases now involve the autism spectrum. For the most part, schools want to include kids with disabilities into mainstream classes because it's cheaper than forming new, special-education classes with low student-teacher ratios. That economy is lost when a full-time aide is mandated. 'Plug the kids in without the supports,' he said, '[and] you might make the parents happy in the short term because they want their kid to look normal, but the pressures on the parents and the child are enormous.'

For one thing, the parents often want their child to pass for normal, and that's a lot of work. The emotional toll is great when you are worrying about whether your child is going to have a tantrum or act oddly. So if a school system is not going to provide a trained aide, then inclusion may not be the right answer, especially in middle and high school when the school systems try to pull back on the early-intervention services, arguing that it's no longer 'early'.

Many parents of young children, this attorney said, are uncomfortable with diagnostic terms. 'A big problem, actually, is the fathers,' the lawyer told me. 'Nine times out of ten, the mother has a balanced view of her child's needs and wants the school to provide both inclusion and intensive special-education services. But almost as often, the fathers say "There is nothing wrong with my kid". Sometimes we have to bring in a third party to give an objective view.' Some parents will not permit the use of a diagnostic label in meetings to decide a child's placement and educational programme. They fear that the label will remain forever, marking their child as unintelligent and limiting his progress in school. In some immigrant or insular communities, such as ultra-orthodox Jews in New York and Baltimore, said child psychiatrist Lance Clawson, 'The parents say directly, "Don't ever mention a diagnostic label in any of your letters of support because the word will get out. Our child will never find a marriage partner, and neither will his siblings."'

More commonly, parents reject the term 'autism' because it sounds too stigmatising, in favour of the current term of art, 'high-functioning PDD'. The problem is that there is no school code for 'high-functioning PDD', and it is the code that drives the services that will be delivered. In the end, many parents opt for the code 'multiple disabilities' because, as the attorney put it, 'it's easier to swallow'. But, he stressed, an autism code will usually get your child more services that benefit him – more hours of speech therapy, more aide support, more of almost everything the school has to give.

All of this is in flux, though, and I've met families who wanted the autism code but had to try their luck with other diagnostic labels. When the Medicaid waiver was first introduced in Virginia, for example, a diagnosis of autism yielded excellent care. But by 2005, the waiting list for that waiver exceeded 300, meaning that a family might have to wait at least three years to get free autism services from the state. Even if their number came up, the funds might no longer be available. In that same year, a diagnosis of mental retardation yielded more services because there were fewer applicants. The mental retardation programmes in Virginia had more money than the autism programmes did. Clawson said, 'This is why a patient's diagnosis can change from year to year depending on where the money is.' A few years ago, one of Clawson's patients with autism from Virginia, who was also mentally retarded, needed services immediately. Clawson knew that in the long run the patient would be better served by programmes tailored to autism treatment and education, so he arranged for the MR services and at the same time put his patient on the autism programme waiting list. The state told him that he couldn't have it both ways and refused to put the child's name on the waitlist for autism services.

Some parents plead with their child's school system for a private-school placement at the district's expense. These parents tend to be those with children on the ends of the spectrum, either the mildly impaired – those who might fit in at a school for bright children with learning disabilities – or the severely impaired – those who might fit in at a school for children with moderate to severe mental retardation. Both kinds of schools are expensive, ranging from $50,000 to as much as $250,000 a year for the best residential schools. The districts almost always say no. To win a residential placement, the parents have to prove that the child cannot get an appropriate education during the day unless he or she is in a special facility at night. Simply proving that your child wakes frequently or wanders off at night or may pose a danger to himself or others doesn't mean that what happens at night is the responsibility of the schools. In these cases, the US Department of Health and Human Services sometimes steps in to help.

But the biggest problem is the courts. When parents end up filing a lawsuit, usually for private placement or for more expensive services, like in-home behavioural therapies, they tend to lose. In Montgomery County, parents often lose because the school system can usually show that it has a programme somewhere in the county that can provide services the law considers 'appropriate'. The courts tell the parents that the state only has to provide free and appropriate services, not optimal services; legal precedent has established that school districts can always claim budgetary constraints when faced with parents' requests for better or more services.

In our county, parents prevailed in 9.5 per cent of the cases brought before a court in 2000 and in 25 per cent of the cases in both 2003 and 2004. But the cases in which they prevailed were simple cases – where, say, a parent wanted the child moved to another school elsewhere in the county, or wanted reimbursement for an inexpensive consultation with an outside expert. Parents rarely won a case in which they asked for reimbursement for private-school placement. On 14 November 2005, the US Supreme Court made it even harder for parents. By a 6–2 vote, the justices made it clear that in disputes about special-education services, the parents have the burden of proof.

In Washington, DC, the attorney's fees in cases involving the Individuals with Disabilities Education Act can be quite costly. A typical three-day hearing may cost up to $50,000 in legal and expert fees. It used to be that many lawyers took special-education cases on contingency, much the way malpractice suits are handled. If you won the case against the school system, the loser paid your attorney; if you lost, the attorney simply didn't get paid.

But attorney fee reimbursements for IDEA cases in DC are now capped at $4,000. So these days, special-education lawyers don't work on contingency. They may take on an extraordinary case pro bono, but it's a rare occurrence. You might be able to get an attorney to sue for something small, like getting your child tested by psychologists, but for a placement dispute, $4,000 is insufficient. Sometimes parents and schools go through mediation, but it's not common, and both parties have to agree to mediate. Because the school system employs its own lawyers anyway, it has little interest in mediation.

The attorney I interviewed told me, 'Almost everyone I've represented who has gone through the hearing process says they would have settled for almost anything.' Parents and guardians feel that they're not on an even playing field with the state, not only because they are often unfamiliar with their rights, but because they are so emotionally invested and fragile. They sometimes leave a hearing feeling that they've been punished. One parent told me, 'They make you relive all you've experienced, and you end up talking about how impaired your kid is, and the attorneys can be belligerent.'

Sometimes parents are so traumatised by the experience, and so dissatisfied with the services provided, that rather than attempt a futile and expensive lawsuit they move to a school district or state that has better services. I've heard many stories of people with autistic children who, after protracted and difficult legal battles, decided to move from Maryland to New Jersey, a state reputed to provide excellent care for children in the autism spectrum. Parents of children with autism in Saskatchewan, Canada, are beginning to move to Alberta, the province next door, because Alberta provides more financial assistance and they are simply too tired of fighting to get help.

Kari Dunn, a special-education consultant who has worked for the state of Minnesota since the early 1980s, told me another reason why some families with a child with autism move away. Until recently, parents in small towns in Minnesota couldn't get an autism coding even if they tried. 'The school administrators knew that if they used that label they would be required by law to provide an instructor with autism training,' she said. If the district officials could prove that they did not have a trained instructor, they were then permitted to code the student with multiple disabilities and place him or her in a preexisting classroom with children who'd been given a host of different diagnoses.

IDEA, which was intended to ensure that the government would provide an appropriate education for all children, wasn't set up with the expectation that parents would be involved in extensive litigation, or that pit-bull attorneys would try to reduce witnesses to tears over the correct placement of a child with special needs. The plan was that parents and schools would work together to form educational programmes, and that parents or guardians who needed hearings would be able to participate without legal counsel. Nonetheless, IDEA has become a litigious arena that parents shouldn't attend without a lawyer.

The attorney I interviewed said, 'There is a firm in the Washington area known for its scorched-earth policy of stopping at nothing, and they usually work for the school systems.' One of his clients, who was suing DC to get his autistic son placed in a private school, noticed a black SUV parked outside his house when he got home from work one afternoon. The driver sat in the car for hours. At about 10 P.M., his client went out to the car and asked the driver if he needed any help with anything. The man said, 'I'm a private investigator for a law firm trying to find out if you actually live in DC.' His client was so intimidated that he almost dropped the suit.

As autism diagnosis rates began to rise during the 1990s, parents started to put more pressure on their schools to come up with special programmes. This was particularly true for the parents of higher-functioning children with PDD-NOS or Asperger's Disorder, because they represented the largest increase in autism cases at that time. It took the school systems in my area several years to realise that having a specialised programme for the children in this group would be more efficient and economical for them than having separate placements for each one: If they had a class devoted to Asperger's Disorder, they wouldn't have to have ten completely different IEPs to write and implement (even though the schools will always insist that every IEP is, by definition, individualised), and if they could place children with Asperger's Disorder within the school district, they might not have to consider funding an expensive placement in a private school (or be sued to do so). Clearly this was a vast improvement over the days when children with autism were lumped together with other 'misfits'.

To be sure, debate is brewing about whether some of these higher-functioning children should be classified as autistic or even disabled. Some disability experts contend that the problems encountered in educating children with Asperger's Disorder lie less with the individual child than with the educational system. The US educational system, they suggest, has disseminated Asperger's Disorder as a category because it is useful to its attempt to make the student body as homogeneous as possible. The paradox they identify is that a child who doesn't fit in has to be seen as somehow impaired in order to justify an effort to normalise him. A cynic might even suggest that there is an economic motive behind the rise of autism codings, and that autism spectrum diagnosis is complicit with the rise of a cadre of special education services, such as speech, occupational, and art therapy.

I think it is indisputable that autism, like any medical condition, exists within a complex network of professional relationships and agendas. But this doesn't mean that these children don't need help. In fact, it's the children at the border that can most often go unnoticed – and then, so, too, does their suffering.

THE GREATEST CHALLENGES for the schools, it seems to me, are calibration and adaptation to change: They need to find the best mix between self-contained special-education classrooms and schools (in which children are educated apart from the mainstream) and full inclusion into the mainstream, while being open to the possibility that the right mix today may not be right tomorrow. Joyce and I found ourselves in the position of fighting for more inclusion only to fight for more special-education support a few months later.

We always try to err on the side of inclusion, because Isabel usually can rise to a challenge, especially during the summers when the stakes are low. In typical summer day camps, there are no grades or exams and no changes to her school programme if she fails to fit in. Some summer camp directors have said, 'We simply don't have the ability to accept special-needs kids right now,' but others have welcomed her. This is why many parents will hide the fact that their child has autism until the first day of camp, or until the camp director expresses concern. Some parents of high-functioning children with autism refuse to use the term 'autism' or even to attempt to describe their child's special needs for fear that their child will be marginalised or rejected. I'm not surprised that parents behave this way. Even after all these years, and having written a book on autism, I'm not confident about how to describe Isabel to people who are in a position of authority. Yet research shows that both teachers and 'normal' students are more supportive to children with autism when they are aware of the diagnosis.

Once Isabel has been accepted into a mainstream environment, I sometimes still feel like I'm on the defensive, or at least anxious. It's not the other children I worry about; it's the adults. Fortunately, though, the anthropologist Elinor Ochs and her colleagues at the University of California at Los Angeles found that successful inclusion of children with autism into mainstream classes at school depends more on the classmates than the teachers, and children these days are more accommodating than ever, especially if they understand something about autism. Every time I put Isabel into a mainstream setting, I begin to wait. I wait for the telephone call from some adult – a teacher or an administrator – to tell me that Isabel had a tantrum, or that she threw something, or that she wouldn't stay where she was supposed to. When the phone rings, your heart sinks.

In 2002, Isabel and Olivia both attended a local summer day camp at a private K–12 school near our home. Although most of the time the campers did sports and arts and crafts, we made sure to sign Isabel into a language-arts class that met for about one hour each morning, the goal being to improve her reading and writing. The teacher agreed to let me stay the whole hour for the first three days, after which I would cut back my participation until Isabel could stay by herself. On the first day that Isabel was alone in the class, the mother of another camper decided to observe. And the story of the experience that followed, which was not unusual for parents of autistic children, will give you a sense of how Joyce and I sometimes spend our days.

The camp director called me that day at about 11 A.M. 'Apparently, Mr Grinker, your daughter took her clothes off in the classroom, and the mother of another girl is demanding that your daughter be removed from the class because she is so disruptive. What do you think we should do?'

'That doesn't sound like something Isabel would do. What did the teacher say?' I asked.

The director answered, 'We haven't talked to her yet.'

'I don't understand why you are telling me something a parent said without having talked to the teacher, and why are you asking *me* what you're supposed to do? Can you call me back after you've talked to the teacher?'

An hour later, at noon: 'Mr Grinker, the teacher said that the air conditioning was on really high and it was cold in the classroom, so Isabel took her arms out of her sleeves and put them under her shirt so she could warm herself. She didn't take off her shirt but she did walk around the room during a class exercise.'

Okay, I thought. So now the problem is over.

But then the director said, 'So what about Isabel leaving the class? Would you like to find another class for her?'

'No!' I said. 'Clearly, this parent doesn't like my daughter being in the same class with hers, but why should that be my problem? It's not like Isabel violated camp policies. So isn't it your problem and the mother's problem?'

Two-and-a-half hours later, at 2:30 P.M.: 'Mr Grinker, we told the mother that Isabel is entitled to stay in the classroom but that we would help her find another activity for her daughter during that same period.'

One hour later: 'Mr Grinker, the mother withdrew her child.'

THE OLDER ISABEL GOT, the more everyone expected of her, and eventually the day arrived when she could not fulfil the expectations. In early 2001, when Isabel was in third grade, the principal established a rule that during announcements made at lunchtime, the children had to be completely silent. But Isabel giggled or talked to herself. When the staff tried to reason with Isabel, she tended not to respond. There were children in the school more difficult than Isabel – a few aggressive and destructive children, and many argumentative and disrespectful children – but the staff actually felt more comfortable with them because they were at least capable of having a dialogue, even if it was an argument. Isabel wasn't that disruptive, but her inability to engage in anything but the most simple social interactions increased their frustrations.

One night that year I returned home and heard the following message on the phone machine. 'This is Jackson. I am in Isabel's third-grade class. Today I saw something at school that I think is what is called child abuse. I am telling you because I know that Isabel can't tell you herself. You can call me or my mother.'

The phone rang before I could even start to dial.

'Richard Grinker? This is Christine. My son Will came home very upset about something he saw today in the lunchroom and I'm really calling on his behalf because he wanted to make sure Isabel was okay.'

Every other child in Isabel's class would have been capable of talking about their day at school in a meaningful way. But if you said to Isabel, 'Tell me about your day at school,' she'd give the same long reply: 'I went to school. Then I went to my class. Then I went to lunch. Then I went to class. Then I got on the bus. Then I came home.' This is why children with speech and language problems, or other cognitive deficits, are so vulnerable. They can't tell you if something bad happens. You have to figure it out for yourself.

Joyce and I first called Jackson and his mother. We heard from him that Isabel had been making noise in the lunchroom during the quiet time. The principal told her to be quiet or her whole table wouldn't get recess in the afternoon. A tall, imposing woman with high heels that slapped the floor loudly, the principal terrified a lot of the students, but apparently not Isabel. Isabel didn't respond to her, or quiet down, and so the principal asked her to leave the lunchroom. Isabel refused.

Jackson continued, 'Everyone in the cafeteria saw her grab Isabel and drag her out of the lunchroom. Isabel didn't want to go. She screamed and she fell on the floor and she tried to lift Isabel up, but Isabel fell back down, and then she pulled her arm and dragged her into the hallway.'

Other children told us the same story that night, but from Isabel I could learn little. 'Isabel!' I called for her. 'What happened to you today? Did someone hurt you?'

She answered, 'Nothing.'

After the calls, Joyce examined Isabel. None of her clothes were ripped, but underneath Isabel's black turtleneck and purple velvet overalls Joyce found fingernail scratches. There were small bruises, in the pattern of fingers, on her chest, back, and arms. I brought Isabel to our paediatrician's office so she could document the marks on her body. Next, we called the county, threatened to press criminal charges against the principal and the school system, and told them we were keeping Isabel home. A few hours later, a county administrator called to inform me that by not sending Isabel to school I was violating state law. By the time we went to bed that night, there would be three more telephone calls and one visit from a neighbour, all to check on Isabel.

The county administrators, fearful of a lawsuit, hastily arranged a meeting with us, the principal, and the director and deputy director of special education for Montgomery County. By this time we had in hand five letters from children who had seen the events, all consistent in their observations, all poignant and touching in their expressions of caring for Isabel. The director said little, letting his deputy look through the letters and act the bad cop.

'I could go out and get my own five letters that say something different,' he said.

'Why would you want to do that?' I asked.

He didn't answer and just kept reading.

'How did she get all the marks on her body?' I asked.

'I have here,' he said, holding a piece of paper, 'a letter from the only other adult who witnessed the events, the janitor.' Quoting the janitor, he said, 'On that date, I saw Isabel Grinker being a harm to self or others.'

Joyce and I almost laughed.

Joyce said, 'No one writes about someone being "a harm to self or others" unless they are instructed to write that way. You are refusing to acknowledge the obvious. Isabel was assaulted by her own principal in front of the entire school.'

The deputy tried to counter, but the director stopped him.

Then the principal burst into tears.

She said, 'I love Izzy. I wouldn't want to hurt Izzy. I am sorry. I apologize. I care about her.'

Joyce said, 'We're going to press charges unless you apologise directly to her and assure us that she is safe going back to school. Also, you and your teachers have to receive training on autism.'

'I will, I will,' the principal said.

'And we want this in the record,' Joyce said.

I looked at the principal: 'I think you have a problem, which is that you are so nervous and anxious that you take it out on the kids, and they are terrified of you. But I'm not terrified of you. And I am willing to take this case as far as it can go because your bosses apparently don't take it seriously. The problem is: You might do this to some other child in the future.'

We kept Isabel home for several more days before bringing her back to school and escorting her to the principal's office, where, as Isabel expected, the principal would apologise. We watched as she sat down with Isabel, said she was sorry for hurting her, and that she wanted to take good care of her.

Isabel said, 'Okay.'

THAT SUMMER OF 2001, when Isabel was nine years old, and in the third grade, Joyce came up with what I now think was a stroke of genius. 'I want her to learn music,' she said, 'and I want her to learn an instrument that she will have to play with a group.' After our experience with her third-grade principal, we had initiated a transfer. In September, Isabel would switch schools and enter a combined fourth- and fifth-grade classroom for bright children with special needs. The idea was that if Isabel played music with a group, she would be compelled to have social interactions; she might be more easily accepted into her new social environment at school, and she might even make a friend or two. At any rate, she'd have to pay attention to other children.

But there was more to Joyce's decision than just that. By the time she had started elementary school, Isabel had become extremely sensitive to a variety of different nonmusical sounds, including certain speech rhythms. These sensitivities have continued to this day. She reacts with defensiveness, covering her ears, if you speak with a rhythm, an intonation, or a volume or pitch she doesn't like, and she covers her ears when a toilet flushes, when a baby cries, or when she hears a word she doesn't like. She detests the 'Happy Birthday' song. Recently, when I was interviewing a woman whose son has autism, I showed her a Polaroid of Isabel taken on her twelfth birthday. In the picture, Isabel is sitting in front of a chocolate cake blowing out twelve candles, while Olivia and two girls from Isabel's sixth-grade class sing 'Happy Birthday'. Isabel looks mildly happy, but she's stuffed her forefingers in her ears to block out the sound. The woman shrieked with laughter and said,

'Oh, I have one of those too!' This is a common posture in autism, not only when people feel overwhelmed by sound, but also when they experience emotions like happiness, anger, and surprise.

Joyce suggested a stringed instrument, and she had an interesting reason for it. Isabel hated things that vibrated. She didn't like pressure on her fingertips so much that she refused to even try to learn to button her clothing or tie her shoelaces. This got in the way of her schoolwork. She didn't want to use her fingertips to hold a pen or pencil, so she couldn't get a correct grip, or even one that would allow her to write clearly. Teaching her a stringed instrument would be a kind of exposure therapy, having her do the things that made her anxious in order to extinguish the aversion. It was sensory integration, for lack of a better term.

We began a three-week day camp at the Levine School of Music in Washington, conceived to introduce elementary-school children to musical instruments. We faced the same predicament as always. The school worried about how to handle Isabel. They were uncomfortable with allowing one of us to shadow her, insisting that they'd never had a child with autism in their programme. Isabel went, nonetheless, and the teachers told us that of all the instruments she tried, she had preferred the cello. We thought it had something to do with the fact that, despite her aversion to vibration, she enjoyed feeling it against her legs.

The teacher who introduced the children to the cello was a thin, quiet, mild-mannered man with whom Isabel immediately felt comfortable. Although he'd worked at a residential school for children with autism while he was in college, he had never taught cello to them. He agreed to do it, but after the first two lessons he told us that he wasn't sure she understood anything. Isabel at first refused to use her left hand and even tried to hold her ears while playing the cello. To his credit, though, he stuck with it; we kept pushing Isabel, and eventually she stuck with it too. The sound and touch sensitivities didn't go away, but they lost their grip on her.

Within a year after her introduction to the cello, Isabel participated in a small recital. When she finished the piece, and the applause died down, she stood on the stage, stunned, and asked the audience, 'Did I win?' Joyce and I were so worried about even getting Isabel to go out onto the stage that we had forgotten to tell her that people would clap afterward. Joyce had to usher her off stage. Several months later, her cello playing had improved dramatically, and she performed in a second recital. This time we made sure she expected the clapping, and we also told her several times that when she was done playing she had to leave. After her performance, she dutifully left the stage, and the building too. After a tense search, looking in bathrooms and classrooms, I found her in the parking lot, cello in hand.

Isabel can't go to a Broadway musical and then come home and write the score from memory, or play two songs on the piano simultaneously, one with the left hand and the other with the right. There are people in the world who are capable of this, many of them with autism. They can repeat exactly what they've heard or seen, although they are not creative. But not long after her music lessons began, Isabel suddenly piped up 'B flat' in response to a tap on a crystal wine glass at a family celebration. I tapped on my glass and she said, 'A'. I don't have perfect pitch – it's rare – so I had to wait until the next day to find a piano I could use to test her. I had her turn away from the piano as I played notes, and she identified every one, even if they were in the very lowest or highest octaves. She didn't enjoy the task. She kept holding her ears. But I continued. I asked her to sing an A flat, and a C and a D, and then I'd hit those notes to see if she was right. She was dead on.

Perfect pitch, also known as 'absolute pitch', is estimated to occur in about 0.05 per cent of the population. People with a skill like this don't necessarily make good musicians, and it doesn't mean they can sing in tune – a recent study of full-time adult music conservatory students showed perfect pitch in only four out of 625 tested – but it does explain a few things about Isabel. For one thing, she doesn't like anyone to sing a song if it's not sung in the same key in which she heard it on a CD or on the radio. She also doesn't mind if she loses her place while playing the cello with other musicians or in an orchestra. She can find her place easily, because she knows exactly which notes the others are playing. Recently, she's been able to hear chords and dis-embed the sounds, naming the various notes that make up the chord, and just by listening to a song she can tell you what key it's in. She also has the ability to memorise musical pieces from sheet music after playing them only a few times. It's a challenge for her to remember which sections are loud or soft, which notes are sustained or staccato, but she knows the tune and seldom looks at the page.

It's still an open question whether there is any link between autism and musical ability. But some surveys in England have found that music is a special interest of at least 40 per cent of people with autism there. These findings are energising neuroscientists to look more closely at the way music influences brain function in autism. They are especially interested in why so-called 'musical savants' do not have numerous talents, but rather tend to excel just in that one area. Unfortunately, neuroscientists have yet to explain how savant skills develop, although it is sometimes hypothesised that the skills are associated with savants' extraordinary ability to concentrate on a narrow topic, and an inability to shift concentration.

One group of researchers from Brown and Tufts universities found that 46 per cent of musicians with perfect pitch scored as 'socially eccentric', as compared with just 15 per cent of the controls. The authors suggested that perfect pitch shows the ability to 'perceive, encode, and remember a stimulus in isolation from its surroundings'. This kind of isolation of sound is consistent with what we know about people with autism: that they have problems with what is sometimes called 'central coherence', seeing the full picture. The neurological reasons for this are not entirely clear, but using functional Magnetic Resonance Imaging (fMRI), researchers have found significantly different types of blood flow in the brains of autistic and nonautistic controls when given auditory stimuli. When listening to complex sounds like speech, the speech-related areas of the brain were less activated in the autistic test subjects than in the control group subjects. Perhaps this is why a simple sound like a single musical note causes so much less disturbance than speech in the autistic brain.

But though Isabel will never astound audiences who hear her play, she is still a wonder to us. And rather than view her musical interests and abilities as part of the 'abnormal', it might be better to see them as skills, as a certain kind of intelligence, or at least as an expression of the glory of the human brain, in itself an unimaginably complex symphony. When it comes to a child with a disability, doctors and educators, and parents too, can easily spend too much time on what the child cannot do, meanwhile not noticing what he can do. We can be so busy dealing with what is absent that we ignore what is right before our eyes. It's often difficult to understand that what we need to make visible is not darkness, but light.

FRANKIE BALL HAD SPENT his entire adult life directing middle-school orchestras and jazz bands, winning numerous awards. A talented musician, and nearing retirement, he was a devoted member of his local congregation, where he also directed the church orchestra. One Sunday, not too long ago, the pastor gave a sermon in which he made the point that everyone has a talent, even though it might not always be obvious or visible. To empha-sise this, he asked everyone to present at least one. Frankie Ball decided that when it was his turn, he'd talk about how he plays several instruments, arranges scores, and conducts the local mid-dleschool orchestra in Bethesda, Maryland.

By the time Isabel Grinker had come to his classroom as a sixth-grader on the first day of school, cello in hand, Mr Ball already knew her. The school staff had talked with him. Joyce and I had met with him, on the advice of the school, and a mother whose son was in the orchestra had talked to Mr Ball about Isabel's skills.

'You know,' Mr Ball had told me that day, 'even ten years ago I wouldn't have seen a kid like Isabel in my class. She wouldn't have been in the school, and if she had been in the school, they probably wouldn't have let her join an orchestra. And if they did let her join the orchestra for some reason, I wouldn't know much about her. Now how can I help a kid like Isabel if I don't know anything about her?'

As the pastor went round the congregation that Sunday, Mr Ball thought about Isabel on stage with the rest of the orchestra dur-ing a recent performance in New Jersey, the audience's applause, and the special award the judges gave the cello section. And he thought about another child at the school, a violinist so hyperac-tive that the other teachers didn't know how to handle him. Then he thought about another violinist, a shy boy who had just arrived from Japan and spoke no English. When it was Mr Ball's turn to speak, he didn't mention his musical talents. Instead he turned to the pastor and said, 'My talent is communicating with children.'

I haven't painted a pretty picture of the battles parents must wage for our children's education. Yet I believe things have improved since autism became a more popular diagnosis. The more chil-dren that are given the diagnosis, the more the schools will have to confront it, and the more knowledgeable administrators and teachers will be about how to support and educate children with autism. When Isabel entered her new school in the autumn of 2001, we met with the team of teachers and the principal. We met with the orchestra conductor and the school bus driver. With them we worked to organise educational plans and improve communication between them and us. Ever since then, we've worked as a team with those who are teaching Isabel, rather than as adversaries. I think that other parents can get to this point too, but it means never leaving your child to people with conflicting loyalties, or worse, closed minds.

And if the school systems begin to appreciate the mounting evidence that early interventions lead to better prognoses and less cost to the government, it is more likely that our children will get more and better services. Beyond these practical approaches, however, I deeply believe that the arrival of these 'difficult' children gives teachers like Frankie Ball new opportunities. He is a remarkable person, with a very special gift, but he's probably not that unusual anymore. How many other educators are developing new teaching skills because of inclusion in the schools and increased awareness of the abilities of people with autism? It's anybody's guess, but I'm certain the numbers are growing.

Beyond the Curve

PEOPLE WITH AUTISM CAN TEACH US A LOT ABOUT VISION.
On a midsummer walk in 2003, after a morning rain, Isabel
stopped to focus on an unremarkable section of the pavement.
She cried out: 'Indonesia!' She glowed with joy but, unable to use
language effectively, couldn't explain. It took me a minute, but
eventually I saw that the puddle of water in front of us formed the
shape of Indonesia.

I've learned to expect Isabel's uncanny observations. She's seen
New Guinea in a cloud formation, Tennessee on a woodpile,
Korea in the fur of a cat. She uses her visual powers to assemble
complicated jigsaw puzzles, memorising the shape and image of
each piece – sometimes making her favourite puzzle, the Japanese
bridge in Monet's garden, with the picture side down. Periodically,
she rubs the surface of a puzzle piece with her fingers. I imagine
that she senses something through the cardboard, that she knows
this piece is a willow, that piece is a water lily.

Isabel's visual skills are similar to those of Temple Grandin, a
well-known person with autism. Grandin once told me that her
mind is like an extensive library of videos and photographs, and
that this is why language is so challenging for her. She thinks
in pictures. Peace is a dove, honesty a picture of someone with

his hand over a Bible. This reminded me of how hard it was for Isabel to conceive of the Vikings as Scandinavian warriors; the only image in her mind was of Daunte Culpepper and his football team in Minnesota.

Once when I spoke with Grandin on the telephone, she had just checked into the Dallas–Fort Worth Hyatt, and all she could talk about was a drop ceiling under construction in the hotel lobby with two modern chandeliers, each with nine spotlights arranged in three levels – red, green, and grey fixtures hanging over the centre of the lobby – a fragment of the environment that few guests would consider a topic of conversation, let alone notice.

And so it is with our everyday lives, in which so much remains invisible unless it is brought to our attention. Our powers of sight seem endless, but they are as limiting as they are liberating. Not long ago when I took Isabel to the deck of a skyscraper in Chicago, I realised how little I had been able to see just minutes before on the ground. This is such a simple observation that it seems almost unmentionable. When we look at something, we always look from somewhere else, whether it be from a particular place, a cardinal direction, a below or an above. There is no pure, natural, or singularly correct way of seeing. Our vision is structured by habit, routine, and consensus. Just because people with autism don't share that consensus doesn't mean that their visions are less valuable. The ability to find Indonesia in a puddle or New Guinea in the sky may be just as important as being able to find them on a map.

Through her powers of sight, Isabel has challenged my assumptions about the world I thought I knew. She's taught me not to expect that life will proceed in a straight line, that the road has many curves. And through her unique personality, she's challenged my assumptions about the most elemental aspects of social life – like the belief that friends should be similar ages, or the idea that children should all live independently when they grow up. When you have a child with autism, you start to think more creatively about the kinds of meaningful relationships that are possible, and beneficial.

Perhaps not surprisingly, once Isabel was diagnosed, I started to see autism all around me. Before that time, I knew virtually nothing about it and had never met anyone with the diagnosis. But afterward, I began to see people with autism at the local swimming pool, at school functions, in shopping malls, at playgrounds. They were there all along; I just wasn't primed to see them. Now, more than a decade later, the world is also primed to see and understand autism. But when the many children diagnosed with autism grow up, will we also be ready to see autistic adults?

I taught a freshman seminar on autism during the spring semester of 2006. On the first day, I asked the students to say why they had enrolled. One student said, 'I took the class because I have autism.' He told the class that he had been diagnosed with Asperger's Disorder in his junior year in high school only after receiving numerous other diagnoses over the years. I was taken aback, but I used the opportunity to ask the students to talk about what kinds of cultural changes had taken place in the United States to make it possible for a student at a major university to tell his peers that he has autism (or, for that matter, any behavioural disorder). The students were quiet at first. They were taken aback too, but less by the man's statement than by my question. They didn't know that in earlier times children with autism were needlessly confined in institutions, demeaned as social misfits, and never integrated into community life, let alone educated.

In this book, I've argued that the so-called autism 'epidemic', and its increased prevalence and visibility, is a sign of changes in our culture that have enabled us to begin the process of integrating people with autism – and other disabilities and differences – into our communities. I can't think of a better example of how far we have come than the nineteen freshmen in my university who took for granted that an adult with autism is part of their world.

WHEN I TALK TO PARENTS who have children with autism and ask them what they are most afraid of, they usually answer with a question: 'What will happen to our child when we're gone?' The assumption underlying that question is that there is no one else who will be able to care for their child. Some mothers say simply, 'Without me, my child would die.' In the Korean film, *Malaton*, Cho-Won's mother, who lives with her two children in a Seoul high-rise with no relatives nearby, makes this clear: 'I want him to die a day before I do; so I better live until I'm at least 100.'

On a rural family farm, or in an African village, there may be numerous relatives who can potentially take care of an adult with autism. In such communities, there may also be less demand for good communication and social skills. These are two of the reasons why, according to several large-scale World Health Organisation studies, people with psychiatric disorders generally fare better over time in rural, nonindustrial societies than they do anywhere in the United States. (Unfortunately, the WHO study didn't include a rural American site.) In fact, the three sites in which psychiatric patients had the poorest outcomes were in Aarhus (Denmark), London, and Washington, DC The three sites with the best outcomes were Agra (India), Cali (Colombia), and Ibadan (Nigeria). The WHO study didn't argue that mental disorders were absent in developing countries like India or Nigeria, but rather, that non-Western, and especially rural, communities were better able to include people with a variety of disabilities, both physical and mental, into social and economic life with less stress and isolation. This is a pattern that was demonstrated as early as the 1930s in studies that compared mental illness in urban and rural America.

Clearly, society has a lot of influence over the outcomes of mental illness.

Over the past two decades, Dr C.T. Gordon, a paediatrician and psychiatrist who specialises in autism, has seen thousands of people with autism in rural Maryland and Pennsylvania. From the home, to the school, to the main street of the nearest town, people in these rural areas seem more understanding than their counterparts in the city, more likely to bend and accommodate. 'In the most rural places I've been in America,' he told me, 'the school meetings to determine placement and services go so beautifully because these kids are truly seen as individuals.' Gordon is himself the parent of an autistic teenager, and the Gordon family has found solace and tolerance outside the city, in a rural religious community. Although he and his family attended an urban church for several years, they felt they were no longer welcome when his son became larger, louder, and more disruptive. They found a place where the entire family could worship at 'The Haven', a rural church in Maryland that invites children and adults with disabilities.

The members of the Haven like to quote 1 Corinthians 12, which suggests that the community is like the body of God: 'As a body is one though it has many parts, and all the parts of the body, though many, are one body, so also Christ.' Phrased differently, there are parts of any body, or community, that we don't want to look at – the parts that are dirty, ugly, or shameful. But to truly embrace the spirit of community, the members of the Haven say, means looking at them as the body of Christ, and making them part of our lives. 'If one part suffers, all the parts suffer with it; if one part is honoured, all the parts share its joy.'

Compared with those living in the cities of Korea, India, or South Africa, rural dwellers in those countries often have more relatives around, and thus more people to care for those with autism.

But in the United States, extended families rarely live together, even in rural areas. Households are smaller, because people have fewer children, and divorce is common. Many people don't own the same home or live in the same neighbourhood for more than a few years, and relatives are increasingly separated by long distances. Maureen Fanning in Long Island, who lost her husband in the World Trade Center attacks in 2001, has many relatives, but she still had to hire a babysitter in order to get some respite from caring for her two autistic sons. Those relatives eager to help her live far away, in North Carolina. Families with an autistic child tend to be more isolated than others. A family taking care of someone with autism has little time to maintain the social and family networks necessary to ensure future support. And the more severely impaired someone is, the more likely the extended family is to avoid contact because of the extraordinary burden of care.

Families with disabled children are not the only ones in this predicament – those caring for an elderly parent face a similar problem. In times past, the elderly lived out their days with their children, but the two-career, mobile family of the past several decades has changed all that. Few people in the United States today are willing or able to live with their ageing parents. Even the ageing parents themselves resist the idea, fearing they will become a burden to their children. This change in family structure – and other changes, too, such as the growth of Medicare to pay for the care of the elderly, and the fact that people simply live longer today than in the past – has been accompanied by an explosion of assisted-living facilities and nursing homes to take care of the people who can no longer live independently and who have nowhere else to go. Of course, few elderly people stay in nursing homes for decades. Maureen Fanning's boys will likely live in group homes for at least 60 years.

THERE ARE MORE GROUP HOMES today for the disabled than ever before, more vocational training for young adults with autism, and more job opportunities. Some of the adult group homes that are reputed to be the best – such as Somerset in England, Bittersweet Farms in northwestern Ohio, the Dunfirth Community in Ireland, and Camphill Farms in South Africa – are modelled after rural, cooperative farms. In France, adults with autism continue to be placed in psychiatric institutions or residential-care facilities, along with people who have chronic psychoses. Fortunately, among industrialised nations, France is the exception, not the rule.

Situations like the one Lily Mayo encountered in 1970s Peru, when she found people with autism were being kept in cages at a church-run hospital (as I recounted in the introduction), are now extremely rare. Of course, there are still sad stories to be told. In 2002 in a suburb of East London, South Africa, I visited a group home for six severely autistic men. The married couple who started the home took me for a tour. At first glance, it looked admirable. In the back of the house, however, there was a free-standing iron cage, like something from a zoo. The founders had no training in psychology or special education. They were committed to helping these men, but they have neither the expertise nor the money to manage the behaviours they sometimes see. The men are locked in their bedrooms at night, and there are bars on the windows to prevent them from running away. If one of the men becomes violent, he is put in the cage, sometimes for many hours, until he calms down.

I asked them why the home wasn't managed by a health-care organisation that could employ well-trained staff, staff that might be able to detect the signs of a violent episode before it occurred. They looked at me as if I was stupid. The husband said, 'There is no such organisation, and there is not enough money. No one in their right mind would want to do this job. And we don't know how long we will last. But if you think the cage is bad, you should see the state institutions.'

And I did. The South African government refused to let me in to see their adult facilities, but a doctor I interviewed near Cape Town took me in anyway under the pretence that I was one of his students. The rooms were not well lit, but there wasn't much to illuminate – pale, bare, yellow walls with mattresses lined up in rows on a cement floor. The place was packed with long-term patients, all of them mentally ill, some of them severely so. Most were black. Men and women were mixed together during the day but separated at night into barracks. They were medicated with antipsychotic medications that made them look sleepy. A woman sat facing a corner, playing with her saliva; a man in another part of the room was masturbating.

The doctor was apologetic. He said he was doing the best he could, donating his time as the sole psychiatrist for the nearly 100 patients on the ward. The patients basically live there permanently – all poor, all urban, and most abandoned by their families. He suggested that if researchers came to study these patients, they would no doubt find many people who qualify for a diagnosis of autism. But most are called psychotic or mentally retarded, and those conditions are widely seen as permanent and untreatable.

SOMETIMES IN THE PANIC of the 'epidemic' we forget how lucky we are in North America – lucky to have a label that doesn't stigmatise the way it used to. I remember how, in late February 2006, a boy with autism from New York named Jason McElwain who attends a regular high school made national news when he scored seven baskets – six of them three pointers – in four minutes during a basketball game. The headlines read 'Autistic Boy Drops 20 Points'. With the exception of media reports about the Special

Olympics, which is a non-mainstream event, we'd never have seen such a headline even a decade ago. That's not only because a child with autism would have never been able to play in a basketball game, but because the child probably wouldn't have even been able to attend that school. Autism is now set apart from other disorders. Even today, it's unlikely we'd see a headline like 'Schizophrenic Scores 20 Points' or 'Mentally Retarded Boy Scores 20 Points', because those labels continue to isolate and stigmatise.

We're lucky that we are finally getting more accurate prevalence rates, that we have medications and treatments that help people with autism, and that we can now imagine positive and productive futures for them. The children diagnosed with autism throughout the 1980s and 1990s have already grown up and are being treated more humanely than autistic adults were in the past. Some live in institutions, some live in group homes (if they can get into one of the few that exist), some spend their days in sheltered workshops and day programmes, and many live with their parents. But many adults with autism have full-time jobs.

Some high-functioning adults with autism live independently with minimal supervision. For example, a Peruvian man named Julio, at 32, is an assistant to Lily Mayo. He has understood the symptoms of autism since he was a teenager, and he's incredibly bright and perceptive. When terrorists were active in Lima during the 1980s, Lily depended on Julio. Water and electricity were scarce commodities and had to be closely monitored and turned off and on at regular intervals. Julio was in charge because he was the only person obsessive enough to be consistent at the tasks. Because he was treated with respect, he became comfortable with his diagnosis.

In 1986, when Lily went to an international psychiatric congress in Lima, Julio tagged along to help her carry her papers and equipment for her presentation. Before the session on autism began, he told her that there were four other people with autism at the conference. 'Where?' she asked. Julio pointed to a man playing with his hair, another who was nervous and rocking slightly, and two others sitting side by side at the presenter's table, talking to each other but staring straight ahead, and rarely making eye contact. The four were all scientists, there to present their research, but they were, perhaps, also victims of some of the disorders they were trying so hard to understand. Today, Julio works full-time at the centre entering data into computer programs. He never makes a mistake. And he proudly says, 'I am autistic.'

Lily Mayo is convinced that Julio's job lessened the severity of his autism and that his experience is a lesson for us all. Remember what the World Health Organisation found: that the symptoms of people disabled by schizophrenia in rural areas were more benign than those experienced by people with schizophrenia in urban areas because the former could play an important economic and social role, even if it was simply ploughing a field or herding sheep. And Julio's case shows that in order to help people with autism, we don't always need to fully mainstream them, or pretend that they are not different, and we don't need to simply reduce stigma. Rather, we need to provide roles in our communities for people with autism, some of which they may, in fact, be able to perform better than anyone else, just like Julio.

UNFORTUNATELY, ONLY A FEW longitudinal studies have followed children with autism into adulthood. The studies that do exist suggest that only a small number of the people diagnosed with autism during the 1980s, before the criteria broadened to include higher-functioning people, have been able to live independently. Scientists generally agree that the best predictor of autistic children's outcomes in adulthood is the IQ score at the time of diagnosis, but this conclusion is not based on extensive research. In addition, outcomes vary considerably depending on the individual case or on how one defines 'outcome'. Some adults with Asperger's Disorder and high IQs cannot hold a job and are aloof, while some adults, like Julio or the scientists he pointed out, or even those with mental retardation, hold down jobs and have long-term, intimate relationships.

For most of the parents I've interviewed, a good outcome means that their child will be able to live independently without close supervision. But I am not particularly invested in the idea of independence. I want Isabel to have minimal emotional distress, to be able to continue learning as an adult, to know how to advocate for her needs, and to make friends. Even more importantly, my idea of a good outcome for Isabel is that people other than Joyce and me will contribute to her care. I know that it takes more than a village to raise a child; it takes a village *and* comprehensive mental-health care *and* educational policies to raise a child with autism. But no policy or parent can transform society. That is why it is so important to cultivate a stable network of family and friends. I don't want to just find comfortable holding patterns, this school or that institution that will care for her at different stages of her life. In that kind of life, she wouldn't have the opportunity to understand the world – or to get to be a part of it – any more than someone who travelled the globe without ever leaving an airport would be able to understand the countries he's landed in.

Joyce has three sisters who, together, have eight children, and we visit them as often as possible. The youngest of the cousins, Daniel, born in 1998, is Isabel's favourite. She cannot keep up socially or intellectually with the older ones, who, despite being compassionate and loving toward her, inhabit another social universe, the universe of gossip, instant messaging, and long and detailed discussions about fashion, make-up, and TV dramas. So Isabel plays with

Daniel. They talk to each other about the topics appropriate to his age, watch *Sponge Bob Square Pants* together, or play the video games he likes. Of course, we want her to interact with her peers, but more than that we want her to *interact*. It has taken a while, but Joyce and I appreciate the relationships Isabel forges, even if some of them are different from what our society expects. Once, when Isabel started to fight with a boy for the only available swing at a playground, another parent asked me, 'Aren't you going to intervene?' 'No!' I said, emphatically. 'It's social interaction.'

We spend lots of time helping Isabel's little sister learn how to help her, and preparing her for the future. I say 'little sister' because Olivia is two years younger than Isabel, and because there was a time when Olivia was the baby in the family. But Olivia soon caught up with Isabel, and then she developed in ways Isabel couldn't. Olivia surpassed her, playing games that Isabel couldn't play, reading books Isabel couldn't read, and needing more sophisticated social interactions than Isabel could offer. I regret that she didn't get as much attention from us as she wanted, especially at night when Joyce and I were occupied with the demands of taking care of Isabel. By the time she was four, Olivia had already become, in essence, the older sibling, stepping up to help take care of Isabel, speak for her, and anticipate her needs.

Wherever we went – to playgrounds, water parks, beaches, and birthday parties – Olivia would be the one to search out and play with the child on crutches or in a wheelchair. Over the years, Olivia learned how to engage Isabel in play, and this means that Olivia is resourceful enough today, as a teenager, to be a friend to just about anyone of any age or ability. She participates in Junior Olympic diving and is as comfortable with elementary and high-school divers as she is with children her own age. At school, she appears to have no need to belong to a clique and has a reputation as a mediator.

PAUL MCENROE, a 55-year-old award-winning reporter for the *Minneapolis Star-Tribune*, knows what it's like to be a sibling of a person with autism. His brothers – Peter, 52, and David, 49 – both have fragile X syndrome and are mentally retarded, but David has autism as well. Paul remembers that during their childhood in Virginia in the early 1960s, there were few special-education programmes so David stayed at home with his mom, a full time housewife who was dedicated to an intensive and rigorous therapy called 'psychomotor patterning', or the 'Doman-Delacato method', named after its inventors, physical therapist Glenn Doman and psychologist Carl Delacato. 'We had a big massage table,' Paul told me, 'and when they were gangly preteens, Peter or David would be on that table while volunteers, often with me, moved their arms or legs like a child crawling.'

The idea behind the unusual method, never shown to be effective and now rarely used, was that the brains of mentally retarded people had not developed properly along an evolutionary trajectory. Normal brains, Doman and Delacato argued, followed a pattern of growth in childhood that was similar to the growth and development of the species over millions of years. The brains of mentally retarded children hadn't followed that pattern, so you needed to manipulate their limbs to mirror the evolutionary stages, from amphibian, to reptile, to mammal. Their mother also put plastic bags over their mouths and noses for precise periods of time. Peter and David would then breathe only through a straw attached to the front of the bag. The idea behind that exercise was that a lack of oxygen would force the brain's neurons to retrain themselves.

Paul's parents used these and other methods for years without success. There was a steady stream of volunteers from the neighbourhood Catholic church who came to the house to help pattern the boys, from 10 A.M. to 9 P.M., even on weekends and holidays. The complicated schedule for therapies and staffing was detailed on a chart that hung in the kitchen. In the evenings, Paul's friends would often wait outside for him until he finished helping with the patterning for that day. He sometimes felt like an only child. But he didn't question the burden placed on him until he was sixteen. Then, he told his father, 'When I graduate from high school, I'm going to buy a Harley and ride across the country.' His father didn't even have to think about how to respond. He said instantly, 'No you're not. Who would take care of Peter and David if you got killed?'

Paul rebelled against his perceived obligations, got poor grades, was suspended from school for defiant behaviours, and went to college as far away as he could imagine at the time, in Marquette, Michigan. Though his parents, Peter, and David eventually moved to Minnesota, where Paul had settled as a newspaper reporter, Paul lived independent of them for more than twenty years, until 1993. That year, his mother died from lung cancer. In the car on the way to the funeral home, his father turned to him and said, 'Paul, you're taking over now.' Paul knew that day would come, and he willingly became the legal guardian of Peter and David, in charge of everything from providing medical care, clothing, and aide support to arranging field trips to New York, Washington, and elsewhere. 'It's a burden I've now accepted,' he said, 'and I'm everything to Peter and David. They would be devastated if something happened to me.'

But his brothers' dependence on him hasn't kept Paul from pursuing his own dreams of travelling the world and taking risks. By the time he was 53, Paul had worked as a reporter in three war zones. In 2003, he narrowly escaped from two Iraqi soldiers who tried to kill him in the northern Iraqi city of Kirkuk. Of course, it might be just as accurate to say that it was his brothers' dependence on him that stimulated him to travel far away and take risks, as a way of resisting his obligations. Either way, Paul has adapted to his predicament with an ingenious solution, making himself as free as possible without ever shirking his duties. 'This year,' Paul told me, 'I'm buying a Harley and I'm driving across the country.' The only decision left to make is what shade of black he wants.

Peter can live independently because he doesn't have autism, but David lives in an apartment with a counsellor. David can speak, but he mumbles, and he usually talks only about his two loves: genealogies, which he can memorise quickly, and religious rituals. When the family lived for a time in Michigan during the 1980s, David used to listen to the radio broadcasts of the Dutch Reformed Church, and he would set out his mother's best silver and pewter on felt runners on the dining-room table as if it were an altar. So now, as an adult, he talks often about how much he wants to go to Catholic churches, but Paul has never agreed to take him.

One Sunday night, in November 2005, Paul fell back on his bed, exhausted after a difficult week at the newspaper and feeling a bit guilty that he hadn't checked in on David for a while. While channel-surfing, he paused on a rebroadcast of the 10 A.M. liturgy from the St Olaf Catholic Church in Minneapolis. He watched for a few minutes, recalling all the reasons why he didn't like Catholicism, and then he saw David. The camera showed him sitting next to his counsellor, rising to go to the centre aisle, and proceeding forward to take Communion. David was smiling as he bowed to take the wafer and wine. And then he quickly disappeared, blending into the line of people returning to their seats. Paul felt a rush of satisfaction and pride.

A month later, Peter, David, Paul, and his wife and two children sat down to Christmas Eve dinner with more than a dozen extended family members. Paul poured a little wine for David, who stood up, as if to give a toast. He raised his goblet high above his head and in a clear and booming voice, like a priest presiding at Mass, said: 'I am the body.'

Paul laughed. But it was a comforting moment. Paul saw that David was at peace, content with his world. A more religious person might have heard in David's words a deeper truth, that David is more than simply a human body, bounded by his own skin and bones, that he is, in a spiritual sense, the body of all of us, imperfect and suffering but also capable of great joy. I heard a deeper truth, extending across cultures. It was an echo of the voices heard throughout this book: of the Indian women from Open Door who talk about how their children resemble the gods and saints; of Seung-Mee, who takes comfort in her church's conviction that her daughter, Soo-Yong, is more pure than others, and closer to God; of the congregation at the Haven, in rural Maryland, where children with autism are, in fact, worshipped as the body of Christ; and of the ultra-orthodox Jews in Israel, who see a child with autism as a vessel containing the untold words of God.

I KNOW THERE ARE PARENTS who think the sibling of their child with autism should be able to pursue a career and a social life unencumbered and free of the burden they shoulder. In addition to being a particularly modern attitude, this view also suggests that the person with autism is a burden only, rather than an asset. Olivia is the first to acknowledge that she feels true affection for her sister, that she learns from her, and that she enjoys her companionship. In many non-Western countries, siblings are expected to assume such responsibilities in much the same way they assume responsibility for the care of their parents. In fact, the psychologist Tamara Daley found that, in India, numerous parents often choose to have additional children after having a child with autism for the explicit purpose of having someone available to take care of the first child after they die. I believe that Olivia has a responsibility to support her sister to some extent in the future, both emotionally and financially, and I believe she will embrace this responsibility, even if, like Paul McEnroe, she is ambivalent about it.

Olivia is just entering her teenage years, but we already know how much she's gained from her sister. Not long ago, there was a remarkable moment in our house. Olivia went into Isabel's room and sat down next to her with a book. Isabel yelled at her, 'Get out!' Olivia said she wasn't going to leave because she'd come in to read with her. Isabel's voice got even louder. 'Get out!!' She grabbed Olivia's feet and tried, unsuccessfully, to drag her off the bed. When that didn't work, she went to her sister's bedroom and grabbed her prized teddy bear, named Sweetheart, returned to her own room, and then threw it out the door into the hallway, yelling, 'Olivia, fetch!'

Olivia picked up Sweetheart and raced down the stairs to Joyce and me. She was holding her stomach, laughing so hard that it hurt. She said it was the funniest thing she'd ever seen.

If we were a so-called 'normal' family, things might have played out differently. We might have chastised Olivia for provoking Isabel. We might have disciplined Isabel for trying to use physical force, for taking something so precious from her sister, and for denigrating her sister as a dog. In a family with autism, there are different expectations, different meanings, and even different kinds of happiness. Instead, I admired Olivia for seeing humour where others might have seen malice, and I admired Isabel for being capable of such a complicated social skill. Not only did she advocate for herself by communicating with Olivia, but she showed evidence of something children with autism usually don't have: theory of mind. This is the ability to understand someone else's mind, what another person understands, values, and wants. In order to act the way she did, Isabel had to appreciate Olivia's feelings about her bear and foresee the possibility that Olivia would go to the bear if it was in danger. Before that day, I wasn't certain if Isabel was capable of holding a theory of mind. Such moments remind us that the symptoms of autism can change over time and give us hope for Isabel's future as an adult and a contributing member of a human community. They also remind us how important it is to think 'outside the box' and learn how to see the world differently, perhaps even as a person with autism sees it.

This past year, Isabel made her first friend at school, a girl who is in the same educational programme. Her friend is a highly skilled artist, and she taught Isabel how to draw cartoons. She is much more verbal and creative than Isabel, so she narrates stories, and Isabel writes them. They've had sleepovers together, and when they say goodbye they hug and say, 'I'll miss you'. Isabel lets her friend sing, but she'll never let me, Joyce, or Olivia even hum a tune. She'll put her hands over her ears and scream if we try. Isabel will even sing along with her friend, though she'll never sing for anyone else.

Then there's her 'best friend', Janeen. (Who says a best friend has to be your own age?) Janeen and her husband Michael, in their mid-forties and with no children of their own, live in the house next door to us. One day, just after they first moved in, Isabel was walking our dog, Linnea. As Janeen left her house, Isabel started peppering her with questions. 'Is this a dog?' 'Is he brown?' 'Does he have fur?' 'Do dogs have tails?' 'Are they vertebrates or invertebrates?' 'Are their tails not prehensile?' 'Who is their ancestor?' 'Are wolves the dogs' ancestors?' 'Is the scientific name *Canis*?'

Janeen invited Isabel to play with her six cats, and it became a daily event. One day Isabel arrived wearing a cowgirl hat and boots, announcing that she was there to 'wrangle' the cats. When Janeen's eldest cat, BooBear, died one day, Isabel came over with a wand as if she were Harry Potter. She asked, 'Who killed BooBear?' 'Was it he, who must not be named?' 'Can I protect the other felines from he who must not be named?'

Janeen likes Isabel and enjoys having her over to hang around the house, play with the cats, and draw pictures. So she bought an expensive set of coloured pencils for Isabel to use at her house. One of Isabel's first pictures with the new pencils was of BooBear in a spacesuit visiting Saturn, and the other cats, who were still living, each bearing the insignia from the respective houses in which she had placed them at Harry Potter's school of wizardry. Unlike a peer, Janeen doesn't ask much of Isabel. Nonetheless, Isabel provides her with a semblance of loyal friendship. Perhaps Isabel's worth should be measured not only by what she is capable of doing but by what she brings to the lives of others, whether human, vertebrate or invertebrate. 'When BooBear died,' Janeen said, 'Isabel was the only person I could really talk to about his death. My friends just didn't understand how upset I could be about a cat. I can't say that Isabel really shared in my grief, but she gave me a Kleenex to wipe my tears, and she was really mad about him dying. She blamed Voldemort [the evil wizard from Harry Potter] and wanted to kill him. Somehow that made me feel better.'

Olivia, our extended families, and friends and neighbours like Janeen are the foundation of Isabel's existence, and possibly her future. Don't ask Isabel to talk about how important these people are to her. She could only tell you the last thing she's done with them. And don't ask her whether she would miss them if they were gone, because as far as I know, she's not capable of envisioning abandonment. Don't even ask her to give a simple description of Janeen or Olivia. She'd probably tell you that they are mammals, primates, or *Homo sapiens*. But we shouldn't underestimate these relationships just because she cannot convey the kind of feelings *we* want her to have. Without them, Isabel would be lost.

JUST WHEN WE THINK Isabel's development has stalled, she surprises us. Sometimes the surprises are subtle, like the time she suddenly held the door open for someone, or when she first moved aside when she sensed she might be in someone's way. Such behaviour is an example of how she is becoming more attuned to the social world around her. Other surprises are easier to see. Isabel has learned to laugh at some of her compulsions (like the way she repeatedly arranges and rearranges her sheets at night before going to sleep), and she is learning to control them by saying out loud, 'No O.C.D.!' (Obsessive Compulsive Disorder), a phrase Joyce taught her.

As she's gotten older, she's learned to negotiate, to compromise, and to work with us to alleviate some of the symptoms of autism that trouble her. For example, she still hates certain sounds, like a baby crying, the car alarm that tells you your seat belt isn't fastened, or the sound of a bathtub draining. When she hears them, she gets agitated, holds her hands over her ears, and vocalises to block out the sound. She has the same reaction when she hears me clear my throat, or when someone says words associated with bathing, such as 'bath', 'shower', or 'shampoo'. It was hard to see her suffer, and also hard to be with her in public when she made a fuss about a crying baby. Her teachers struggled as well when she had tantrums over the sound of the bell marking the beginning and end of class periods. So we went to Isabel's psychiatrist to ask for medications that might help her. He suggested, instead, that we try a game.

He said, 'Give her one point for every time she can hear those sounds or words without getting agitated, and when she gets 100 points she gets something she wants.' So we explained the game to Isabel and told her that when she got 100 points she could visit the new baby panda bear at the National Zoo. Within just a few hours she was begging me to clear my throat and to say 'bath' and 'shower'. She got her prize, and the game's over. Isabel still hates those sounds, but she no longer reacts defensively. It was a simple example of how effective it can be to use a reward system, but it felt like a miracle.

In January 2006, Isabel and Joyce went on a long walk after school, and Isabel liked it so much she decided to make it a habit. On the second outing, Isabel announced that their walks had a name, 'Consideration, Compliments, and Conversation Time'. They are words Isabel learned from the speech therapist at school, who taught her how to be considerate and wait for lulls in conversation before interrupting. Joyce says that, somehow, Isabel is easier to talk to when she's walking, as if the movement helps her social abilities, like when she was just a toddler and would make better eye contact with me when she was on a swing.

She's learning algebra now, teaching herself to play the piano, rollerblading, skiing, and doing daily tests on the chemical values of our saltwater fish tank. Her knowledge of the animal world is astounding. She gets us credit at a nearby pet store that gives coupons if you can correctly answer trivia questions about obscure aspects of nature. She even stumped a Smithsonian scientist. After a lecture by the curator of mammals at the National Zoo, Isabel asked him, 'Are Malayan tapirs related to horses and rhinos?' He said he didn't think so. I jumped in: 'She doesn't ask questions if she doesn't already know the answer. If you find out anything different, here's my card.' The next day he e-mailed me to say that Isabel was right. And after we bought her an elaborate poster of the earth, depicting hundreds of animals and their habitats, Isabel noticed that the Beluga whale was drawn, incorrectly, with a dorsal fin. 'Beluga whales don't have dorsal fins!' she said contemptuously. She never looked at the poster again.

And if we are concerned about her future, she isn't. Her lifelong goal is to visit every zoo in the world. We've already visited zoos in

San Diego, Columbus, Chicago, Denver, Copenhagen, Barcelona, Verona, and Paris, among others. She looks at zoo websites and memorises the maps of the grounds so that by the time we get there, she'll know exactly where to go. When she grows up, she says, she wants to be a zookeeper, preferably at SeaWorld or the National Zoo.

THERE ARE MANY OTHER CHILDREN in the world like Isabel, in every country on every continent, and with each day they are less strange, less foreign. Community organisations, charities, research foundations, and parent groups are responding quickly to the new visibility of autism. The renovations to Maureen Fanning's group homes have started now, and Merry Barua has moved into the newly built National Centre for Autism in New Delhi. Neighbourhood organisations in South Korea no longer fight to keep children with autism off their streets and out of their schools, and under the direction of just a few tireless mothers and fathers of children with autism, South Africa and Kenya are both renovating their institutions and working to integrate people with autism into their schools.

Maureen Fanning likes to quote the anthropologist Margaret Mead every chance she gets. 'Never doubt that a small group of thoughtful, committed citizens can change the world; indeed, it's the only thing that ever has.'

Acknowledgments

THIS BOOK WAS SUPPORTED by numerous people who are part of my life, either on a personal or a professional level, and I am grateful for the many ways that they helped to make this book a reality.

My wife, Joyce, a partner in everything I do, is the most generous and selfless person I know. When I decided to write a book about autism, she worried about protecting Isabel's privacy, and she was concerned that I would blur the line between our professional and personal lives, that our lives would become consumed by autism and that I might begin to see Isabel more as a condition or a category than as our daughter. But together we worked through each of these challenges because we both believed that Isabel had something to say to the world, even if she couldn't yet represent herself.

In April 2004, when Joyce was diagnosed with breast cancer, our professional lives suddenly came to a halt. For much of the next year, through chemotherapy, immunotherapy, and radiation therapy, neither of us had the focus to read even a newspaper article from start to finish. Despite fear and sickness, Joyce had the strength to encourage me to write. If we left the house to go to chemotherapy or radiation, she made sure I took my books or computer. She urged me to visit other countries, and she even made travel arrangements for me when I procrastinated. To Joyce, I extend my deepest love and gratitude.

Alison Brooks, chair of the Anthropology Department at the George Washington University, where I teach, Bill Frawley, former dean of the Columbian School of Arts and Sciences, and Joel Kuipers of the Anthropology Department at GWU believed that a cross cultural study of autism needed to be written, and had confidence in me. Alison and Bill helped me arrange my teaching and administrative duties so that I would have time to research and write, encouraging me at every step of the way. I offer my heartfelt thanks to them, as well as to Jonathan Higman, our department administrator, and to the George Washington University as a whole. The research on which this book is based was funded entirely by the George Washington University Facilitating Fund, the George Washington University Columbian Fellows Program, and the National Alliance for Autism Research/Autism Speaks.

Paul Brodwin, Lance Clawson, C.T. Gordon, and Michelle Marks read the manuscript in its entirety, and spent hours discussing its strengths and weaknesses with me. At the very early stages of writing, Steve Olson offered invaluable advice about how to construct a book for a general rather than an academic audience.

Dan Pine at the National Institutes of Mental Health, Deborah Blacker at Harvard University, Eric Fombonne at McGill University, and Young-Shin Kim of Yale University gave much needed advice. In addition, I wish to thank my research assistants and proofreaders at GWU and in my field sites: Tong-Geun Chun, Michaela Grillo, Anthony Gualtierri, Rachel Harvey, Catarina Kim, Melissa Kronfeld, Bit Nala Park, Hannah Park, Hae-Min Pyun, and Diana Santillan. I extend my gratitude to my supportive colleagues at GWU: Cheryl Beil, Peter Caws, J. Jeffery Cohen, Alex Dent, Daniel Gutstein, Jonathan Higman, Alf Hiltebeitel, Susan Johnston, Young-Key Kim-Renaud, Jennifer Korjus, Brian Richmond, Robert Shepherd, and Carol Sigelman.

I also wish to thank the large number of parents and professionals whom I interviewed or who gave me articles, books, references, and other information. In some cases, people asked me to use their real names, but often – for example, for Shubhra in India, for the Khumalos in South Africa, and for all the Korean families described in this book – I provided pseudonyms. The list includes all those who follow, listed by continent or country. I apologise if I have omitted anyone.

In North America: David Amaral, Tami Amiri, Thomas Anders, Deborah Baker, the Bakken family, Brian Bonfardin, Leah Brasch, John R. Brown, Emily Campbell, Stella Chess, Kristina Chew, Carol Chung, Patricia Cohen, Jeanne Connors, Tamara Daley, Anne M. Donnellan, Kari Dunn, Tina Dyches, Leon Eisenberg, Maureen Fanning, Uta Frith, Amy Gardner, Morton Ann Gernsbacher, Jude Gillespie, Byron Good, Edie Gordon, Temple Grandin, Lori Grinker, Roy R. Grinker, Jr, Ian Hacking, Tanya Harvey, Jr, Robert Hendren, Margaret Hertzig, Robert Johnston, Susan Johnston, Christy Jones, Gary Kaplan, Lynn Katz, Catherine Kim, Arthur Kleinman, Andrew Lakoff, Rebecca Landa, Bennett Leventhal, Jill Mankowitz, Lisa Matthews, James and Marlene McConnell, James McKenna, Michelle McKinley, Gary McMillan, Mary Michael, Mary and Tony Nelson, Ralph Nicholas, Pam Olek, Terry O'Nell, Marie Pribyl, Judith Rapoport, Steve Rasin, Janeen Reutemann, Don Rosenstein, Mary Rosenstein, Kirsten Sandberg, Sharon Shafer, Theodore Shapiro, Andy Shih, Jane Shore, Chloe Silverman, Marjorie Solomon, Bridget Stokes, Barry Tharp, Ann Turnbull, Fred Volkmar, Joyce West, Anna-Marie Wilmsfloet, Gail Leondar-Wright, Deborah Zarin, and Jun Zhang.

In Croatia: Lidija Penko. *In India*: Action for Autism, Priyam Ahuja, Merry Barua, Shirshendu Charkrabarti, Indu Chaswal, Deepak Gupta, Shubhra Gupta, Lekha Nair, Sonya Philip, Nalin Punt, Amit Sen, Nidhi Singhal, Madhusudan Srinivas, Shubhangi

Vaidya, Anne Varuvakala, and the many mothers who gave me so much time but who did not want their names mentioned. *In Kenya*: Monica Mburu. *In Korea*: Kyung-Jin Cho, Kyung-Soo Chun, Tong-Geun Chun, Michael Hong, Chang-Ju Kim, Dong-Ho Song, Hee-Jeong Yoo, and the many mothers and fathers in Seoul, Jinju, Ilsan, and Sunch'ang County who were so generous but did not want me to publish their names. Much of my work in South Korea was made possible by my close friends, Dong-Ik Lee and Hye-Yeon Kim, who gave me a place to stay, and helped me arrange my schedule. *In Peru*: Liliana Mayo. *In South Africa*: The Vera School, Brown's School, Anna Atkins, Lorna Jacklin, Christine Koudstaal, Suzanne LeClerc, Denbigh Maurer, Aletta Pearce, Elizabeth Peter, Gerhard Pieterse, Paul Pratt, Jill Stacy, Dan Stein, Julie Treloar, and the many parents who talked with me and invited me into their homes, but who chose to remain anonymous. *In Trinidad*: Wayne James and Teresina Sieunarine. *In Venezuela*: Lilia Negron.

Of course, I take full responsibility for all errors.

I could not imagine a better agent than Anne Edelstein, someone who can follow through with great skill on the business side of publishing but who provides the good judgment and constructive criticism that stimulates you to keep writing, and to feel good about it. I also thank my editor at Basic Books, Jo Ann Miller, for helping me clarify the goals of this book, and for providing roadmaps for its completion; and Katherine Streckfus and Carol Smith for superb copyediting and production.

Special thanks go to the many therapists and doctors who have helped Isabel – and our whole family – over the years, and the outstanding teachers, special educators, and aides who have worked with her at the Smithsonian Early Enrichment Center in Washington, DC, and in the Montgomery County, Maryland, schools. I reserve a special appreciation for Isabel's classmates, especially those in the mainstream classes, for recognising her strengths, standing up for her on the few occasions when she was bullied, and helping her feel at home in the chaos of a crowded classroom, cafeteria, or schoolyard.

Finally, I thank my daughter, Olivia, barely a teenager but wise beyond her years, and most of all, Isabel, who is the reason I wrote this book in the first place. One day, when she can read this book, I hope she recognises herself and sees how much she's grown.

Notes

Introduction

page

1   Scientists now report ... Centers for Disease Control 2005, http://www.cdc.gov/ncbddd/autism (accessed 28 November 2005).

8   In the winter of 2005 ... Interview with 'Mamta', 20 January 2005, New Delhi, India.

8   In KwaZulu-Natal ... Interview with 'Golden' and 'Suzanna Khumalo' (pseudonyms), Cape Town, South Africa, 5 July 2003.

9   Just outside Lima ... Interview with Lily Mayo, 5 May 2005, Baltimore.

10 The US Department of Education figures ... Individuals with Disabilities Education Act (IDEA) data. 'Number of Children Served under IDEA by Disability and Age Group', 1994–2003, http://www.ideadata.org/tables27th/ar_aa9.xls (accessed 28 November 2005).

11 In the United Kingdom, the National Autistic Society ... National Autistic Society 2007. Trustees Annual Reports and Accounts. London: National Autistic Society.

12 ... Many autisms ... Robert Hendren, quoted in Seligman 2005, 13.

13 World Health Organisation (WHO) studies ... World Health Organisation 1979.

15 In the United States, white children ... Mandell et al. 2002.

15 The anthropologist Marshall Sahlins ... Sahlins 1976, 20.

16 Autism was first defined ... American Psychiatric Association 1980.

18 In 1993, the state of Maryland ... Maryland State Department of Education/Early Intervention Services Census Data 1994.

19 4,084 children ... Individuals with Disabilities Education Act Data, www.ideadata.org; US Office of Special Education Programs.

21 'Traumatic brain injury' ... Gernsbacher et al. 2005.

CHAPTER ONE

36 He had in his office ... American Psychiatric Association, 1987.

40 Someone I never met ... Grinker, 2000.

CHAPTER TWO

43 American institutions for the insane ... Shorter 1997.

43 By mid-century, more than 500,000 ... Ibid., 33–68; see also Whitaker 2002.

44 Werner Heinz ... Shorter 1997, 17.

45 Leo Kanner was born ... Kanner n.d.; Neumarker 2003; Sanua 1990; Schopler et al. 1981.

46 Kanner did prosper in Berlin ... Leon Eisenberg, 2 June 2005, 'Kanner Lecture', the Johns Hopkins University.

49 He could repeat the poem ... Interview with Leon Eisenberg, 9 June 2005.

49 Blau made grand arguments ... Ibid., and Blau, A. 1943.

50 He destroyed Blau's argument ... Kanner 1945.

50 American Indians ... Adams and Kanner 1926.

51 'Let us try to recall' ... Kanner 1942–1943.

51 In his article 'Autistic Disturbances' ... Kanner 1943.

51 Sigmund Freud ... Freud 1921, 69.

52 He contrasted the 'social' ... Freud 1921.

52 This is uncanny ... Silverman 2004, 238.

52 'I do not believe' ... Kanner 1949, 419.

53 'Since 1938' ... Kanner 1943, 11.

55 'Hyperamnesia' ... Attributed to Theodule Ribot, *Les maladies de la memoire*, by Ian Hacking. Lectures, College de France, http://www. college-de-france.fr (accessed 28 November 2005).

58 In Lima, Peru ... Interview with Lily Mayo, 5 May 2005, Baltimore, Maryland.

61 'Nit-ku-bon' ... Ellenberger 1968.

61 Navajo Indian children ... Connors and Donnellan 1995.

62 Green children ... Jeffrey Jerome Cohen, personal communication. See also Cohen 1996.

63 Brother Juniper ... Frith 1989, 40–3.

63 Majia Nadeson ... Nadesan 2005, 46–9.

63 Victor ... Lane 1977; Shattuck 1994.

63 Kamala and Amala ... Singh and Zingg 1966.

64 Many such creatures ... Bradford and Blume 1992.

65 Down, after whom ... Darold A. Treffert, 'Dr. J. Landon Down and "Developmental" Disorders', Wisconsinmedicalsociety.org/savant/doctordown.cfm (accessed 17 September 2005).

66 Alfred Tredgold's classic ... Tredgold and Soddy 1963.

71 The two psychiatrists never met ... Frith 1991; Asperger 1991 [1944], 37–9; Wing 1991.

73 'Theory of mind' ... Baron-Cohen 1997, 3.

73 As two experts in the field put it ... Rutter and Schopler 1987, 182.

73 Systematising ... Simon Baron-Cohen 2003, 3.

74 Silicon Valley ... Silberman 2001.

74 'The largest sheltered workshop in the world' ... Grandin quoted in Silberman 1001.

CHAPTER THREE

78 One mother recalled ... 'Interview with Maria', Simpson et al. 2002.

79 'Nothing,' she wrote ... Sontag 2001 [1977], 58.

79 'Now twice victimized' ... Scheper-Hughes and Lock 1986, 137–40.

80 This was the situation ... Prefaut 1999.

82 'Got to know their parents' ... Asperger 1991 [1944], 84.

83   Three twin studies ... Bailey et al. 1995; Steffenburg et al. 1989; Folstein and Rutter 1977.

83   Rate increased to 82 per cent ... Folstein and Rutter 1987.

84   As a result of Kanner's observations ... Dunham 1964; Ginsburg 1958.

85   The typical case ... Eisenberg 1957.

87   What psychiatrists did not anticipate ... Constantino and Todd 2003.

90   Sent his son Neil ... Friedman 1999, 208–20.

91   When Freud first visited ...Turkle 1992.

92   American individualsm ... Ibid., 7.

92   Bettelheim wrote ... Bettelheim 1972.

93   Harlow conducted ... Blum 2002.

93   In 1956 the Ford Foundation ... Pollak 1997, 253, 267.

93   Also called them child schizophrenics ... Silverman 2004, 288.

94   Two other books ... Rimland 1964; Park 1967.

96   The only real difference ... McDonnell 1998, 224.

96   Puritans sometimes attached wooden rods ... Mintz 2004, 11–17.

CHAPTER FOUR

100   Many different kinds of bad mothers ... Ladd-Taylor and Umansky 1998.

100   The guru of child guidance ... Mintz 2004, 191.

101   John Watson ... Ibid., 191–2.

101   Breast-feeding ... US Department of Health, Education, and Welfare 1973; Ryan et al. 1991; Fomon 2001.

103   They were joined by Hillary Clinton ... Bruer 1999, 4–5.

103   Kotulak argued ... Kotulak 1996.

103   Remarkably few neuroscientists ... Bruer 1999.

104   Cross-cultural evidence ... Kagan 1975.

105   Judith Rapoport ... see, for example, Gogtny et al. 2004;Thompson et al. 2001.

105   A team of Korean psychiatrists ... Shin et al. 1999.

108 Hwa-byung ... Lim 1983, 105–7.

109 The French initially ... Turkle 1992.

109 'Psychoanalysis threatened' ... Ibid., 32.

111 Eight years earlier ... De Baecque and Toubiana 1999.

113 Among all European countries ... Sanua 1986.

113 The CFTMEA ... Lanzi et al. 1996.

114 French analysts are not concerned ... Oliner 1988, 11; see also Lebovici and Widlöcher 1980.

115 The work of parent advocacy groups ... Chamak and Cohen 2003.

116 American obsession with quick fixes ... Le Monde 2004, 3.

116 And in Argentina ... Lakoff 2006.

CHAPTER FIVE

119 Lightner Witmer ... Cantor 1988, 17.

119 A little boy named Arnold ... Esman 1960.

120 It was a low-prestige ... Lakoff 2000, 157–8.

120 Lauretta Bender ... *Biological Psychiatry* 1987.

120 More than 600 cases ... Bender 1969.

121 Of the thousands of cases ... Interview with Judith Rapoport, National Institute of Mental Health, 11 March 2005.

122 In contrast to children ... Freedman, Kaplan, and Sadock 1972, 640–1.

123 the State of New York asked Chess ... Chess and Stella 1971.

123 One treatment was prefrontal lobotomy ... Freeman and Watts 1950, 436.

124 French scientists ... Pichot 1997.

124 LSD ... Bender et al. 1961; Freedman, Ebin, and Wilson 1962.

125 A hundred such children ... Bender 1947.

125 Child psychiatry's shift ... Kandel 1998.

125 Membership in the American Academy ... Personal communication, Christy Jones, American Academy of Child and Adolescent Psychiatry, 21 September 2005.

127 In several articles ... See Taylor and Green 2001.

129 Schizophrenia, Childhood Type ... American Psychiatric Association 1968.

129 David Rosenhan's account ... Rosenhan 1972.

130 Differences between British and American ... Kendell et al. 1971.

130 Philip Ash, an American psychologist ... Spiegel 2005.

131 'There was little more than a random chance' ... Wilson 1993, 403.

131 Government funding for psychiatric research ... Ibid.

131 In academic conferences ... Ibid.

131 In 1964, he published ... Grinker 1964, 228.

133 Return psychiatry to the pre-Freudian days ... Pichot 1997, 48.

134 Reliably diagnosed 'homosexuality' ... See, for example, Holemon and Winokur 1965.

135 The *DSM-III* would transform mental health ... Kutchins, Herb and Stuart A. Kirk. 1997.

136 'Hysterical psychoses' ... Spiegel 2005.

137 Spitzer's committee wrote ... Wilson 1993, 405.

139 Abnormalities on almost every chromosome ... Veenstra-Vander Weele and Cook 2004.

139 The most plausible genetic model ... Risch et al. 1999; see also Pickles et al. 1995.

139 Geraldine Dawson ... Quoted by Reuters, August 3, 2006; see also Schellenberg et al. 2006.

140 Recent review essay ... Wong and Van Tol 2003.

140 'In some ways ...' ... Ibid., 292.

CHAPTER SIX

141 Two of the leaders ... Cohen and Volkmar 1997, 947.

142 Arthur Kleinman ... Kleinman 1988, 11.

143 The Salish ... O'Nell 1998.

144 African American men ... Whaley 1997; Strakowski et al. 1996.

145 Among the mentally ill ... Whitaker 2002.

145 Navajo Indians ... Connors and Donnellan 1995.

147 In a case that Connors followed closely ... Interview with Jeanne L. Connors, 25 May 2005.

150 'I am incredibly disciplined' ... Interview with Judith Rapoport, National Institute of Mental Health, 11 March 2005.

151 Differences between researchers and clinicians ... Prendergast et al. 1988.

154 According to Margaret Hertzig ... Interview with Margaret Hertzig, Cornell University Medical School, New York, 9 September 2005.

155 'A mother and father' ... Interview with Daniel Pine, MD, National Institute of Health, 7 October 2005.

156 Significantly affected by a host of factors ... Williams et al. 2006.

158 Many psychiatrists were pleased with the *DSM-III* ... Volkmar, Klin, and Cohen 1997.

159 In one study of 194 children ... Waterhouse et al. 1996; see also Rutter and Schopler 1992.

162 There was an error ... Volkmar, Shaffer, and First 1991, 74.

CHAPTER SEVEN

166 On 9 February 2005 ... Speech on the House Floor Concerning Thiomersal and Mercury in Childhood Vaccinations, 9 February 2005, Congressman Dan Burton (IN–5), http://www.house.gov/burton/autism.htm.

166 A recent book on the subject ... Kirby 2005; Kennedy 2005; Olmsted, 'The Age of Autism' (United Press International series, multiple dates beginning 26 January 2005).

166 The passion behind this movement ... Durbach 2005, 204–5.

168 ... relationship between vaccines and autism ... Schecter and Grether, 2008; DeStefano, 2007.

169 0 per cent of two-year-olds ... 'Cases of Mumps Soaring Across UK'. British Broadcasting Corporation, 13 May 2005, http://news.bbc.co.uk/1/hi/health/4539887.stm (accessed 14 January 2006).

169 The British government reported ... 'Notifications of Infectious Diseases Confirmed by Salivary Antibody Detection', Health Protection Agency, Centre for Infections, 1995–2005, http://

www.hpa.org.uk/infections/topics_az/mumps/data_quarter.htm (accessed 12 December 2005).

169 Centers for Disease Control ... http://www.cdc.gov/nip/vacsafe/concerns/autism/autism-mmr.htm#2 (accessed 26 December 2005).

170 Rise in rates of autism after thiomersal was removed ... Fombonne et al. 2006.

170 Methodological quibbles ... Silverman and Hebert 2003, 7.

173 Golden Square, London ... Murphy et al. 1999; Snow 1855.

175 In a third stage ... Lord et al. n.d; Rutter et al. n.d.

176 'Ideas and products' ... Gladwell 2002.

177 Alzheimer's ... National Institute of Mental Health, http://www.ninds.nih.gov/disorders/alzheimersdisease/detail_alzheimersdisease.htm (accessed 26 December 2005).

178 Foetal alcohol syndrome ... Centers for Disease Control, http://www.cdc.gov/ncbddd/factsheets/FAS_monitoring.pdf (accessed 26 December 2005).

178 Showalter ... Showalter 1998.

179 Economic influences at work ... Lakoff 2006.

180 'Illness of Western civilization' ... Lotter 1978; Sanua 1984.

181 English-language epidemiological studies ... Fombonne 2003.

181 Conducted in Australia ... DeMyer et al. 1981.

181 We do not know what the rate ... Tonge and Brereton 1997, 951–3.

184 Multiple informants ... Gould et al. 1981; Shaffer et al. 1996.

185 Three researchers working in northern Finland ... Kielinen et al. 2000.

186 Morton Ann Gernsbacher and colleagues ... Gernsbacher et al. 2005.

186 It's PDD-NOS and Asperger ... Chakrabarti and Fombonne 2005.

186 1 in 100 school-aged children ... Yeargin-Allsopp and Boyle 2002.

187 Mentally retarded or learning disabled dropped in tandem ... Shattuck 2006.

189 Centers for Disease control study in Atlanta ... Yeargin-Allsopp et al. 2003.

190 Anywhere from 1 per cent to 4 per cent ... Filipek et al. 2000; Filipek et al. 1999, 439.

190 Widely accepted *conservative* estimates ... Fombonne 2005.

192 Confirmed the 1 in 166 rate ... Chakrabarti and Fombonne 2005.

195 'The number of persons' ... State of California Department of Developmental Services 1999.

196 Fombonne did the simple maths ... Fombonne 2001.

197 Among seven-year-olds ... Gurney 2003.

197 James Laidler of Portland State ... Laidler 2005; see also Shattuck 2006.

197 One study in Texas ... Palmer et al. 2005.

199 Department of Education officials wrote ... US Department of Education Office of Special Education Programs 1996, http://www.ed.gov/pubs/OSEP96AnlRpt/chap1b.html (accessed 26 December 2005).

199 In the 1992–1993 school year ... Department of Education Annual Reports to the US Congress (Children with a Diagnosis of Autism, Aged 6–21 Served by the Individuals with Disabilities Education Act), US Individuals with Disabilities Education Act Data, http://www.IDEAdata.org/tables/ar_aa2.htm.

199 The Centers for Disease Control estimated ... www.cdc.gov/od/oc/media/transcripts/t060504.

200 Incidence of Melanoma ... Welch, Woloshin, and Schwartz, 2005:481.

CHAPTER EIGHT

206 Diagnose autism in infants ... Maestro et al. 2002; see also Chawarska et al. 2005.

207 Church members tried to exorcise ... 'Autistic Boy's Death at Church Ruled Homicide', CNN.com Law Center, 26 August 2003, http://www.cnn.com/2003/LAW/08/25/autistic.boy.death (accessed 4 January 2006).

207 Most commonly used therapy ... see Cooper et al. 1987.

207 ABA is supposed to help … Lovaas 1987; Macheachin and Lovaas 1993.

207 Debates about ABA … Rogers 1998; Schreibman 2005, 23.

208 Floortime … Greenspan 2006.

210 Smithsonian … www.seec.si.edu (accessed 4 January 2006).

211 Philosophy behind the preschool curriculum … Vygotsky 1986; Gardner 1993.

211 Science of education … Marzano 2004.

214 An emotionally charged scene … Klin et al. 2002; see also Gladwell 2005.

215 She pored over … Conrad 1989.

217 Uta Frith and others … Frith 1989.

222 Mental retardation is defined …Yeargin-Allsopp and Boyle 2002.

222 In unstructured classrooms … Schopler 1987.

222 Leiter … Roid and Miller 1997.

225 Book about Monet … Bjork and Anderson 1985.

227 'Topic elaboration' … Siegel 1998, 67, 270–1.

CHAPTER NINE

231 Portia Iversen and Jon Shestack … Cure Autism Now, www.cureautismnow.org; National Alliance for Autism Research, www.naar.org.

234 Jack Fanning … Interview with Maureen Fanning, 10 November 2005. See also www.angelsforautism.org.

238 Six-year-old Big Boy … Interview with 'Golden and Suzanna Khumalo' (pseudonyms), Cape Town, South Africa, 5 July 2003.

240 Families may also pay … Ngubane 1977.

243 Psychiatric hospitals in South Africa … Emsley 2001.

250 According to UNICEF … http://www.unicef.org/india/children_166.htm (accessed 27 December 2005).

251 Merry is the director … Autism-india.org (accessed 9 January 2006).

CHAPTER TEN

253 'Grandparents routinely' ... Interview with Amit Sen, MD, New Delhi, India, 20 January 2005.

254 A diagnosis of mental retardation ... Daley 2004, 1334.

255 Consider the case ... Interview with 'Rohit' (pseudonym), his family, and psychiatrist, New Delhi, India, 26 January 2005.

256 As a child, he wore girls' clothing ... Dimmitt and van Buitenen 1978, 160–1; O'Flaherty 1973, 5–8, 211–15.

258 There are ascetics ... Obeyesekere 1984.

258 Ultra-orthodox Jews in Israel ... Bilu and Goodman 1997.

259 Among all Hindu communities ... Dube 1955; see also Kakar 1982, Kurtz 1992.

260 Mothers tease their children ... Kurtz 1992, 80–1.

260 'You had your milk' ... Roland 1988.

CHAPTER ELEVEN

269 The writer Susan Sontag ... Sontag 2001 [1977].

270 'Disease' and 'illness' ... Kleinman 1988, 7.

270 Seung-Mee ... Interviews with 'Seung-Mee' (pseudonym), July 3–15, 2003, Seoul, South Korea.

281 Unification ... Grinker 1998.

283 The only study I know of ... Seo 1991.

287 1,500 psychiatrists ... Interviews with Michael Hong, MD, 16 December 2005; Hee-Jeong Yoo, MD, 16 December 2005; and Dong-Ho Song, MD, 17 December 2005, Seoul, South Korea.

287 The term 'inclusion' ... Kwon 2005.

290 'Education fever' ... Seth 2002.

291 Classrooms were standing room only ... Seth 2004.

CHAPTER TWELVE

295 On a winter morning ... Interview, Vera School, Cape Town, South Africa, 6 July 2002.

298 Sung-Hee Kim ... Interview with 'Sung-Hee' and 'Kyung-Soo' (pseudonyms), Suwon, South Korea, 7 July 2003.

CHAPTER THIRTEEN

314 'The parents say directly' ... Interview with Lance Clawson, MD 11 January 2006.

316 The courts tell the parents ... Mandlawitz 2005.

316 In our county ... http://www.montgomerycountymd.gov (accessed 3 May 2005).

316 By a 6–2 vote ... *Schaffer v. Weast*, US Supreme Court Opinion: http://www.mcps.k12.md.us/info/pdf/SupremeCourtOpinion. pdf (accessed 29 December 2005).

318 Kari Dunn ... Interview with Kari Dunn, 3 May 2005.

319 An effort to normalize him ... Molloy and Vasil 2002.

321 More supportive to autistic children ... Ochs et al. 2001.

321 Inclusion of children with autism ... Ibid.

328 Perfect pitch ... Baharloo et al. 2000.

329 Music is a special interest ... Heaton 2003.

329 One group of researchers from Brown and Tufts ... Brown 2003.

CHAPTER FOURTEEN

333 Grandin once told me ... Grandin 1996, 2–4; 9–10.

336 This is a pattern ... Faris and Dunham 1939.

348 Extending across cultures ... Warner 1985.

References

Adams, G.S., and Leo Kanner. 1926. 'General Paralysis among the North American Indians: A Contribution to Racial Psychiatry'. *American Journal of Psychiatry* 83 (1): 125–33.

American Psychiatric Association. 1968. *Diagnostic and Statistical Manual of Mental Disorders*, 2d ed. Washington, DC: American Psychiatric Association.

———. 1980. *Diagnostic and Statistical Manual of Mental Disorders*, 3rd ed. Washington, DC: American Psychiatric Association.

———. 1987. *Diagnostic and Statistical Manual of Mental Disorders*, 3rd ed., rev. Washington, DC: American Psychiatric Association.

———. 1994. *Diagnostic and Statistical Manual of Mental Disorders*, 4th ed. Washington, DC: American Psychiatric Association.

———. 2000. *Diagnostic and Statistical Manual of Mental Disorders*, 4th ed., rev. Washington, DC: American Psychiatric Association.

Asperger, Hans. 1991 [1944]. '"Autistic Psychopathy" in Childhood'. Trans. Uta Frith. Pp. 37–92 in Uta Frith, *Autism and Asperger Syndrome*. Cambridge: Cambridge University Press.

Baharloo, S., P.A. Johnson, S.K. Service, J. Gitschier, and N.B. Freimer. 2000. 'Absolute Pitch: An Approach for Identification of Genetic and Non-Genetic Components'. *American Journal of Human Genetics* 62: 224–31.

Bailey, A., A. LeCouteur, I. Gottesman, P. Bolton, E. Simonoff, E. Yuzdr, and M. Rutter. 1995. 'Autism as a Strongly Genetic Disorder: Evidence from a British Twin Study'. *Psychological Medicine* 25 (1): 53–77.

Baird, G. et al. 2007. 'Measles Vaccination and Antibody Response in Autism Spectrum Disorders'. *Archives of Diseases in Childhood*. doi: 10.1136/adc.2007.122937.

Baron-Cohen, Simon. 1997. *Mindblindness: An Essay on Autism and Theory of Mind*. Cambridge, Mass.: M.I.T. Press.

_____. 2000. 'Theory of Mind and Autism: A Fifteen Year View'. Pp. 3–20 in Simon Baron-Cohen, ed., *Understanding Other Minds: Perspectives from Developmental Cognitive Neuroscience*. Oxford: Oxford University Press.

_____. 2003. *The Essential Difference: The Truth about the Male and Female Brain*. New York: Basic Books.

Barrett, Louise, Robin Dunbar, and John Lycett. 2002. *Human Evolutionary Psychology*. Princeton, NJ: Princeton University Press.

Bender, Lauretta. 1947. 'One Hundred Cases of Childhood Schizophrenia Treated with Electric Shock'. *Transactions of the American Neurological Association,* 72: 165–9.

_____. 1969. 'A Longitudinal Study of Schizophrenic Children with Autism'. *Hospital and Community Psychiatry* 20 (8): 230–7.

Bender, Lauretta, Lothar Goldschmidt, and D.V. Siva Sankar. 1961. 'Treatment of Autistic Schizophrenic Children with LSD–25 and UML–491'. *Recent Advances in Biological Psychiatry* 4: 170–9.

Bettelheim, Bruno. 1972. *The Empty Fortress: Infantile Autism and the Birth of the Self*. New York: Free Press.

Bilu, Yoram, and Yehuda C. Goodman. 1997. 'What Does the Soul Say? Metaphysical Uses of Facilitated Communication in the Jewish Ultraorthodox Community'. *Ethos* 25 (4): 375–407.

Biological Psychiatry. 1987. 'Lauretta Bender, 1899–1987. In Memoriam'. *Biological Psychiatry* 22: 1040–2.

Bjork, Christina, and Lena Anderson. 1985. *Linnea in Monet's Garden*. Stockholm: R&S Books.

Blau, A. 1943. 'A Philological Note on a Defect in Sex Organ Nomenclature'. *Psychoanalytic Quarterly*, 12: 481–5.

Blum, Deborah. 2002. *Love at Goon Park: Harry Harlow and the Science of Affection*. New York: Perseus.

Bradford, P.V., and H. Blume. 1992. *Ota Benga: Pygmy in a Zoo*. New York: St. Martin's Press.

Brown, Walter A., Karen Commuso, Henry Sachs, Brian Winklasky, Julie Mullane, Raphael Bernier, Sarah Svenson, Deborah Arin, Beth Rosen-Sheindley, and Susan Folstein. 2003. 'Autism Related Language, Personality, and Cognition in People with Absolute Pitch'. *Journal of Autism and Developmental Disorders* 33 (2): 163–7.

Bruer, John T. 1999. *The Myth of the First Three Years: A New Understanding of Early Brain Development and Lifelong Learning*. New York: Free Press.

Cantor, Sheila. 1988. *Childhood Schizophrenia*. New York: Guilford.

Castaneda. Claudia. 2002. *Figurations: Child, Bodies, Worlds*. Durham: Duke University Press.

Chakrabarti, Suniti, and Eric Fombonne. 2005. 'Pervasive Developmental Disorders in Preschool Children: Confirmation of Higher Prevalence'. *American Journal of Psychiatry* 162 (6): 1133–41.

Chamak, Brigitte, and David Cohen. 2003. 'L'autisme: Vers une nécessaire revolution culturelle'. *Medecine/Sciences* 19: 1152–9.

Chawarska, Katarzyna, and Fred R. Volkmar. 2005. 'Autism in Infancy and Early Childhood'. Pp. 223–46 in Fred Volkmar et al., eds., *Handbook of Autism and Pervasive Developmental Disorders*, 3rd ed. New York: John Wiley.

Chess, Stella. 1971. 'Autism in Children with Congenital Rubella'. *Journal of Autism and Childhood Schizophrenia*, 1 (1): 33–47.

Cohen, Donald J., and Fred R. Volkmar. 1997. 'Conceptualizations of Autism and Intervention Practices: International Perspectives'. Pp. 947–50 in Donald J. Cohen and Fred R. Volkmar, eds., *Handbook of Autism and Pervasive Developmental Disorders*, 2nd ed. New York: John Wiley and Sons.

Cohen, J.J. 1996. *Monster Theory: Reading Culture*. Minneapolis: University of Minnesota Press. Connors, Jeanne L., and Anne M. Donnellan. 1995. 'Walk in Beauty: Western Perspectives on Disability and Navajo Family/Cultural Resilience'. Pp. 159–82 in H. McCubbin, E. Thomson, A. Thompspon, and J. Fromer, eds., *Resiliency in Ethnic Minority Families: Native and Immigrant American Families*, vol. 1. New York: Sage.

Conrad, Pam. Illustrated by Richard Egielski. 1989. *The Tub People*. New York: Harper Trophy.

Constantino, John N., and Richard D. Todd. 2003. 'Autistic Traits in the General Population: A Twin Study'. *Archives of General Psychiatry* 60 (May): 524–53.

Cooper, John O., Timothy E. Heron, and William L. Heward. 1987. *Applied Behavioral Analysis*. Upper Saddle River, NJ: Prentice-Hall.

Daley, Tamara. 2004. 'From Symptom Recognition to Diagnosis: Children with Autism in Urban India'. *Social Science and Medicine* 58: 1323–35.

De Baecque, Antoine, and Serge Toubiana. 1999. *Truffaut*. Catherine Temeson, trans. New York: Knopf.

DeMyer, M.K., J.N. Hington, and R.K. Jackson. 1981. 'Infantile Autism Reviewed: A Decade of Research'. *Schizophrenia Bulletin* 7: 388–451.

DeStefano, F. 2007. 'Vaccines and Autism: Evidence does not Support Causal Association'. *Clinical Pharmacology and Therapeutics*, 82 (6): 756–9.

Dimmitt, Cornelia, and A.B. van Buitenen, eds. and trans. 1978. *Classical Hindu Mythology: A Reader in the Sanskrit Puranas*. Philadelphia: Temple University Press.

Dube, S.C. 1955. *Indian Village*. London: Routledge and Kegan Paul.

Dunham, Warren H. 1964. 'Social Class and Schizophrenia'. *American Journal of Orthopsychiatry* 34 (July): 634–42.

Durbach, Nadja. 2005. *Bodily Matters: The Anti-Vaccination Movement in England, 1853–1907*. Durham, NC: Duke University Press.

Eisenberg, Leon. 1957. 'The Fathers of Autistic Children'. *American Journal of Orthopsychiatry* 27 (October): 715–24.

Ellenberger, H.F. 1968. 'Psychiatric Impressions from a Trip to Dakar'. *Canadian Psychiatric Association Journal* 13: 539–45.

Emsley, Robin. 2001. 'Focus on Psychiatry in South Africa'. *British Journal of Psychiatry* 178 (April): 382–6.

Esman, Aaron H. 1960. 'Childhood Psychosis and "Childhood Schizophrenia"'. *American Journal of Orthopsychiatry* 30: 391–6.

Faris, Robert E.L., and H. Warren Dunham. 1939. *Mental Disorders in Urban Areas: An Ecological Study of Schizophrenia and Other Psychoses.* New York: Hafner.

Filipek P.A., P.J. Arcado, S. Ashwal, G.T. Baranek, E.H. Cook, Jr, G. Dawson, B. Gordon, et al. 1999. 'The Screening and Diagnosis of Autistic Spectrum Disorders'. *Journal of Autism and Developmental Disorders* 29 (2): 439–84.

Filipek P.A., P.J. Arcado, S. Ashwal, G.T. Baranek, E. H. Cook, Jr, G. Dawson, B. Gordon, et al. 2000. 'Report of the Quality Standards Subcommittee of the American Academy of Neurology and the Child Neurology Society: Practice Parameter, Screening and Diagnosis of Autism'. *Neurology* 55: 468–79.

Folstein S., and M. Rutter. 1977. 'Infantile Autism: A Genetic Study of 21 Twin Pairs'. *Journal of Child Psychology and Psychiatry* 18 (4): 297–321.

————. 1987. 'Autism: Familial Aggregation and Genetic Implications'. *Journal of Autism and Developmental Disorders* 18: 3–29.

Folstein, Susan, and Susan L. Santangelo. 2000. 'Does Asperger Syndrome Aggregate in Families?' Pp. 159–71 in Ami Klin, Fred R. Volkmar, and Sara S. Sparrow, eds., *Asperger Syndrome.* New York: Guilford.

Fombonne, Eric. 2001. 'Is There an Epidemic of Autism?' *Pediatrics* 107 (2): 111–12.

————. 2003. 'Epidemiological Surveys of Autism and Other Pervasive Developmental Disorders: An Update'. *Journal of Autism and Developmental Disorders* 33 (4): 365–82.

————. 2005. 'The Changing Epidemiology of Autism'. *Journal of Applied Research in Intellectual Disabilities* 18 (4): 281–94.

Fombonne, Eric, Rita Zakarian, Andrew Bennett, Linyan Meng, and Diane Mclean-Heywood. 2006. 'Pervasive Developmental Disorders in Montreal, Quebec, Canada: Prevalence and Links with Immunizations'. *Pediatrics,* 188: 139–50.

Fomon, Samuel J. 2001. 'Infant Feeding in the 20th Century'. *Journal of Nutrition* 131 (supplement): 409–20.

Freud, Sigmund. 1921. *Group Psychology and the Analysis of the Ego.* Standard Edition. 18, 67–143. New York: Norton.

_____. 1921. 'Introduction to J. Varendonck's The Psychology of Day-Dreams'. Standard Edition, 18: 271. James Strachey, ed. London: Hogarth.

Freedman, Alfred M., Eva V. Ebin, and Ethel A. Wilson. 1962. 'Autistic Schizophrenic Children'. *Archives of General Psychiatry* 6: 35–45.

Freedman, Alfred M., Harold I. Kaplan, and Benjamin J. Sadock. 1972. *Modern Synopsis of Comprehensive Textbook of Psychiatry*. New York: Williams and Wilkins.

Freeman, Walter, and James Watts. 1950. *Psychosurgery in the Treatment of Mental Disorders and Intractable Pain*. Springfield, Ill.: Charles C. Thomas.

Friedman, Lawrence J. 1999. *Identity's Architect: A Biography of Erik H. Erikson*. New York: Scribner.

Frith, Uta. 1989. *Autism: Explaining the Enigma*. Oxford: Blackwell.

Frith, Uta, ed. 1991. *Autism and Asperger Syndrome*. Cambridge: Cambridge University Press.

Gardner, Howard. 1993. *Frames of Mind: The Theory of Multiple Intelligences*. New York: Basic Books.

Gernsbacher, Morton Ann, Michelle Dawson, and H. Hill Goldsmith. 2005. 'Three Reasons Not to Believe in an Autism Epidemic'. *Current Directions in Psychological Science* 14 (2): 55–8.

Ginsburg, Sol W. 1958. 'Social Class and Mental Illness: A Community Study'. Pp. 192–201 in August Hollingshead and Frederick C. Redlich, *Social Class and Mental Illness: A Community Study*. New York: John Wiley and Sons.

Gladwell, Malcolm. 2002. *The Tipping Point: How Little Things Can Make a Big Difference*. New York: Back Bay Books.

_____. 2005. *Blink: The Power of Thinking Without Thinking*. New York: Little, Brown.

Gogtay, N., A. Sporn, L. Clasen, T. Nugent III, D. Greenstein, R. Nicolson, J. Giedd, M. Lenane, P. Gochman, A. Evans, and J.L. Rapoport. 2004. 'Comparison of Progressive Cortical Gray Matter Loss in Childhood-Onset Schizophrenia with that in Childhood-Onset Atypical Psychoses', *Archives of General Psychiatry* 61: 17–22.

Gould, M.S., R. Wunsch–Hitzig, and B. Dohrenwend. 1981. 'Estimating the Prevalence of Childhood Psychopathology: A Critical Review'. *Journal of the American Academy of Child and Adolescent Psychiatry* 20: 462–75.

Grandin, Temple. 1996. *Thinking in Pictures: And Other Reports from My Life with Autism.* New York: Vintage.

Greenspan, Stanley. 2006. *Engaging Autism: Helping Children Relate, Communicate and Think with the DIR Floortime Approach.* New York: Da Capo Press.

Grinker, Roy R., Sr. 1964. 'Psychiatry Rides Madly in All Directions'. *Archives of General Psychiatry* 10: 228.

Grinker, Roy Richard. 1998. *Korea and Its Futures: Unification and the Unfinished War.* New York: St. Martin's Press.

————. 2000. *In the Arms of Africa: The Life of Colin M. Turnbull.* New York: St. Martin's Press. Gurney, James. 2003. 'Analysis of Prevalence Trends of Autism Spectrum Disorder in Minnesota'. *Archives of Pediatrics and Adolescent Medicine* 157 (7): 622–7.

Heaton, Pamela. 2003. 'Pitch Memory, Labelling and Disembedding in Autism'. *Journal of Child Psychology and Psychiatry* 44 (4): 543–51.

Holemon, R. Eugene, and George Winokur. 1965. 'Effeminate Homosexuality: A Disease of Childhood'. *Journal of Orthopsychiatry* 35 (January): 48–56.

Kagan, Jerome. 1975. 'Resilience in Cognitive Development'. *Ethos* 3 (2): 231–47.

Kakar, Sudhir. 1982. *The Inner World: A Psycho-Analytic Study of Childhood and Society in India.* Oxford: Oxford University Press.

Kandel, Eric. 1998. 'A New Intellectual Framework for Psychiatry'. *American Journal of Psychiatry* 155 (4): 457–66.

Kanner, Leo. 1942–1943. 'The Exoneration of the Feebleminded'. *American Journal of Psychiatry* 99: 17–22.

————. 1943. 'Autistic Disturbances of Affective Contact'. *Nervous Child* 2: 217–50.

————. 1945. 'A Philological Note on Sex Organ Nomenclature'. *Psychoanalytic Quarterly* 14: 228–33.

_____. 1949. 'Problems of Nosology and Psychodynamics of Early Infantile Autism'. *American Journal of Orthopsychiatry* 19: 416–26.

_____. N.d. 'Freedom from Within'. Unpublished autobiography, American Psychiatric Association library, Arlington, VA.

Kendell, R.E., J.E. Cooper, A.J. Gourlay, J.R. Copeland, L. Sharpe, and B.J. Gurland. 1971. 'Diagnostic Criteria of American and British Psychiatrists'. *Archives of General Psychiatry* 25: 123–30.

Kennedy, Robert F., Jr. 2005. 'Deadly Immunity'. Salon.com, 16 June.

_____ 'Deadly Immunity'. *Rolling Stone*, 30 June 2005. Issue 977/978: 57–66.

Kielinen, S.L., Linna Moilanen, and I. Moilanen. 2000. 'Autism in Northern Finland'. *European Child and Adolescent Psychiatry* 9: 162–7.

Kirby, David. 2005. *Evidence of Harm*. New York: St. Martin's Press.

Kleinman, Arthur. 1988. *Rethinking Psychiatry: From Cultural Category to Personal Experience*. New York: Free Press.

Klin, Ami, Warren Jones, Robert Schultz, Fred Volkmar, and Donald Cohen. 2002. 'Visual Fixation Patterns During Viewing of Naturalistic Social Situations as Predictors of Social Competence in Individuals with Autism'. *Archives of General Psychiatry* 59 (September): 809–16.

Kotulak, R. 1996. *Inside the Brain: Revolutionary Discoveries of How the Mind Works*. Kansas City, Mo.: Andrew McMeel.

Kurtz, Stanley. 1992. *All the Mothers Are One: Hindu India and the Cultural Reshaping of Psychoanalysis*. New York: Columbia University Press.

Kutchins, Herb and Stuart A. Kirk. 1997. *Making Us Crazy: DSM: The Psychiatric Bible and the Creation of Mental Disorders*. New York: The Free Press.

Kwon, Hyunsoo. 2005. 'Inclusion in South Korea: The Current Situation and Future Directions'. *International Journal of Disability, Development and Education* 52 (1): 61–70.

Ladd-Taylor, Molly, and Lauri Umansky, eds. 1998. *'Bad' Mothers: The Politics of Blame in Twentieth Century America*. New York: New York University Press.

Laidler, James R. 2005. 'US Department of Education Data on "Autism" Are Not Reliable for Tracking Autism Prevalence'. *Pediatrics* 116 (1): 120–4.

Lakoff, Andrew. 2000. 'Adaptive Will: The Evolution of Attention Deficit Disorder'. *Journal of the History of the Behavioral Sciences* 36 (2): 149–69.

———. 2006. *Pharmaceutical Reason: Knowledge and Value in Global Psychiatry*. Cambridge: Cambridge University Press.

Lane, Harlan. 1977. *The Wild Boy of Aveyron*. Cambridge: Harvard University Press.

Lanzi, G., et al. 1996. 'A Comparison Between Diagnostic Classificatory Systems for Pervasive Developmental Disorders: A Study of 20 Cases'. Paper presented at the 5th Congress, Autism-Europe. Barcelona, Spain.

Le Monde. 2004. 'Le Gouvernement face au défi de la prise en charge de l'autisme'. *Le Monde,* 24 November 2004, 3.

Lebovici, Serge, and Daniel Widlöcher, eds. 1980. *Psychoanalysis in France*. New York: International Universities Press.

Lim, K. 1983. 'Hwa-Byung: A Korean Culture-Bound Syndrome?' *American Journal of Psychiatry* 140: 105–7.

Lord, Catherine, Michael Rutter, Pamela C. DiLavore, and Susan Risi. N.d. *Autism Diagnostic Observation Schedule (ADOS)*. Los Angeles: Western Psychological Services.

Lotter, V. 1978. 'Childhood Autism in Africa'. *Journal of Child Psychology and Psychiatry* 19 (3): 231–44.

Lovaas, O.I. 1987. 'Behavioral Treatment and Normal Educational and Intellectual Functioning in Young Autistic Children'. *Journal of Consulting and Clinical Psychology* 55: 3–9.

Macheachin, J.J., T. Smith, and O.I. Lovaas. 1993. 'Long-Term Outcome for Children with Autism Who Received Early Intensive Behavioral Treatment'. *American Journal of Mental Retardation* 97: 359–72.

Maestro, S., F. Muratori, M.C. Cavallero, F. Pei, D. Stern, B. Golse, F. Palacio-Espasa. 2002. 'Attentional Skills During the First 6 Months of

Age in Autism Spectrum Disorder'. *Journal of the American Academy of Child and Adolescent Psychiatry* 41 (10): 1239–45.

Mandell, David S., John Listerud, Susan E. Levy, and Jennifer A. Pinto-Martin. 2002. 'Race Differences in the Age at Diagnosis Among Medicaid-Eligible Children with Autism'. *Journal of the American Academy of Child andAdolescent Psychiatry* 41 (12): 1447–53.

Mandlawitz, Myrna. 2005. 'Educating Children with Autism: Current Legal Issues'. Pp. 289–300 in Fred R.Volkmar, et al., eds., *Handbook of Autism and Pervasive Developmental Disorders,* 3rd ed. New York: John Wiley.

Marzano, Robert J. 2004. *Building Background Knowledge for Academic Achievement.* Alexandria, Va.: Association for Supervision and Curriculum Development.

McDonnell, Jane Taylor. 1998. 'On Being the "Bad" Mother of an Autistic Child'. Pp. 220–9 in Molly Ladd-Taylor and Lauri Umansky, eds., *'Bad' Mothers: The Politics of Blame in Twentieth Century America.* New York: New York University Press.

Mintz, Stephen. 2004. *Huck's Raft: A History of American Childhood.* Cambridge: Belknap.

Molloy, Harvey, and Latika Vasil. 2002. 'The Social Construction of Asperger Syndrome: The Pathologizing of Difference?' *Disability and Society* 17: 659–69.

Murphy, Jane M., Mauricio Tohen, and Ming T.Tsuang. 1999. 'Psychiatric Epidemiology'. Pp. 752–77 in Armand M. Nicholi, ed., *The Harvard Guide to Psychiatry.* Cambridge, Mass.: Belknap.

Nadeson, Majia Holmer. 2005. *Constructing Autism: Unraveling the 'Truth' and Understanding the Social.* London: Routledge.

Neumarker, Klaus-Jurgen. 2003. 'Leo Kanner: His Years in Berlin, 1906–24: The Roots of Autistic Disorder'. *History of Psychiatry* 14 (2): 205–48.

Ngubane, Harriet. 1977. *Body and Mind in Zulu Medicine.* London: Academic Press.

Obeyesekere, Gananath. 1984. *Medusa's Hair: An Essay on Personal Symbols and Religious Experience.* Chicago: University of Chicago Press.

Ochs, Elinor, Tamar Kremer-Sadlik, Olga Solomon, and Karen Gainer Sirota. 2001. 'Inclusion as Social Practices: Views of Children with Autism'. *Social Development* 10 (3): 399–418.

O'Flaherty, Wendy D. 1973. *Asceticism and Eroticism in the Mythology of Siva*. London: Oxford University Press.

Oliner, Marion Michel. 1988. *Cultivating Freud's Garden in France*. Northvale, NJ: Jason Aronson.

O'Nell, Theresa Deleane. 1998. *Disciplined Hearts: Hearts, Identity and Depression in an American Indian Community*. Berkeley: University of California Press.

Palmer, R.F., S. Blanchard, C.R. Jean, and D. Mandell. 2005. 'School District Resources and Identification of Children with Autistic Disorder'. *American Journal of Public Health* 95: 125–30.

Park, Clara Clairborne. 1967. *The Siege: A Family's Journey into the World of an Autistic Child*. Boston: Little, Brown.

Peacock, Geraldine, and Hugh Morgan. 1996. *Adults with Autism: A Guide to Theory and Practice*. Cambridge: Cambridge University Press.

Phillips, Helen. 2005. 'Families Share Traits of Autistic Children'. *New Scientist,* 24 November, no. 252: 14.

Pichot, Pierre. 1997. 'DSM-III and Its Reception: A European View'. *American Journal of Psychiatry* 154 (6): 47–54.

Pickles, A., P. Bolton, H. Macdonald, A. Bailey, A. LeCouteur, C.H. Sim, and M. Rutter. 1995. 'Latent-Class Analysis of Recurrence Risks for Complex Phenotypes with Selection and Measurement Error: A Twin and Family History Study of Autism'. *American Journal of Human Genetics* 57 (3): 717–26.

Pollak, Richard. 1997. *The Creation of Dr. B.: A Biography of Bruno Bettelheim*. New York: Simon and Schuster.

Prefaut, Jeanne-Marie. 1999. *Maman, Pas Hopital!* Paris: Robert Laffont.

Prendergast, M., E. Taylor, J.L. Rapoport, J. Bartko, M. Donnelly, A. Zametkin, A.B. Ahearn, G. Dunn, and H.M. Wiselberg. 1988. 'The Diagnosis of Childhood Hyperactivity: A U.S.–U.K. Cross-National Study of DSM-III and ICD-9'. *Journal of Child Psychology and Psychiatry* 29 (3): 289–300.

Rimland, Bernard. 1964. *Autism: The Syndrome and Its Implications for a Neural Theory of Behavior.* Upper Saddle River, NJ: Prentice-Hall.

Rimland, Bernard, and Deborah Fein. 1988. 'Special Talents of Autistic Savants'. Pp. 474–92 in Loraine Obler and Deborah Fein, eds., *The Exceptional Brain.* New York: Guilford.

Risch, N., D. Spiker, L. Lotspeich, N. Nouri, D. Hinds, J. Hallmeyer, L. Kalaydjiova, et al. 1999. 'A Genome Screen of Autism: Evidence for a Multilocus Etiology'. *American Journal of Human Genetics* 65 (2): 493–507.

Rogers, S.J. 1998. 'Empirically Supported Comprehensive Treatments for Young Children with Autism'. *Journal of Clinical Child Psychology* 27: 168–79.

Roid, Gale H., and Lucy J. Miller. 1997. *Leiter International Performance Scale-Revised.* Lutz, Fla.: Psychological Assessment Resources.

Roland, Alan. 1988. *In Search of Self in India and Japan: Toward a Cross-Cultural Psychology.* Princeton, NJ: Princeton University Press.

Rosenhan, D.L. 1972. 'On Being Sane in Insane Places'. *Science* 179: 250–58.

Rutter, Michael, Ann LeCouteur, and Catherine Lord. n.d. *Autism Diagnostic Interview, Revised (ADI-R).* Los Angeles: Western Psychological Services.

Rutter, M., and E. Schopler. 1987. 'Autism and Pervasive Developmental Disorders: Concepts and Diagnostic Issues'. *Journal of Autism and Developmental Disorders* 17: 159–86.

_____. 1992. 'Classification of Pervasive Developmental Disorders: Some Concepts and Practical Considerations'. *Journal of Autism and Developmental Disorders* 22 (4): 459–82.

Ryan, A.S., W.F. Pratt, J.L. Wysong, G. Lewandowski, J.W. McNally, and F.W. Krieger. 1991. 'A Comparison of Breast-Feeding Data from the National Surveys of Family Growth and the Ross Laboratories Mothers Surveys'. *American Journal of Public Health* 81: 1049–52.

Sahlins, Marshall. 1976. *Culture and Practical Reason.* Chicago: University of Chicago Press.

Sanua, Victor D. 1984. 'Is Infantile Autism a Universal Phenomenon? An Open Question'. *International Journal of Social Psychiatry* 30 (3): 163–77.

_____. 1986. 'A Comparative Study of Opinions of U.S.A. and European Professionals on the Etiology of Infantile Autism'. *International Journal of Social Psychiatry* 32 (2): 16–30.

_____. 1990. 'Leo Kanner (1894–1981): The Man and the Scientist'. *Child Psychiatry and Human Development* 21: 3–23.

Schecter, R. and J.K. Grether. 2008. 'Continuing increases in autism reported to California's developmental services system: mercury in retrograde'. *Archives of General Psychiatry*, 65 (1): 19–24.

Schellenberg, G.D.G. Dawson, Y.J. Sung, A. Estes, J. Munson, E. Rosenthal, J. Rothstein et al. 2006. 'Evidence for Multiple Loci from a Genome Scan of Autism Kindreds'. *Molecular Psychiatry*, August 1: 1–12.

Scheper-Hughes, Nancy, and Margaret Lock. 1986. 'Speaking Truth to Illness: Metaphors, Reification, and a Pedagogy for Patients'. *Medical Anthropology Quarterly* 17 (5): 137–40.

Schopler, Eric. 1987. 'Specific and Nonspecific Factors in the Effectiveness of a Treatment System'. *American Psychologist* 42 (4): 376–83.

Schopler, Eric, Stella Chess, and Leon Eisenberg. 1981. 'Our Memorial to Leo Kanner'. *Journal of Autism and Developmental Disorders* 11: 257–69.

Schreibman, Laura. 2005. *The Science and Fiction of Autism*. Cambridge: Harvard University Press.

Seligman, Katherine. 'Chronicles in Autism: A Boy Recovers'. *San Francisco Chronicle*, 13 November 2005, p. 11.

Seo, Gyeong-Hee. 1991. 'Cross-Cultural Study of Autism in South Korea and the United States'. PhD dissertation. University of Texas, Austin.

Seth, Michael J. 2002. *Education Fever: Society, Politics, and the Pursuit of Schooling in South Korea*. Honolulu: University of Hawaii Press.

_____. 2004. 'Korean Education: A Philosophical and Historical Perspective'. Paper presented at the 11th Hahn Moo Sook Colloquium, 23 October 2004, George Washington University, Washington, DC.

Shaffer, David, Prudence Fisher, Mina K. Dulcan, Mark Davies, John Piacentini, Mary Schwab-Stone, Benjamin Lahey, et al. 1996.

'The NIMH Diagnostic Interview Schedule for Children, Version 2.3 (DISC–2.3) Description, Acceptance, Prevalence Rates, and Performance in the MECA Study'. *Journal of the American Academy of Child and Adolescent Psychiatry* 35 (7): 865–77.

Shattuck, Paul. 2006. 'The Contribution of Diagnostic Substitution to the Growing Administrative Prevalence of Autism in U.S. Special Education'. *Pediatrics* 117 (4): 1028–37.

Shattuck, Roger. 1994. *The Forbidden Experiment: The Story of the Wild Boy of Aveyron*. New York: Kodansha Globe.

Shin Yee-Jin, Kyung-Sook Lee, Sung-Kil Min, and Robert N. Emde. 1999. 'A Korean Syndrome of Attachment Disturbance Mimicking Symptoms of Pervasive Developmental Disorder'. *Infant Mental Health Journal* 20 (1): 60–76.

Shorter, Edward. 1997. *A History of Psychiatry: From the Era of the Asylum to the Age of Prozac*. New York: John Wiley.

Showalter, Elaine. 1998. *Hystories: Hysterical Epidemics and Modern Media*. New York: Columbia University Press.

Siegel, Bryna. 1998. *The World of the Autistic Child: Understanding and Treating Autistic Spectrum Disorders*. Oxford: Oxford University Press.

Silberman, Steve. 2001. 'The Geek Syndrome'. *Wired Magazine*, December.

Silverman, Chloe. 2004. 'A Disorder of Affect: Love, Tragedy, Biomedicine, and Citizenship in American Autism Research, 1943–2003'. PhD dissertation. University of Pennsylvania.

Silverman, Chloe, and Martha Hebert. 2003. 'Autism and Genetics'. *Gene Watch* 16 (1): 1–8.

Simpson, David E., J.J. Hanley, and Gordon Quinn. 2002. *Refrigerator Mothers*. Documentary Film. Boston: Fanlight Productions, 2002.

Singh, J.A.L., and Robert M. Zingg. 1966. *Wolf-Children and Feral Man*. New York: Archon Books.

Snow, John. 1855. *On the Mode of Communication of Cholera*. London: Churchill.

Sontag, Susan. 2001 [1977]. *Illness as Metaphor and AIDS and Its Metaphors*. New York: Picador.

Spiegel, Alix. 2005. 'The Dictionary of Disorder'. *New Yorker*, 3 January, 56–63.

State of California Department of Developmental Services. 1999. *Changes in the Population of Persons with Autism and Pervasive Developmental Disorders in California's Developmental Services System, 1987–1998*. A Report to the Legislature. Sacramento, California.

Steffenburg, S., C. Gillberg, and L. Hellgren, and L.C.Anderson. 1989. 'A Twin Study of Autism in Denmark, Finland, Iceland, Norway and Sweden'. *Journal of Child Psychology and Psychiatry* 30 (3): 405–16.

Strakowski, S.M., M. Flaum, X. Amdor, H.S. Bracha, A. K. Pandurangi, D. Robinson, and M. Tohen. 1996. 'Racial Differences in the Diagnosis of Psychosis'. *Schizophrenia Research* 21: 117–24.

Taylor, E., and J. Green, eds. 2001. *Research and Innovation on the Road to Child Psychiatry*, vol. 2: *The Classic Papers of Sir Michael Rutter*. London: Gaskell.

Thompson, P.M., C. Vidal, J.N. Giedd, P. Gochman, J. Blumenthal, R. Nicholson, A.W. Toga, and J.L. Rappoport. 2001. 'From the Cover: Mapping Adolescent Brain Change Reveals Dynamic Wave of Accelerated Gray Matter Loss'. *Proceedings of the National Academy of Sciences of the United States of America* 98 (2): 11650–5.

Tonge, Bruce J., and Avril V. Brereton. 1997. 'Australia'. Pp. 951–3 in Donald J. Cohen and Fred R. Volkmar, eds., *Handbook of Autism and Pervasive Developmental Disorders*, 2nd ed. New York: John Wiley and Sons.

Turkle, Sherry. 1992. *Psychoanalytic Politics: Jacques Lacan and Freud's French Revolution*. New York: Guilford.

Tredgold, R.F., and K. Soddy, with the assistance of E.W. Dunkley. 1908. 1963. *Textbook on Mental Deficiency*, 10th ed. [originally published in 1908 as *Mental Deficiency*]. Baltimore: Williams and Wilkins.

US Department of Health, Education, and Welfare. 1973. 'Trends in Breast Feeding Among American Mothers'. National Survey of Family Growth. US Department of Health, Education, and Welfare, Series 23, no. 3. Veenstra-Vander Weele, J., S.L. Christian, and E.H.J.

Cook. 2004. 'Autism as a Paradigmatic Complex Genetic Disorder'. *Annual Review of Genomics and Human Genetics* 5: 379–405.

Volkmar, Fred R., Ami Klin, and Donald J. Cohen. 1997. 'Diagnosis and Classification of Autism and Related Conditions: Consensus and Issues'. Pp. 5–40 in Donald J. Cohen and Fred

R.Volkmar, eds., *Handbook of Autism and Pervasive Developmental Disorders*, 2nd ed. New York: John Wiley and Sons.

Volkmar, Fred R., David Shaffer, and Michael First. 1991. Letter to the Editor. *Journal of the American Academy of Child and Adolescent Psychiatry* 30 (1): 74.

Vygotsky, Lev S. 1986. *Thought and Language*. Cambridge, Mass.: M.I.T. Press.

Waterhouse, Lynn, Robin Morris, Doris Allen, Michelle Dunn, Deborah Fein, Carl Feinstein, Isabelle Rapin, and Lorna Wing. 1996. 'Diagnosis and Classification in Autism'. *Journal of Autism and Developmental Disorders* 26 (1): 59–86.

Welch, H. Gilbert, Steven Woloshin, and Lisa M. Schwartz. 2005. 'Skin Biopsy Rates and Incidence of Melanoma: Population Based Ecological Study'. *British Medical Journal* 3 September; 331(7515): 481–5; E-publication, August 4, 2005.

Whaley, A.L. 1997. 'Ethnicity/Race, Paranoia, and Psychiatric Diagnoses: Clinician Bias Versus Sociocultural Differences'. *Journal of Psychopathology and Behavioral Assessment* 19: 1–20.

Whitaker, Robert. 2002. *Mad in America: Bad Science, Bad Medicine, and the Enduring Mistreatment of the Mentally Ill*. New York: Perseus.

Williams, J.G., J.P.T. Higgins, and C.E.G. Brayne. 2006. 'Systematic Review of Prevalence Studies of Autism Spectrum Disorders'. *Archives of Disease in Childhood* 91: 8–15.

Wilson, Mitchell. 1993. 'DSM-III and the Transformation of American Psychiatry: A History'. *American Journal of Psychiatry* 150 (3): 399–410.

Wing, Lorna. 1991. 'The Relationship Between Asperger's Syndrome and Kanner's Autism', pp. 93–121 in Uta Frith, ed. *Autism and Asperger Syndrome*. Cambridge: Cambridge University Press.

Wong, Albert, Hung Choy, and Hubert H.M. Van Tol. 2003. 'Schizophrenia: From Phenomenology to Neurobiology'. *Neuroscience and Biobehavioral Reviews* 27: 269–306.

World Health Organisation. 1979. *Schizophrenia: An International Follow-up Study*. New York: Wiley.

Yeargin-Allsopp, Marshalyn, and Coleen Boyle. 2002. 'Overview: The Epidemiology of Neurodevelopmental Disorders'. *Mental Retardation and Developmental Disorders* 8: 113–6.

Yeargin-Allsopp, Marshalyn, et al. 2003. 'Prevalence of Autism in a U.S. Metropolitan Area'. *Journal of the American Medical Association (JAMA)* 289: 49–55.

Index